Walt Kelly's OUR GANG

FANTAGRAPHICS BOOKS

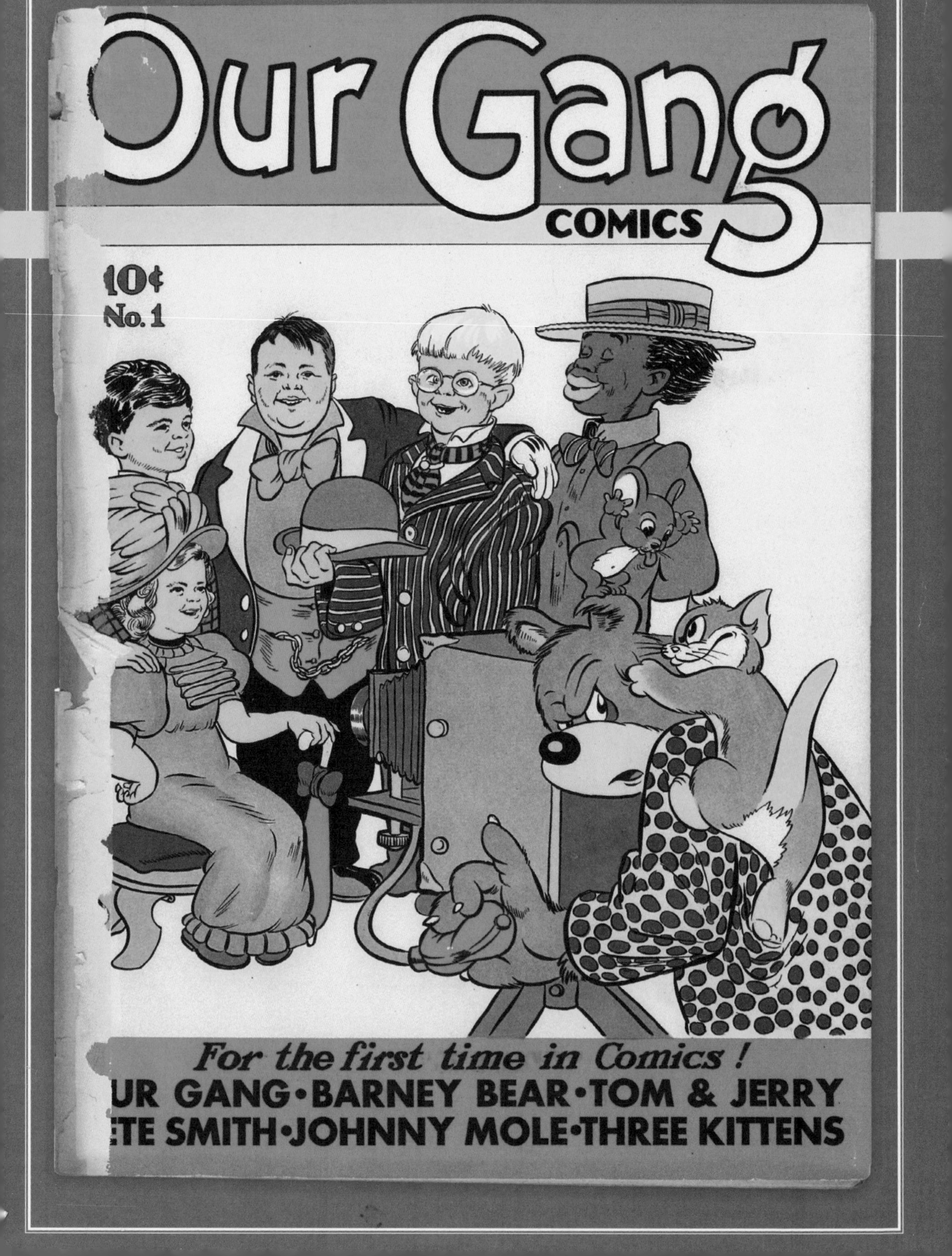
Our Gang
COMICS
10¢
No. 1
For the first time in Comics!
UR GANG • BARNEY BEAR • TOM & JERRY
ETE SMITH • JOHNNY MOLE • THREE KITTENS

OUR GANG: *Evolution of a Comic Book*

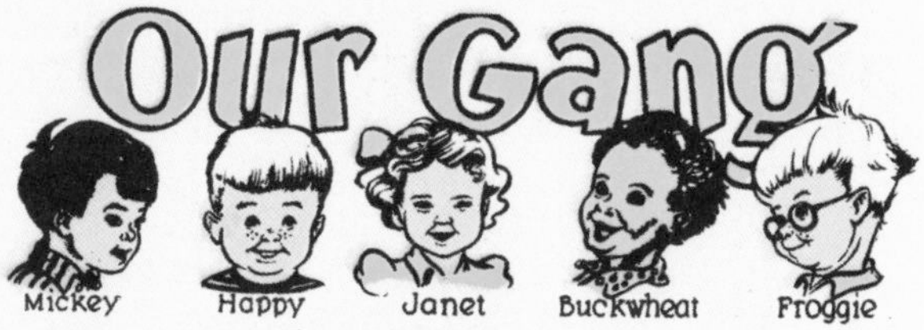
Our Gang
Mickey
Happy
Janet
Buckwheat
Froggie

Leonard Maltin

BY ANY DEFINITION *Our Gang* has had an extraordinary run, in a variety of media, since producer Hal Roach created the comedy series in 1922. Its life as a Dell comic book series is certainly the least-documented aspect of that history; that the series was written and drawn by the great Walt Kelly is icing on the cake for comics fans.

KELLY'S WORK ALSO rescued *Our Gang* from the doldrums of its final days on-screen at the MGM studio...but I'm getting ahead of my story.

HAL ROACH WAS NOT only a movie pioneer and a self-made man, but one of the most important figures in the history of comedy. In the early teens he stumbled, like many others, into the burgeoning film business and found work as an extra. He made friends with another ambitious young man who had his sights set on an acting career, and when Roach inherited some money, he started making comedy short subjects with his friend, Harold Lloyd.

They prospered together, Lloyd becoming one of the biggest stars of the silent screen (and one of the wealthiest men in Hollywood) and Roach taking charge of a studio in Culver City, California where the specialty was comedy. Later, toward the end of the 1920s, a performer-turned-gag-writer named Stan Laurel chanced to work on screen with a journeyman comic actor named Oliver Hardy, and the world's greatest comedy duo came to life.

But in 1921, Roach foresaw great things for an ebullient black boy named Ernie Morrison who'd had scene-stealing roles in several Harold Lloyd comedies. The boy was nicknamed Sunshine Sammy, and Roach put him under contract. His presence at the studio helped sow the seeds for a new comedy series.

As Roach told it for decades to come, the idea for that series solidified in his mind when he was looking out his office window one day and watched some boys fighting over possession of a stick. When he realized that these everyday kids had held him in rapt attention, the idea for *Our Gang* was hatched.

Whether it was really as simple as that or not, we'll never know. We do know that Roach's team of writers and filmmakers had a difficult time crafting an acceptable film. Eventually, the series made its debut in 1922, and before long was pronounced

a success. Its popularity grew with each passing year, even as some of its cast members moved on and others were introduced.

The coming of sound should have spelled disaster for a series that depended on a patient director coaching his youthful actors through every scene as it was being shot. Instead, the kids came through with flying colors (as did the entire Roach studio, which made a smoother transition to sound than any of the "big boys" in Hollywood).

Several budding stars were introduced in the talkies, notably Jackie Cooper, who after one year went on to a major career in feature films, even earning an Academy Award nomination as Best Actor for *Skippy* (based on Percy Crosby's popular comic strip) in 1931. Dickie Moore and Scotty Beckett, who joined the series in the next few years, both went on to enjoy healthy careers in features, usually playing the hero (Gary Cooper, Errol Flynn, et al.) as a boy.

But it was George "Spanky" McFarland, Carl "Alfalfa" Switzer, Darla Hood, Billie "Buckwheat" Thomas, and Eugene "Porky" Lee that composed the series' most durable and memorable cast. (Tommy "Butch" Bond was never put under contract, but was also an integral part of this troupe.)

Hal Roach loved the series, and so did audiences, but the economics of making short-subjects were changing in the 1930s. Double features, promising moviegoers more for their money, crowded shorts off the program. Even theater owners who were loyal to the shorts weren't necessarily willing to pay more for them as production costs went up.

Roach moved his biggest stars, Laurel and Hardy, to feature-length films as a result, but he didn't have similar success with Charley Chase, Patsy Kelly, or Our Gang (who were featured in a Civil War period piece called *General Spanky* in 1936).

Rather than see the series die, Roach sold it, lock, stock, and barrel to his distributor, MGM, in 1938, along with his young stars' contracts.

At first, it seemed as if MGM would continue making *Our Gang* comedies in the same vein as the Roach series, but after a few years it became sadly clear that the people at Metro lacked the light touch when it came to comedy, and weren't prepared to give the films the t.l.c. they required. After all, this was the studio that took away Buster Keaton's autonomy in the 1930s and diluted the work of Laurel and Hardy and the Marx Brothers in the 1940s.

What's more, they were reluctant to part with the youthful stars even though they were literally outgrowing their parts. (Both Spanky and Buckwheat had been three years old when they joined the Gang in the early 1930s.)

With the addition of a whiny Mickey Gubitosi (later known as Bobby, then Robert, Blake), a trick-voiced Billy Laughlin as Froggy, and a syrupy new leading lady named Janet Burston, the series hit rock bottom in the early 1940s. One by one, Darla, Porky, Alfalfa, and Spanky left, while *Our Gang* plodded on doing ten-minute morality plays and World War Two flag-wavers.

IMAGINE, THEN, HOW it must have felt to purchase the first issue of *Our Gang* comics in October of 1942 and see the familiar members of this troupe in a lively, funny, raucous outing, quite unlike the treacle being foisted on audiences by MGM. This was the work of Walt Kelly.

The trail that connected *Our Gang* to Kelly was serendipitous, to say the least. In the late 1920s Hal Roach's secretary, Eleanor Packer, expressed an interest in writing, and when Western Printing and Lithography approached the producer about doing a book about Our Gang, he gave Eleanor the assignment. *A Day With Our Gang*, released under the Whitman imprint, was a great success. Eventually, Packer left Roach to work at MGM in the publicity department, where among other things she arranged for publishing tie-ins for

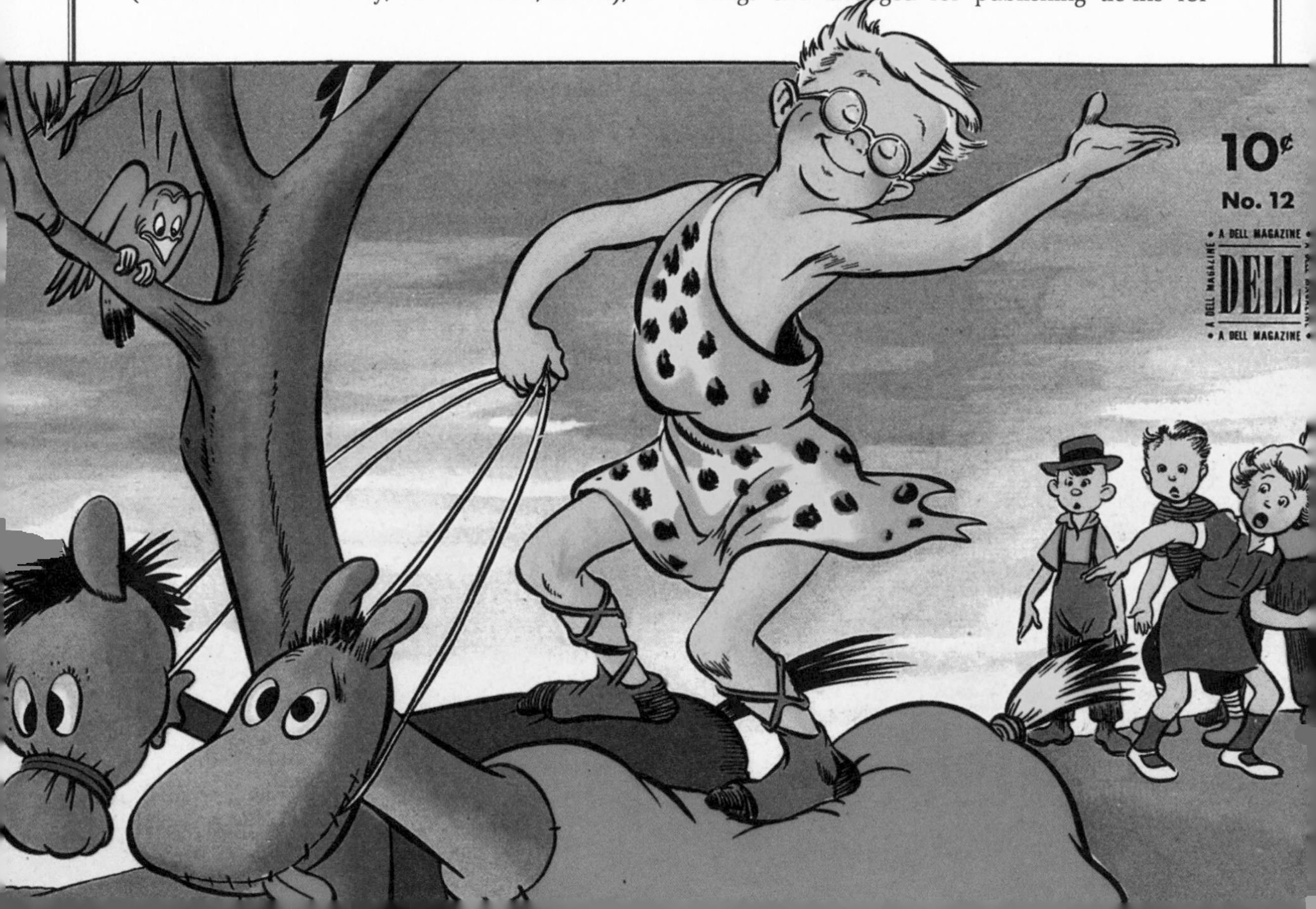

10¢
No. 12
A DELL MAGAZINE
DELL
A DELL MAGAZINE

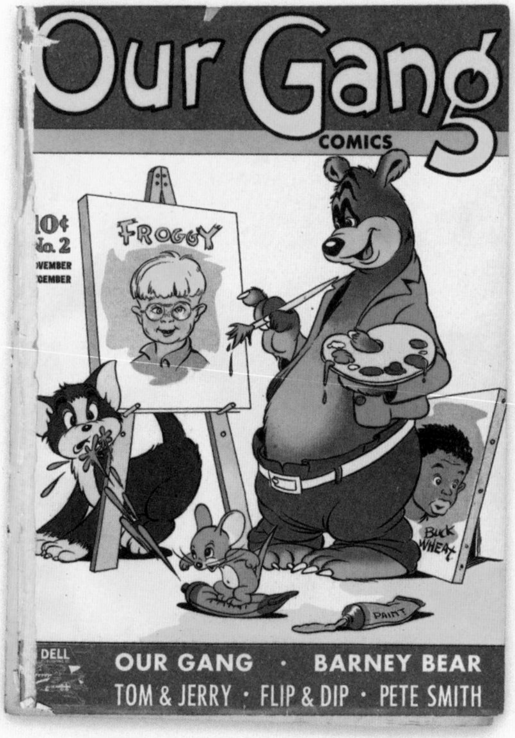
Our Gang
COMICS
10¢
No. 2
FROGGY
BUCK WHEAT
PAINT
DELL
OUR GANG · BARNEY BEAR
TOM & JERRY · FLIP & DIP · PETE SMITH

the studio. She was probably responsible for the existence of an *Our Gang* Big Little Book, published in 1934, as Metro distributed all of Hal Roach's product.

When Western opened a Los Angeles office in 1940, Packer was hired as resident editor because of her movie connections and savvy. MGM, for instance, would have felt secure placing its properties in her hands. She was the editor responsible for hiring Carl Barks, then a staff writer and artist at the Walt Disney studio, to begin his long career in the comic book field. It was common for staffers from all the animation studios to work (and even moonlight) on comic books.

One of Barks' colleagues at Disney was Walt Kelly, who left the company and moved East after the settlement of a bitter labor strike in 1941. Kelly maintained a good relationship with Disney himself, and Walt, who respected Kelly's work, saw that he had work sent to him. Freelancing from his home in Connecticut, Kelly's Disney credential stood him in good stead, and earned him various assignments from Western's New York office from editor Oskar Lebeck. Soon he was contributing to *Walt Disney's Comics and Stories*, and earned the task of turning the *Our Gang* comedies into one component of a new Dell comic book which featured other MGM characters and properties (Tom & Jerry, Barney Bear, even short-subject narrator and personality Pete Smith). Indeed, the cover of issue #1 shows Barney Bear taking a photograph of the kids.

It's clear that Kelly worked from photographs on the early issues of the series to render recognizable likenesses of Spanky, Buckwheat, Janet, Froggy, and Mickey, though Buckwheat seems to have given him the most trouble and his look evolved and improved over time.

What is most striking about Kelly's storytelling is that he managed to create a tangible environment for the Gang, invent a rivalry between them and the Gashouse Gang, stage vivid action scenes both serious and slapsticky, and imbue each member of the cast with individual personalities.

Kelly aficionado Maggie Thompson remembers reading these comics when they were new and admiring his portrayal of Janet, so different from the sickly sweet character seen in the movies. "The girls were just as plucky and smart as the boys, and resistant to 'you're a girl, you can't do that' thinking. Considering the era it's one of the things I admire about Kelly."

He is just as progressive in his treatment of Buckwheat. When Hal Roach integrated *Our Gang* in 1922 he made a fairly bold statement that soon became accepted as the norm in Hollywood movies—for children, not adults.

Says Thompson, "Janet and Bucky are the smartest members of the gang. (He drops Buckwheat fairly soon and becomes Bucky.) This is a comic book where the kids age in real time. He eventually becomes a high school track star; he'll be the one to come in and analyze things, and solve problems. Later we meet Buckwheat's family, who are just as smart as he is; they even outwit a con man."

Oddly, Kelly resorts to caricature for the maid depicted in issue #3, who races from the sight of the kids in circus disguise screaming, "Cannaboils!" On the other hand, no one among the adults was spared indignities in this or any of the other *Our Gang* stories.

Like the MGM shorts, Kelly was careful to include home-front patriotism in almost every issue of the comic for the duration of World War Two; the very first story has the kids gathering scrap metal for a Victory drive. He was obliged to drop Spanky from the cast when the real-life George McFarland left the movie series, so he renamed him Happy and continued on his merry way.

The comic book was a solid success, and quickly shifted from a bimonthly to a monthly schedule. Kelly even wrote and drew Our Gang stories for issues #3 and #26 of the *March of Comics* series. (Perhaps it was conflicting deadlines that diverted Kelly and forced Dell to hire another artist to fill in for him on *Our Gang* #7, although the story seems to have been scripted by Kelly.)

As the months rolled on, Kelly had some of the cast members grow up and move away. In time, he did away with all of the original Gang members and introduced his own characters. Red becomes the tough leader, and younger brothers and sisters came to the fore, including Button-Nose and Two-by-Two (the former black, the latter white, but portrayed as equals—echoing the relationship between Buckwheat and Porky in the Hal Roach comedies of the 1930s).

Kelly presumably had the freedom to do all of this because MGM pulled the plug on *Our Gang* in the spring of 1944. The momentum of the series, a staple of moviegoing for more than twenty years, was more than enough to propel the comic book to the end of the decade—that, and the entertaining stories themselves.

Just the same, the various MGM "stars" jockeyed for position as the comic book continued.

In October 1947, the front cover bore the name *Our Gang with Tom & Jerry,* with a strip of film running down the left side featuring Leo the MGM Lion, Froggy, Janet, Egghead (aka Eggy), Flip and Dip, Benny Burro, and Barney Bear. Tom & Jerry are the lead story inside. In April 1949, the last *Our Gang* story appeared, although the title of the book remained the same for two more issues!

Issue #57 featured the eight-page conclusion of a two-part story in which dishonest carnival workers have stolen Julip the Goat and Hortense the Dog from our heroes, Button-Nose, Two by Two and Anastasia. In the bottom two panels the kids are walking back to their rowboat. The last panel says, "And so as the sun sets over Beautiful Old Shotton's Island we bid a fond farewell to the friends of our gang, and wish them luck."

In another fluke of timing, Hal Roach reacquired the rights to his own *Our Gang* comedies and reissued them to theaters under the name *The Little Rascals*, beginning in 1950. In 1955 they won a new generation of fans, perhaps a bigger audience than ever before, on television, where they served as daily entertainment fodder for several decades. Had Dell held on a little longer they could have ridden that wave of renewed popularity. Instead, the company launched a new Little Rascals comic book in 1956, and kept it running until 1962. But by that time, Walt Kelly wasn't available to call the shots.

He was to the comic books what Hal Roach had been to the movie series: creator and godfather.

Leonard Maltin is the co-author, with Richard W. Bann, of *The Little Rascals: The Life and Times of Our Gang* (Three Rivers Press/Crown), the definitive account of that movie series. He is perhaps best known for his annual paperback reference *Leonard Maltin's Movie Guide* and its companion volume, *Leonard Maltin's Classic Movie Guide.* He has written many other books, including *The Disney Films* and *Of Mice and Magic: A History of American Animated Cartoons,* and since 1982 has appeared on television's *Entertainment Tonight.* He teaches at the University of Southern California School of Cinema-Television, publishes a quarterly newsletter, *Leonard Maltin's Movie Crazy,* and presides over www.leonardmaltin.com.

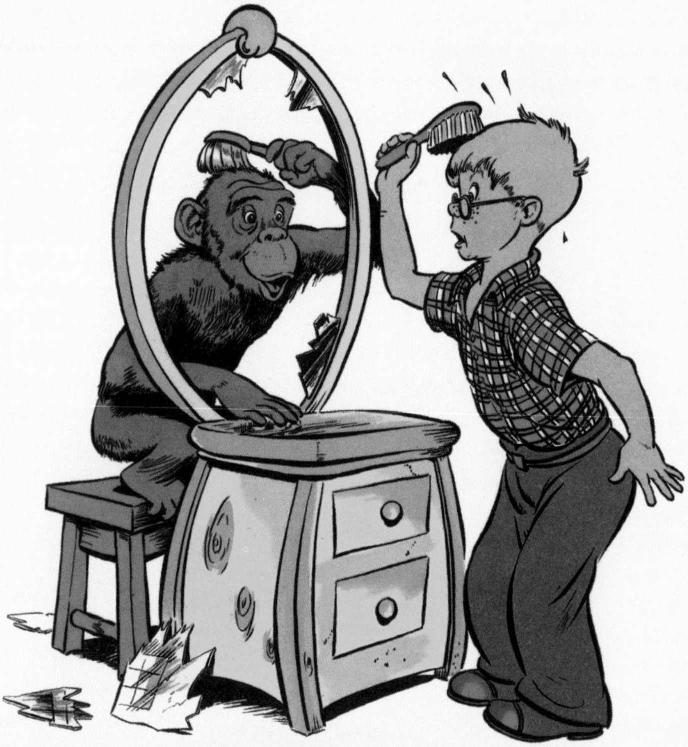

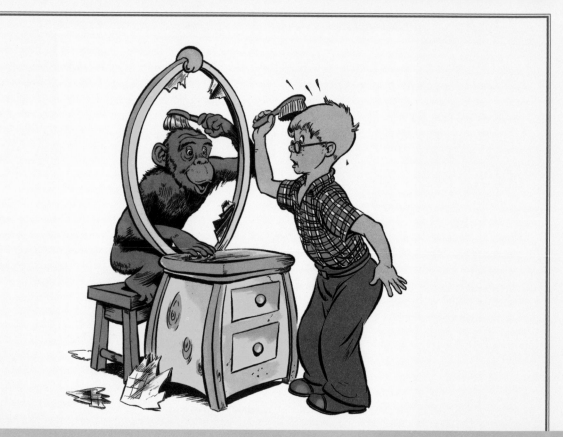

INTRODUCTION TO OUR GANG *by Steve Thompson*

FOR THOSE WHO are only familiar with Walt Kelly's work through *Pogo*, it may come as a surprise to learn that he drew the long-running *Our Gang* series for Dell Comics.

Since Kelly is one of the early inductees into the National Cartoon Museum's Hall of Fame, it's been frustrating for fans that such a major portion (almost 800 pages) of his early career has not been reprinted. Fortunately, that is now being corrected and we have a chance to see Kelly as he draws and writes about real people, and to see him write narrative fiction in addition to his better-known humor.

Not that it's important or even relevant after all this time, but why Kelly? At the time, he certainly wasn't a "name" artist with Dell and it would be some time before he would be publicly credited for his Mother Goose and fairy-tale series. A year before *Our Gang* #1 hit the newsstands in mid-1942 (cover dated Sept.-Oct.), Kelly had left Walt Disney Studios after six years of primarily drawing animals (*Dumbo, Fantasia*) and much of his subsequent work for Dell starred animals as well. However, his first published comic book work involved people, when he drew an adaptation of *Gulliver's Travels* for DC Comics, just before he started work at Disney.

Although some of Kelly's correspondence with Dell regarding various comics survives, there doesn't seem to be any documentation of why he was selected to do *Our Gang*. In addition to the artistic requisites of caricaturing known movie stars, the scripts were also Kelly's responsibility. Since he had already shown his skills in both writing and drawing stories (the first Pogo story was in *Animal Comics* #1, Dec. 1941/Jan. 1942), this may have played a role in his selection. Whether some decision-maker selected him, he asked for the opportunity to do the series, or someone just picked his name out of a hat will probably never be known. All we can do is enjoy the result.

Although it is undoubtedly overly nostalgic, it's possible to look at the Our Gang era from sixty years on and declare that it was a great time to be a kid. Not for them the over-organized and regimented sports, dance and music activities of today's youth. In those days before "stranger danger" and almost daily reports of child abductions, in all but the largest cities during summer, kids could disappear after breakfast, possibly return for lunch, and then vanish again until supper, without panicking their parents. They might get into mischief, but only very rarely would get into trouble.

Note that while the eight stories in this volume appeared over the course of a year and a half, there is no apparent seasonal change in the stories. The absence of any school activities is also interesting. These stories seem to exist in a kind of limbo, an eternal summer where the daily grind of school or the housebound days of winter don't intrude. We don't know exactly where Greenpoint is located, but evidence over the course of the series points to the East Coast, probably the Northeast. In the 1940s, it's unlikely that any group of children in the South would be integrated. Other physical features, such as water access and sizeable hills would argue against the Midwest. Historical elements in later stories dating back over a century preclude most of the West Coast.

Many of the activities in early issues were similar to, if not actually based on, Kelly's own experiences growing up in Bridgeport, Connecticut twenty years earlier, which also encourages us to place Greenpoint in the Northeast. Staging a circus, as the Gang does in issue #3, would have been a natural, since Bridgeport was the home of P.T. Barnum and his circus. In fact, Mickey's opening suggestion, "Say, Gang, let's have a circus in my back yard," is laughably stereotypical today of an entire genre of kid movies.

Early *Our Gang* stories were comparatively light comedies, much like the movies, and reflected much of the necessity of kids finding their own entertainment. If you wanted to play ball, you were probably going to have to find a vacant lot, clean it up, and organize the teams and games without adult assistance. Want a place to gather with your friends and have a little privacy? Better build your own clubhouse, or find a cave. "Going to Press," the title of one of the 1942 films, could just as easily be applied to the story in issue #2.

Not all is fun and games in the Our Gang world, however. The only threat in #1 comes from the Gashouse Gang, and is little more than the typical cross-town rivalry of similar groups of kids. Later stories, however, would involve the Gang with black marketeers, counterfeiters, pirates and other serious villains. Some of these would turn violent and even life-threatening, surprising in stories about and aimed at children.

After sixty-plus years, it's difficult for today's readers to realize that the involvement of the *Our Gang* kids in their community was not particularly unusual. With geography no doubt based in part on that of Bridgeport, children raised before the explosion of countless Levittown suburban developments would have recognized at least parts of their own towns in Greenpoint.

However strange or idealized it may be to those who later grew up in suburban tract housing or urban apartment buildings, small town America provided a wealth of opportunities for juvenile activities. Kids knew the local merchants (and vice versa), and ample locations, exotic to young children, for adventures and exploration. Unlike the costumed crimefighters in other comics, the readers of *Our Gang* could not only identify with the characters but could easily imagine themselves doing almost exactly the same things.

All the stories in this volume take place at the height of WWII, when virtually every youngster in the U.S. looking for adventure could find it almost without looking. Kids participated in all types of war-related efforts, following the news as avidly as their parents, and sometimes even more so. Unlike the wars since, kids were able to actively participate in a wide variety of home-front activities. When they weren't memorizing aircraft silhouettes (so they could spot invaders when they flew over), they would be watching for suspicious activities by the dozens of spies that were no doubt living right next door. Kids usually know their neighborhood better than adults, and can be more attuned to anything unusual or out of place. Of course, it didn't hurt that Nazis and the Japanese were deliciously perfect villains and the lines between good and evil were very clearly drawn.

Many of the stories in this volume have some aspect of this home-front war activity, either as the main plot or side element. In issue #1, the Gang not only gathers up scrap metal to be used for ammunition, but the money they receive for it is donated to the Red Cross. In #2, as neighborhood reporters, they take part in monitoring the blackout (and incidentally stop a minor opportunistic crime wave). While #3 is strictly kid-jinks, #4 makes up for it by making the Gang Air Raid Wardens. (How many of us cringe when we see what gas was selling for in this episode?) This time they help catch a gas bootlegger, but the money they receive as a reward goes to war stamps. Victory gardens take the stage in #6. One children's wartime effort that doesn't show up in these stories is the paper drive, which is perhaps a little ironic since that's one reason so few WWII-era comics have survived.

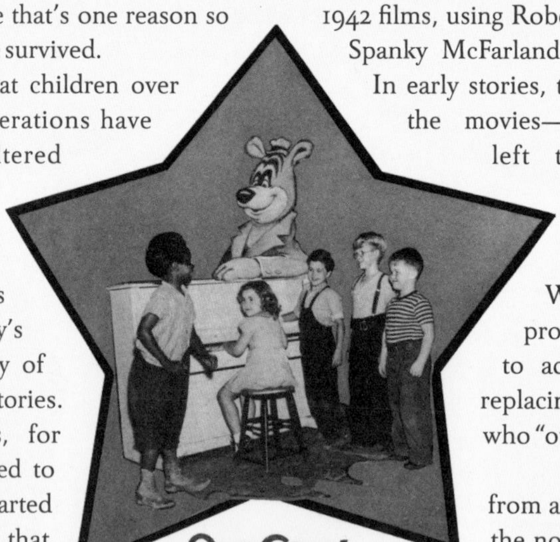
Our Gang

Some have argued that children over the last two or three generations have been increasingly sheltered and that it may work to their disadvantage. While this is not the place for that discussion, it's difficult to imagine today's preteens involved in many of the adventures in these stories. Most of today's parents, for instance, would be appalled to find that their kids had started a fairly sizeable fire (#4) that destroyed their clubhouse. To find they had then been digging, unsupervised, into the base of a hill, might cause a few panic attacks. At least the Gang had the sense to shore up the roof of their "bombproof shelter," but that didn't help when they hit the underground gas tank.

Since the concept of safety-inspected playgrounds was nonexistent and adult supervision apparently absent, it may be amazing that the kids of *Our Gang* survived to become teenagers. For the readers of *Our Gang,* Kelly's stories may have been exaggerated for dramatic purposes, but they could see many elements of their own lives in the stories as well.

The criminals that the Gang runs into are a different breed than those of today, as well. Spanky, Mickey, et al. are not at risk from drive-by shootings; tire thieves and gas bootleggers, while armed, still don't seem to be a serious threat to the life-and-limb of the Gang members. This will change in later stories, when the Gang even manages to acquire a nemesis who, after his escape from jail, returns to wreak revenge on the kids who got him arrested. Even the perceived definition of a "Gang" has changed considerably from these stories. The rivalry between the Gashouse Gang and Our Gang, while real and sometimes violent, does not endanger the members of either outside of an occasional black eye.

Our Gang #1 uses the same main cast as the 1942 films, using Robert Blake, Janet Burston, Spanky McFarland and others as models. In early stories, the cast followed that of the movies—Spanky, for instance, left the movie series by the end of 1942, and was only in the first two stories in the comics. When the movies ceased production, Kelly was able to add his own characters, replacing many of the originals who "outgrew" their roles.

It's interesting to note from an artistic standpoint that the non-Gang characters, such as those in the Gashouse Gang, are somewhat less realistic than the Gang. Since they were not modeled on known personalities, Kelly was able to indulge his love of character exaggeration on these. That didn't stop him from introducing little in-jokes, either. The face of the director in issue #8 bears a close resemblance to that of Kelly himself (albeit considerably pudgier).

SPEAKING OF CARICATURES, however, it is necessary to discuss the portrayal of Buckwheat. Often derided by later movie viewers as an offensive racial stereotype, he didn't fare much better in the early comic book stories. It's difficult to say how much of this is carryover from the films and how much was because this was the way blacks were portrayed in comics. In this volume, for instance, he is shown with the enlarged light lips common to black comic book characters of the time. In "The Great Our Gang Circus," Buckwheat immediately volunteers to be "The Wild Man," decked out in jungle attire. Unfortunately, the representation of Mickey's family maid is even more egregious, and we almost expect to hear her say, "Feets, do your stuff." The maid, as with all adults, would already have been less important to the Gang than were their peers, but the image of Buckwheat in these stories sometimes contradicts the apparently casual integration of *Our Gang*.

Walt Kelly was an early proponent of racial equality, both in his artwork and his personal life. In 1948, for instance, he provided artwork for a fundraising campaign to support the first interracial hospital in the country. In these comics, his portrayal of Buckwheat can only be defended on the basis of the conventions of the time. As the *Our Gang* series progressed, he changed the portrayal of Buckwheat to much less of a stereotype, eventually renaming him Bucky and, in some of the stories, showing him outsmarting the other characters. It may be that Kelly, once he had shown he could do the series successfully, felt he had enough clout to force the changes. It should also be noted that his use of black characters in other comic book work during the 1940s was against the common stereotypes, with art and dialogue that made them much more mainstream.

The *Overstreet Comic Book Price Guide* lists issues #7 and #9 as "no Kelly story." While there are some differences in the appearance of secondary characters, notably the gangsters who are drawn considerably "harder" than those of other stories, the Gang characters don't seem to show non-Kelly lines.

This by itself is no verification, since many of Dell's artists were former Disney animators. I believe it was John Stanley who said, "We all drew like Walt Kelly – and he drew like us." There are no financial or other statements that can settle the question one way or the other.

As far as the script in #7 is concerned, the rivalry between Our Gang and the Gashouse Gang seems more mean-spirited and vicious than earlier stories, where the two groups can manage to work together when it's important. Indeed, the addition of glue to the wash water ends up damaging the storeowner's property, while in other stories the damage is pretty much limited to individual egos and group pride. The dialogue is also less sophisticated than other stories, with more mispronunciations and misspellings. The blackmarketeers the Gang runs into are more on a level with serious gangsters, instead of the somewhat bumbling crooks in #1 and #4. Even if the artwork is Kelly's, the writing and dialogue doesn't feel like his.

In issue #8, with no backstory or explanation, the Gang is suddenly seen on a fairly sizeable movie set, and seems quite at home there. While their interrupting a scene in progress belies familiarity with film work, one can't help but wonder if this is almost breaking the fourth wall, implying that this is a set on which some *Our Gang* movies are filmed. Buckwheat's dialogue descends a little further into patois than earlier stories, but he otherwise plays part of the hero's role. The villainy in this story is closer to that in #7, where we can feel that the Gang is actually in real danger.

In the next volume, we'll see Kelly begin to mold the Gang into more of his own creation. By then the movie series would no longer be in production, and he wouldn't be hampered by having to conform to the screen versions of the characters. Many of the current characters will be replaced, as they move away or go off to school, and the Gang will begin to be more of a cohesive whole, with the kids developing complementary skills and personalities, rather than being a loosely affiliated group of individuals.

Steve Thompson has been collecting and researching Walt Kelly for over 30 years. He is the author of *The Walt Kelly Collector's Guide* and co-author (with Selby Daley Kelly) of *Pogo Files for Pogophiles: A Retrospective on Fifty Years*. He also serves as President of the Pogo Fan Club (www.pogo-fan-club.org) and editor of their bimonthly magazine *The Fort Mudge Most*. He is currently working on a book-length biography of Kelly, due out in 2007 from University Press of Mississippi.

HELLO KIDS !!!
THIS IS OUR FIRST MAGAZINE WE HOPE YOU'LL LIKE IT. WE'RE GOING TO TAKE TURNS BEING EDITOR. I'M FIRST AND FROGGY WILL BE EDITOR NEXT TIME.
WE'VE TRIED TO FIND PICTURES AND STORIES THAT YOU'LL THINK ARE GOOD. HERE'S THE LIST OF WHAT'S IN THIS ~~BOOK~~ MAGAZINE :

Edited *by* GARY GROTH . Art Direction *by* JACOB COVEY . Cover Illustration *by* JEFF SMITH . Coloring *by* STEVE HAMAKER
Promotion *by* ERIC REYNOLDS . Production *by* PAUL BARESH . Published *by* GARY GROTH *&* KIM THOMPSON

 Fantagraphics Books, Inc. 7563 Lake City Way NE, Seattle, WA 98115, United States of America.

ISBN10: 1-56097753-1 . ISBN13: 978-1-56097-753-7 . Printed in Malaysia.
Distributed in the U.S. by W.W. Norton and Company, Inc. (1-212-354-5500)
Distributed in Canada by Raincoast Books (1-800-663-5714)
Distributed in the UK by Turnaround Distribution (1-208-829-3009)
To receive a free catalogue of fine comics and books, call 1-800-657-1100 or visit our website at Fantagraphics.com.

Our Gang

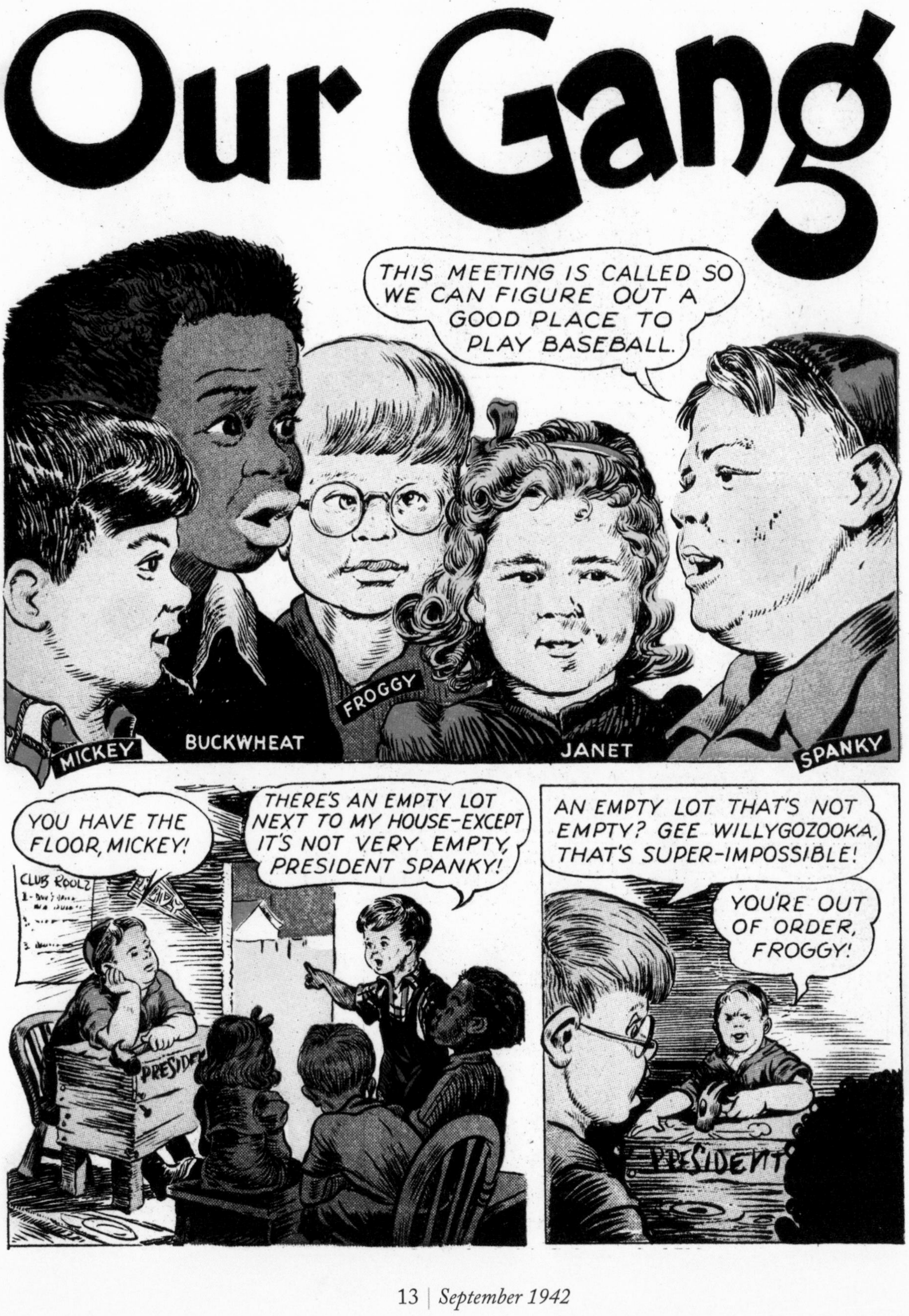
THIS MEETING IS CALLED SO WE CAN FIGURE OUT A GOOD PLACE TO PLAY BASEBALL.
MICKEY
BUCKWHEAT
FROGGY
JANET
SPANKY
YOU HAVE THE FLOOR, MICKEY!
THERE'S AN EMPTY LOT NEXT TO MY HOUSE-EXCEPT IT'S NOT VERY EMPTY, PRESIDENT SPANKY!
CLUB ROOLZ
PRESIDE
AN EMPTY LOT THAT'S NOT EMPTY? GEE WILLYGOZOOKA, THAT'S SUPER-IMPOSSIBLE!
YOU'RE OUT OF ORDER, FROGGY!
PRESIDENT

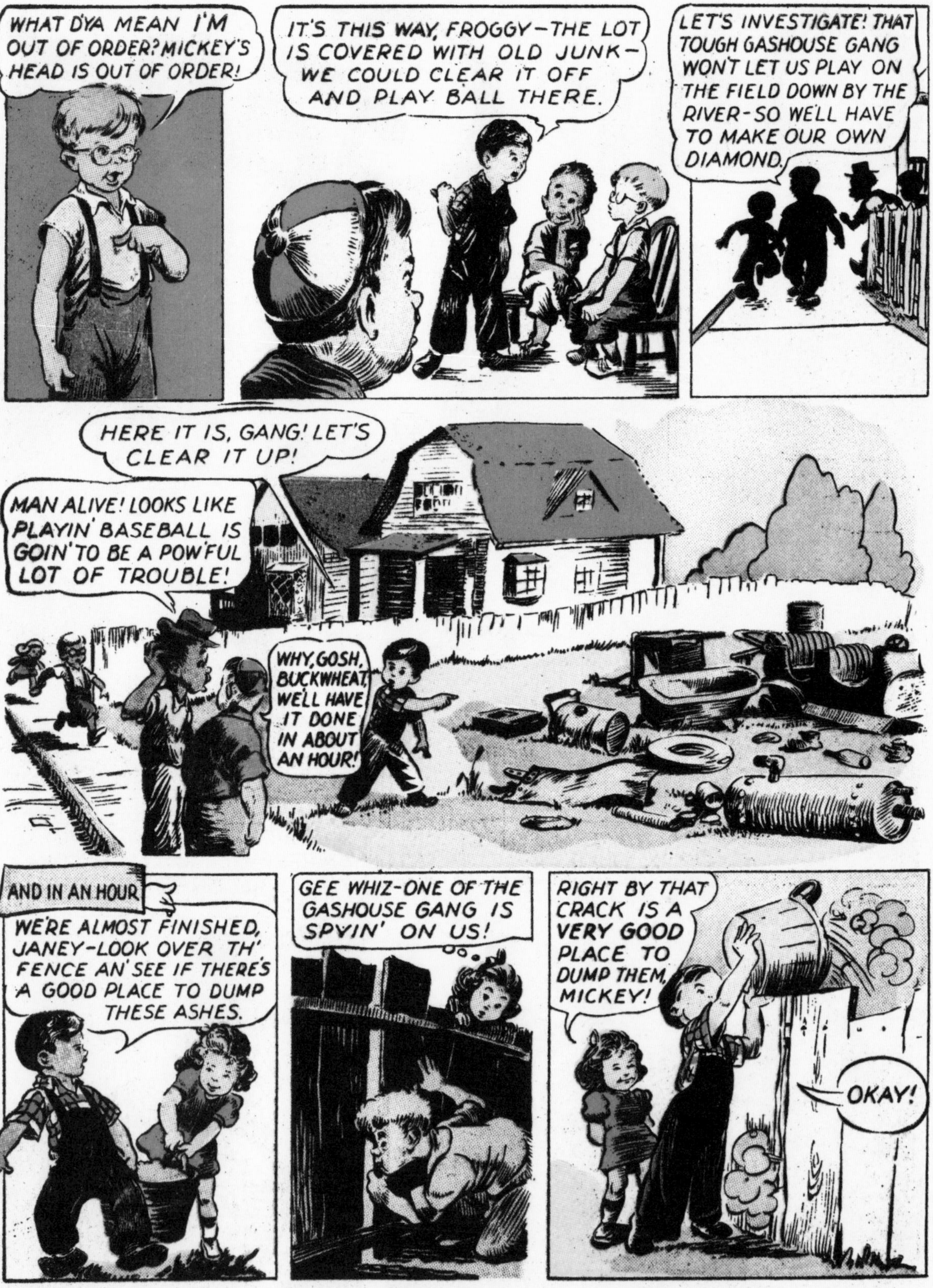
WHAT D'YA MEAN I'M OUT OF ORDER? MICKEY'S HEAD IS OUT OF ORDER!
IT'S THIS WAY, FROGGY—THE LOT IS COVERED WITH OLD JUNK—WE COULD CLEAR IT OFF AND PLAY BALL THERE.
LET'S INVESTIGATE! THAT TOUGH GASHOUSE GANG WON'T LET US PLAY ON THE FIELD DOWN BY THE RIVER—SO WE'LL HAVE TO MAKE OUR OWN DIAMOND.
HERE IT IS, GANG! LET'S CLEAR IT UP!
MAN ALIVE! LOOKS LIKE PLAYIN' BASEBALL IS GOIN' TO BE A POW'FUL LOT OF TROUBLE!
WHY, GOSH, BUCKWHEAT, WE'LL HAVE IT DONE IN ABOUT AN HOUR!
AND IN AN HOUR
WE'RE ALMOST FINISHED, JANEY—LOOK OVER TH' FENCE AN' SEE IF THERE'S A GOOD PLACE TO DUMP THESE ASHES.
GEE WHIZ—ONE OF THE GASHOUSE GANG IS SPYIN' ON US!
RIGHT BY THAT CRACK IS A VERY GOOD PLACE TO DUMP THEM, MICKEY!
OKAY!

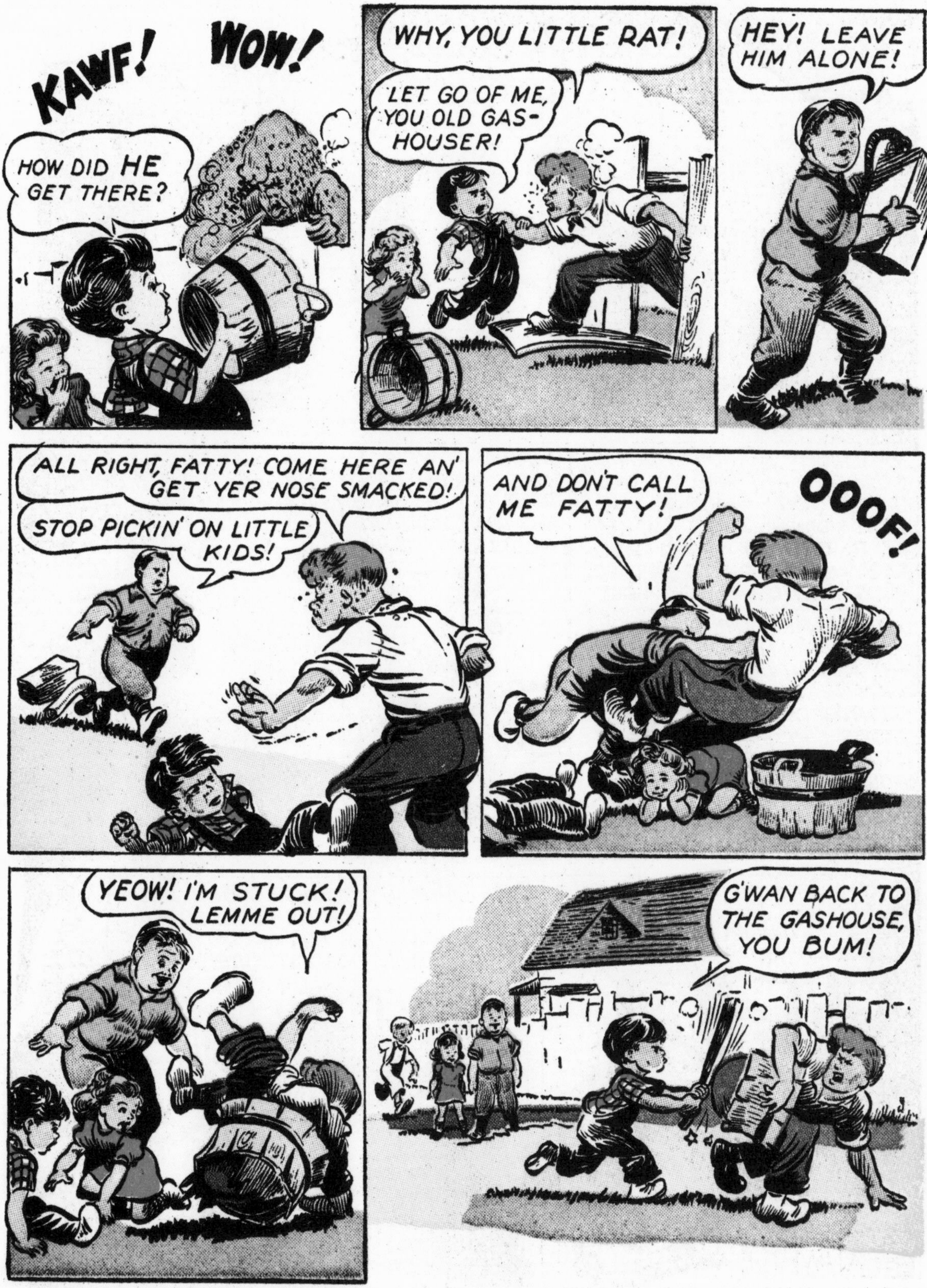
KAWF!
WOW!
HOW DID HE GET THERE?
WHY, YOU LITTLE RAT!
LET GO OF ME, YOU OLD GAS-HOUSER!
HEY! LEAVE HIM ALONE!
ALL RIGHT, FATTY! COME HERE AN' GET YER NOSE SMACKED!
STOP PICKIN' ON LITTLE KIDS!
AND DON'T CALL ME FATTY!
OOOF!
YEOW! I'M STUCK! LEMME OUT!
G'WAN BACK TO THE GASHOUSE, YOU BUM!

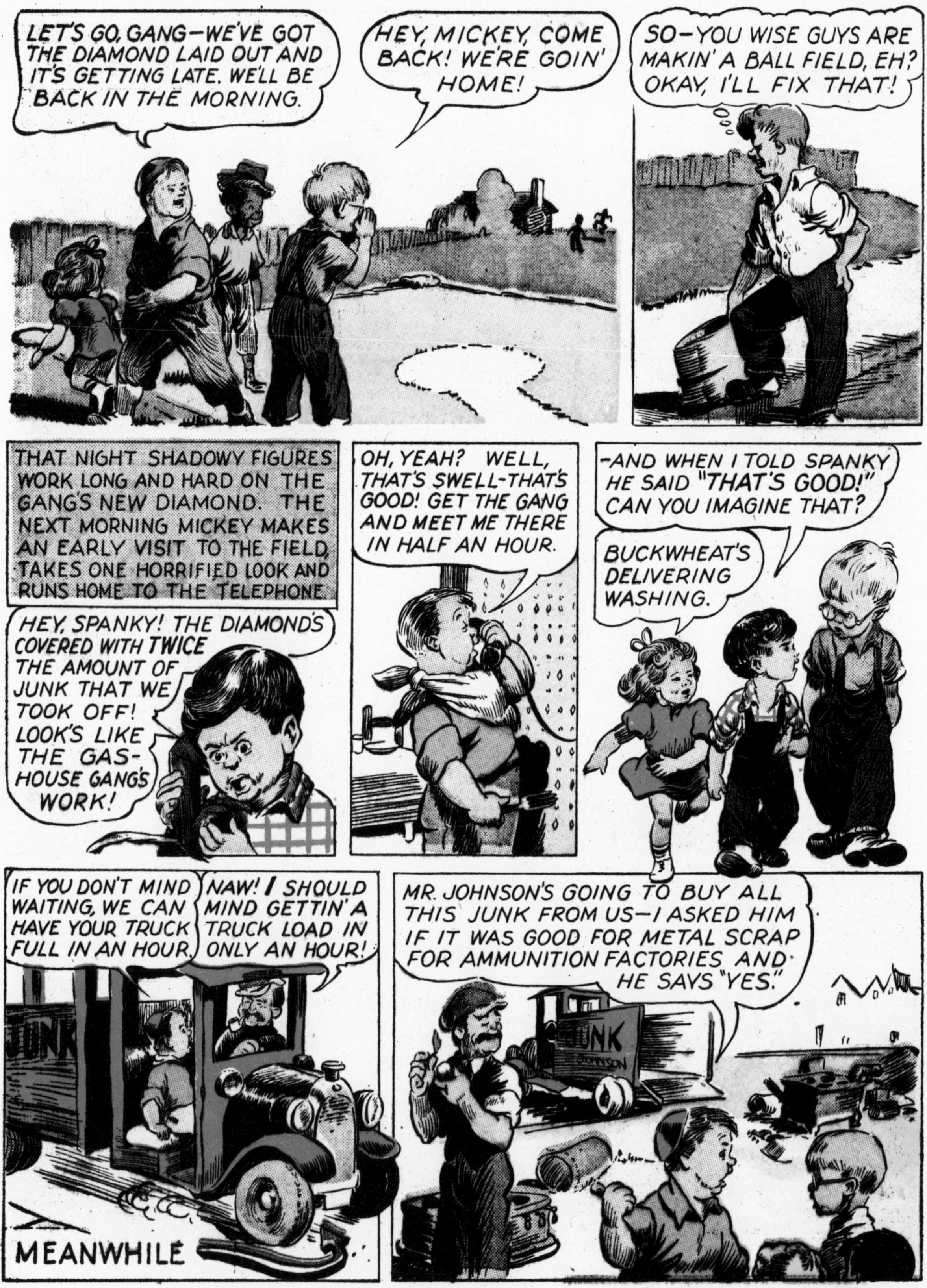

LET'S GO, GANG—WE'VE GOT THE DIAMOND LAID OUT AND IT'S GETTING LATE. WE'LL BE BACK IN THE MORNING.
HEY, MICKEY, COME BACK! WE'RE GOIN' HOME!
SO—YOU WISE GUYS ARE MAKIN' A BALL FIELD, EH? OKAY, I'LL FIX THAT!
THAT NIGHT SHADOWY FIGURES WORK LONG AND HARD ON THE GANG'S NEW DIAMOND. THE NEXT MORNING MICKEY MAKES AN EARLY VISIT TO THE FIELD, TAKES ONE HORRIFIED LOOK AND RUNS HOME TO THE TELEPHONE.
HEY, SPANKY! THE DIAMOND'S COVERED WITH TWICE THE AMOUNT OF JUNK THAT WE TOOK OFF! LOOK'S LIKE THE GAS-HOUSE GANG'S WORK!
OH, YEAH? WELL, THAT'S SWELL-THAT'S GOOD! GET THE GANG AND MEET ME THERE IN HALF AN HOUR.
-AND WHEN I TOLD SPANKY HE SAID "THAT'S GOOD!" CAN YOU IMAGINE THAT?
BUCKWHEAT'S DELIVERING WASHING.
IF YOU DON'T MIND WAITING, WE CAN HAVE YOUR TRUCK FULL IN AN HOUR.
NAW! I SHOULD MIND GETTIN' A TRUCK LOAD IN ONLY AN HOUR!
JUNK
MEANWHILE
MR. JOHNSON'S GOING TO BUY ALL THIS JUNK FROM US—I ASKED HIM IF IT WAS GOOD FOR METAL SCRAP FOR AMMUNITION FACTORIES AND HE SAYS "YES."
JUNK

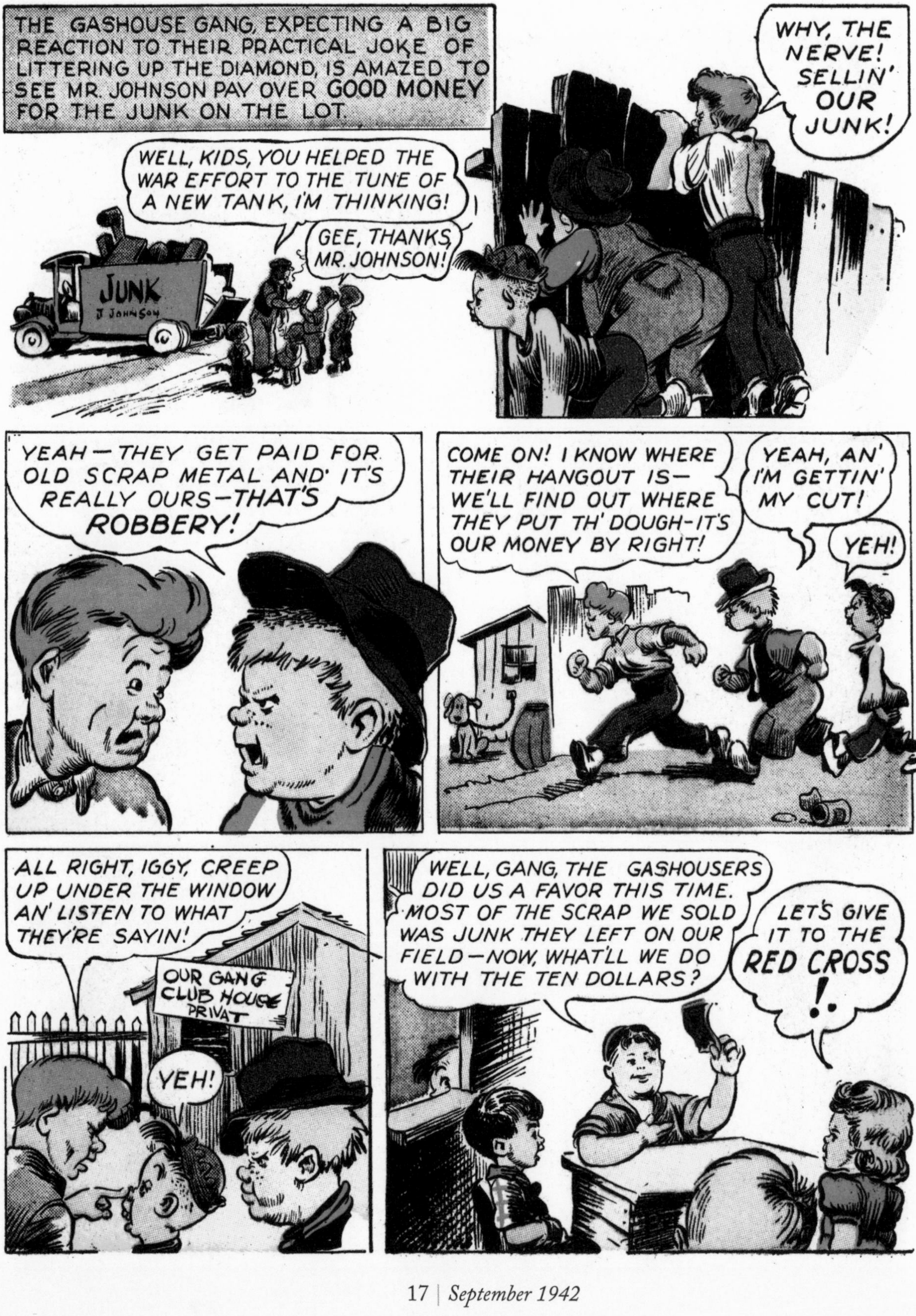
THE GASHOUSE GANG, EXPECTING A BIG REACTION TO THEIR PRACTICAL JOKE OF LITTERING UP THE DIAMOND, IS AMAZED TO SEE MR. JOHNSON PAY OVER GOOD MONEY FOR THE JUNK ON THE LOT.
WELL, KIDS, YOU HELPED THE WAR EFFORT TO THE TUNE OF A NEW TANK, I'M THINKING!
GEE, THANKS, MR. JOHNSON!
JUNK
J JOHNSON
WHY, THE NERVE! SELLIN' OUR JUNK!
YEAH—THEY GET PAID FOR OLD SCRAP METAL AND IT'S REALLY OURS—THAT'S ROBBERY!
COME ON! I KNOW WHERE THEIR HANGOUT IS—WE'LL FIND OUT WHERE THEY PUT TH' DOUGH-IT'S OUR MONEY BY RIGHT!
YEAH, AN' I'M GETTIN' MY CUT!
YEH!
ALL RIGHT, IGGY, CREEP UP UNDER THE WINDOW AN' LISTEN TO WHAT THEY'RE SAYIN!
OUR GANG CLUB HOUSE PRIVAT
YEH!
WELL, GANG, THE GASHOUSERS DID US A FAVOR THIS TIME. MOST OF THE SCRAP WE SOLD WAS JUNK THEY LEFT ON OUR FIELD—NOW, WHAT'LL WE DO WITH THE TEN DOLLARS?
LET'S GIVE IT TO THE RED CROSS!

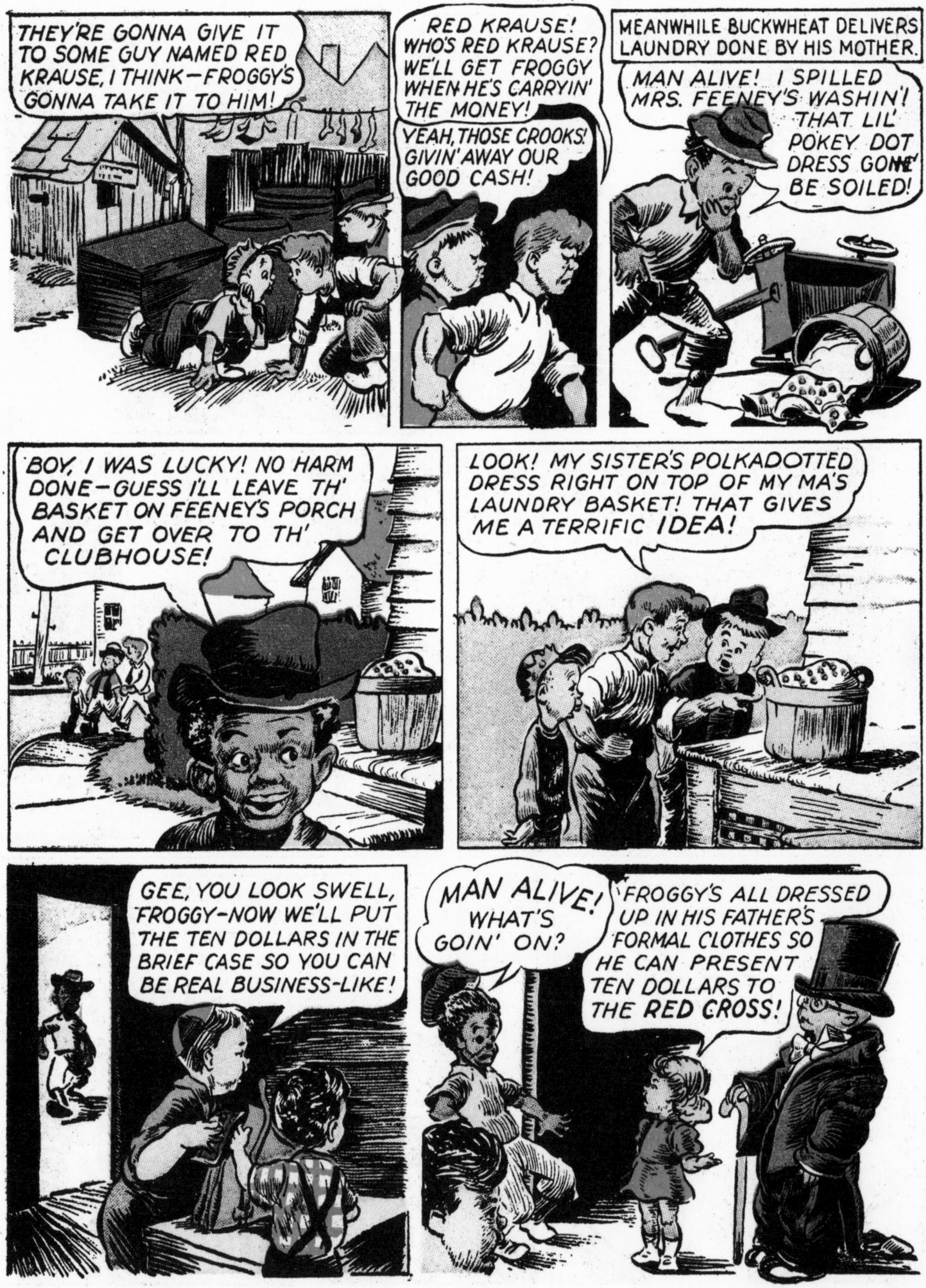
THEY'RE GONNA GIVE IT TO SOME GUY NAMED RED KRAUSE, I THINK—FROGGY'S GONNA TAKE IT TO HIM!
RED KRAUSE! WHO'S RED KRAUSE? WE'LL GET FROGGY WHEN HE'S CARRYIN' THE MONEY!
YEAH, THOSE CROOKS! GIVIN' AWAY OUR GOOD CASH!
MEANWHILE BUCKWHEAT DELIVERS LAUNDRY DONE BY HIS MOTHER.
MAN ALIVE! I SPILLED MRS. FEENEY'S WASHIN'! THAT LIL' POKEY DOT DRESS GONE BE SOILED!
BOY, I WAS LUCKY! NO HARM DONE—GUESS I'LL LEAVE TH' BASKET ON FEENEY'S PORCH AND GET OVER TO TH' CLUBHOUSE!
LOOK! MY SISTER'S POLKADOTTED DRESS RIGHT ON TOP OF MY MA'S LAUNDRY BASKET! THAT GIVES ME A TERRIFIC IDEA!
GEE, YOU LOOK SWELL, FROGGY—NOW WE'LL PUT THE TEN DOLLARS IN THE BRIEF CASE SO YOU CAN BE REAL BUSINESS-LIKE!
MAN ALIVE! WHAT'S GOIN' ON?
FROGGY'S ALL DRESSED UP IN HIS FATHER'S FORMAL CLOTHES SO HE CAN PRESENT TEN DOLLARS TO THE RED CROSS!

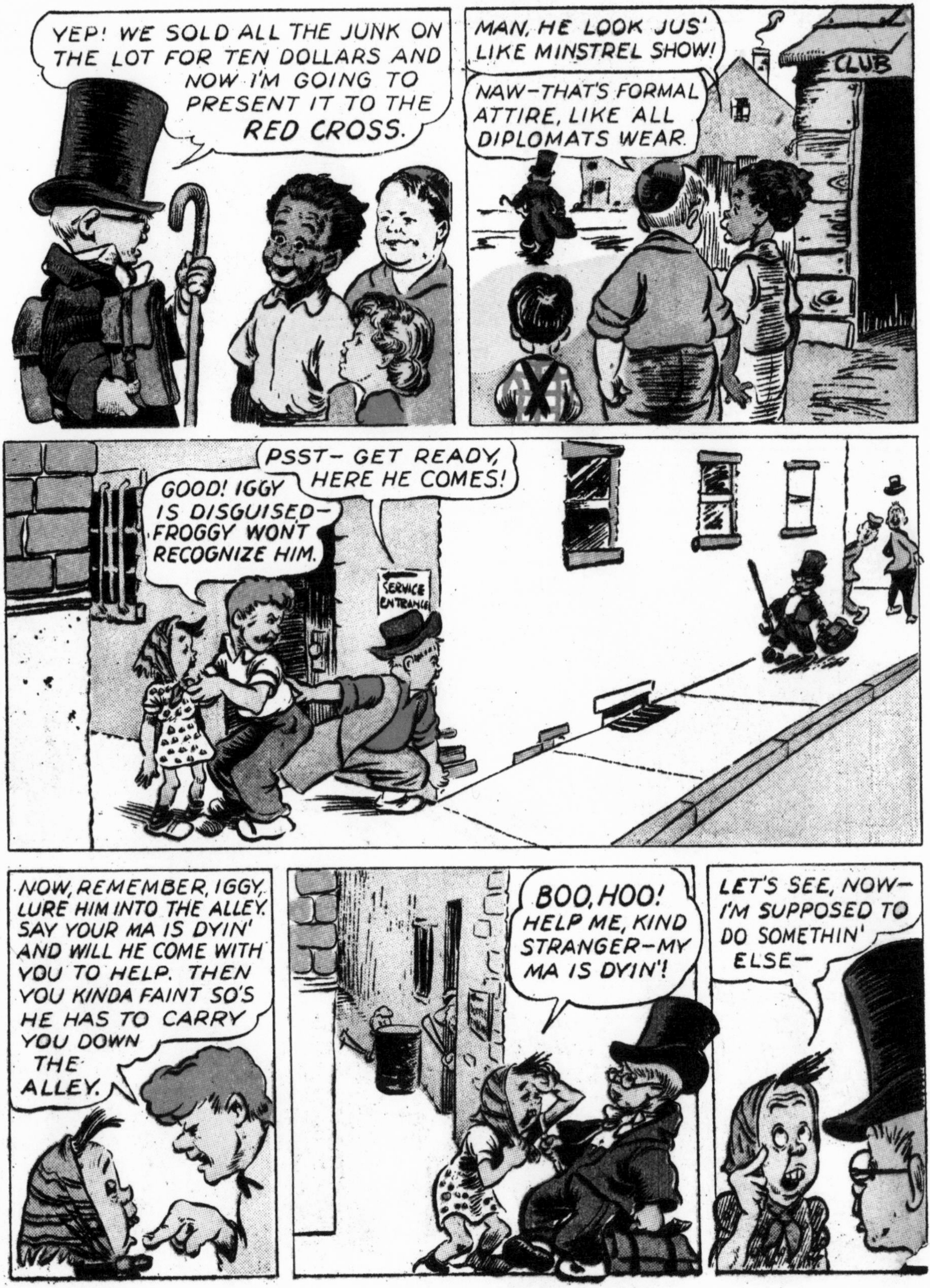
YEP! WE SOLD ALL THE JUNK ON THE LOT FOR TEN DOLLARS AND NOW I'M GOING TO PRESENT IT TO THE RED CROSS.
MAN, HE LOOK JUS' LIKE MINSTREL SHOW!
NAW—THAT'S FORMAL ATTIRE, LIKE ALL DIPLOMATS WEAR.
CLUB
GOOD! IGGY IS DISGUISED—FROGGY WON'T RECOGNIZE HIM.
PSST—GET READY, HERE HE COMES!
SERVICE ENTRANCE
NOW, REMEMBER, IGGY, LURE HIM INTO THE ALLEY. SAY YOUR MA IS DYIN' AND WILL HE COME WITH YOU TO HELP. THEN YOU KINDA FAINT SO'S HE HAS TO CARRY YOU DOWN THE ALLEY.
BOO, HOO! HELP ME, KIND STRANGER—MY MA IS DYIN'!
LET'S SEE, NOW—I'M SUPPOSED TO DO SOMETHIN' ELSE—

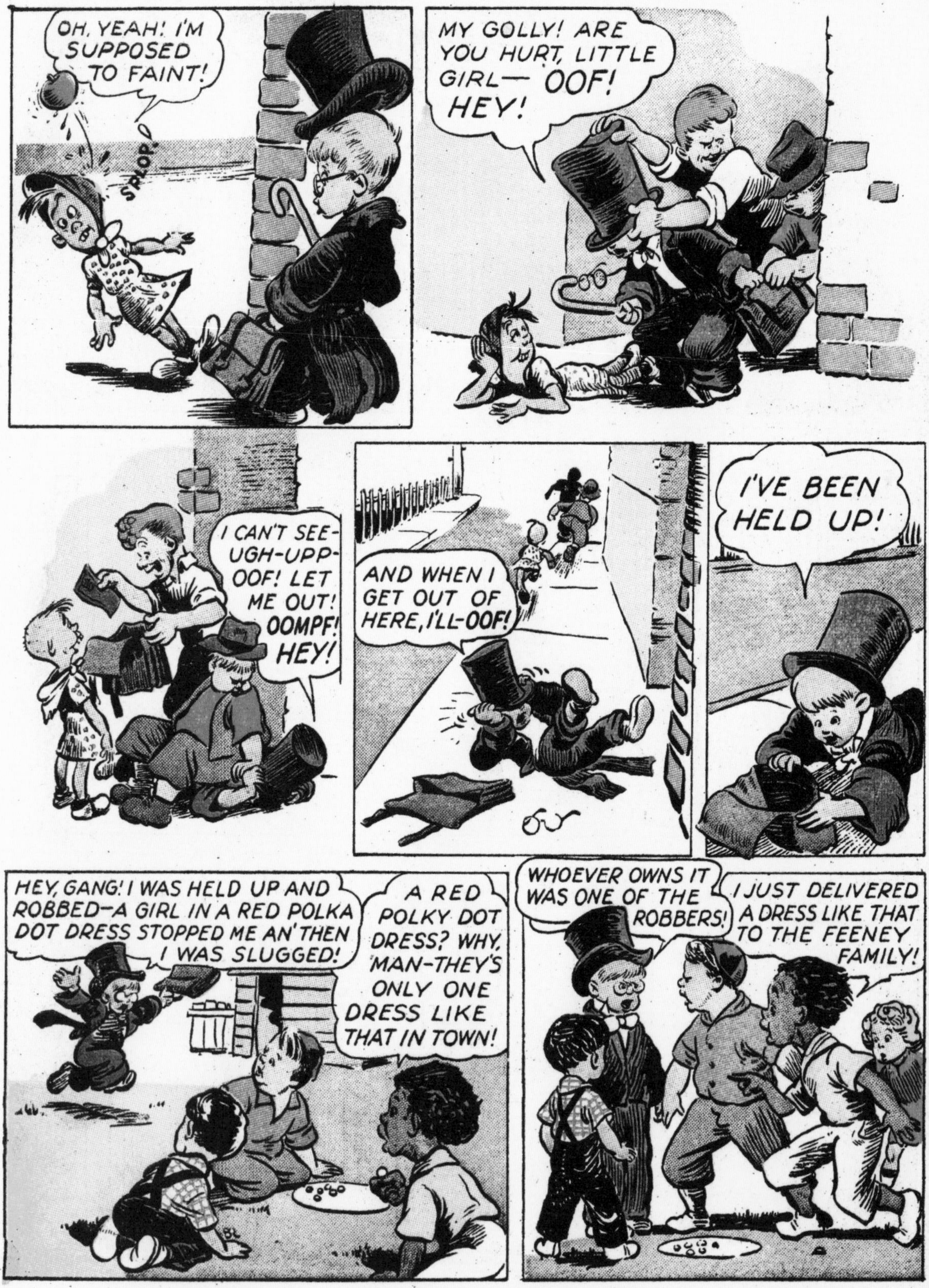
OH, YEAH! I'M SUPPOSED TO FAINT!
SPLOP
MY GOLLY! ARE YOU HURT, LITTLE GIRL— OOF! HEY!
I CAN'T SEE-UGH-UPP-OOF! LET ME OUT! OOMPF! HEY!
AND WHEN I GET OUT OF HERE, I'LL-OOF!
I'VE BEEN HELD UP!
HEY, GANG! I WAS HELD UP AND ROBBED—A GIRL IN A RED POLKA DOT DRESS STOPPED ME AN' THEN I WAS SLUGGED!
A RED POLKY DOT DRESS? WHY, MAN-THEY'S ONLY ONE DRESS LIKE THAT IN TOWN!
WHOEVER OWNS IT WAS ONE OF THE ROBBERS!
I JUST DELIVERED A DRESS LIKE THAT TO THE FEENEY FAMILY!

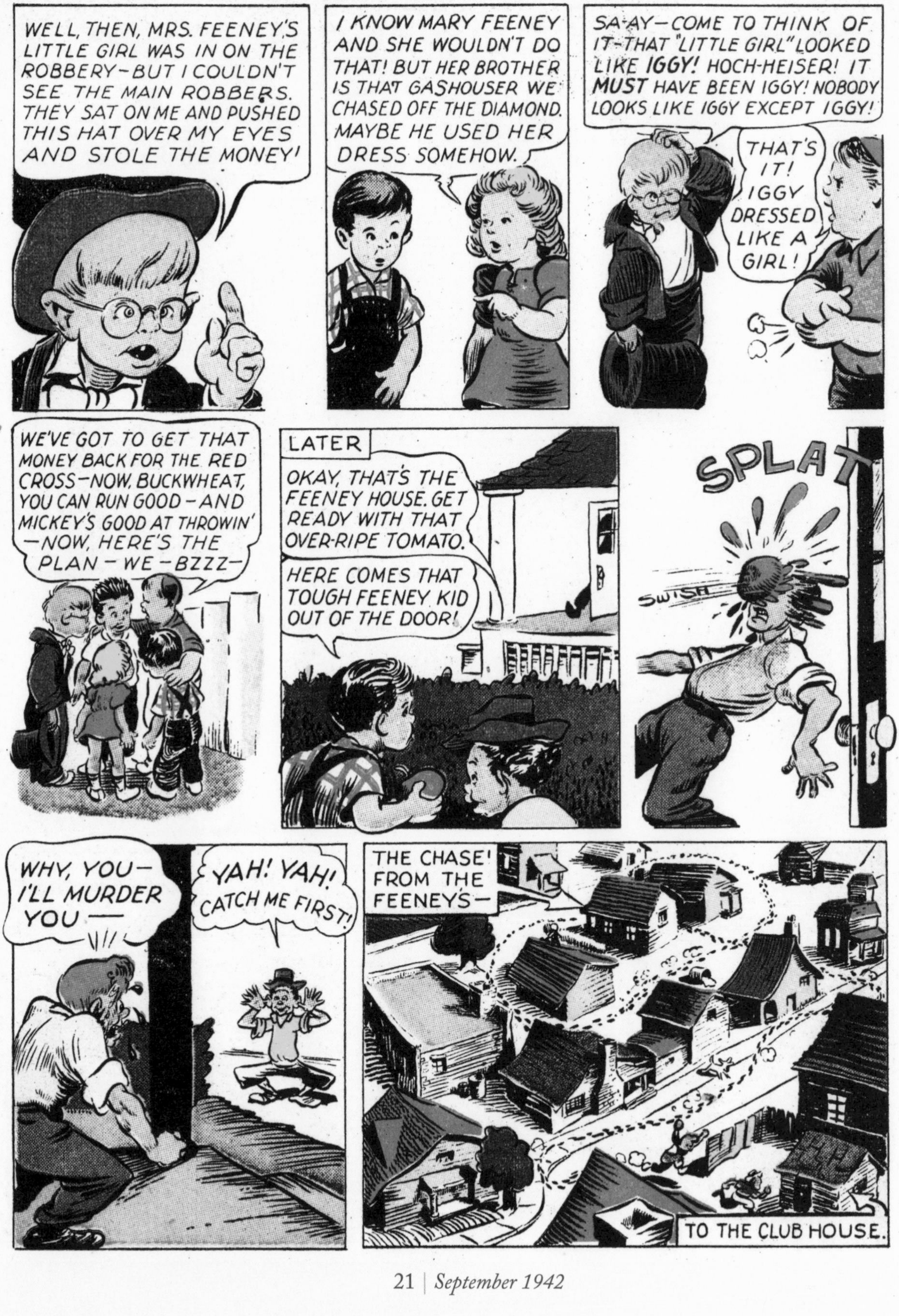

WELL, THEN, MRS. FEENEY'S LITTLE GIRL WAS IN ON THE ROBBERY—BUT I COULDN'T SEE THE MAIN ROBBERS. THEY SAT ON ME AND PUSHED THIS HAT OVER MY EYES AND STOLE THE MONEY!
I KNOW MARY FEENEY AND SHE WOULDN'T DO THAT! BUT HER BROTHER IS THAT GASHOUSER WE CHASED OFF THE DIAMOND. MAYBE HE USED HER DRESS SOMEHOW.
SA-AY—COME TO THINK OF IT—THAT "LITTLE GIRL" LOOKED LIKE IGGY! HOCH-HEISER! IT MUST HAVE BEEN IGGY! NOBODY LOOKS LIKE IGGY EXCEPT IGGY!
THAT'S IT! IGGY DRESSED LIKE A GIRL!
WE'VE GOT TO GET THAT MONEY BACK FOR THE RED CROSS—NOW, BUCKWHEAT, YOU CAN RUN GOOD—AND MICKEY'S GOOD AT THROWIN' —NOW, HERE'S THE PLAN—WE—BZZZ—
LATER
OKAY, THAT'S THE FEENEY HOUSE. GET READY WITH THAT OVER-RIPE TOMATO.
HERE COMES THAT TOUGH FEENEY KID OUT OF THE DOOR!
SPLAT
SWISH
WHY, YOU— I'LL MURDER YOU—
YAH! YAH! CATCH ME FIRST!
THE CHASE! FROM THE FEENEY'S—
TO THE CLUB HOUSE.

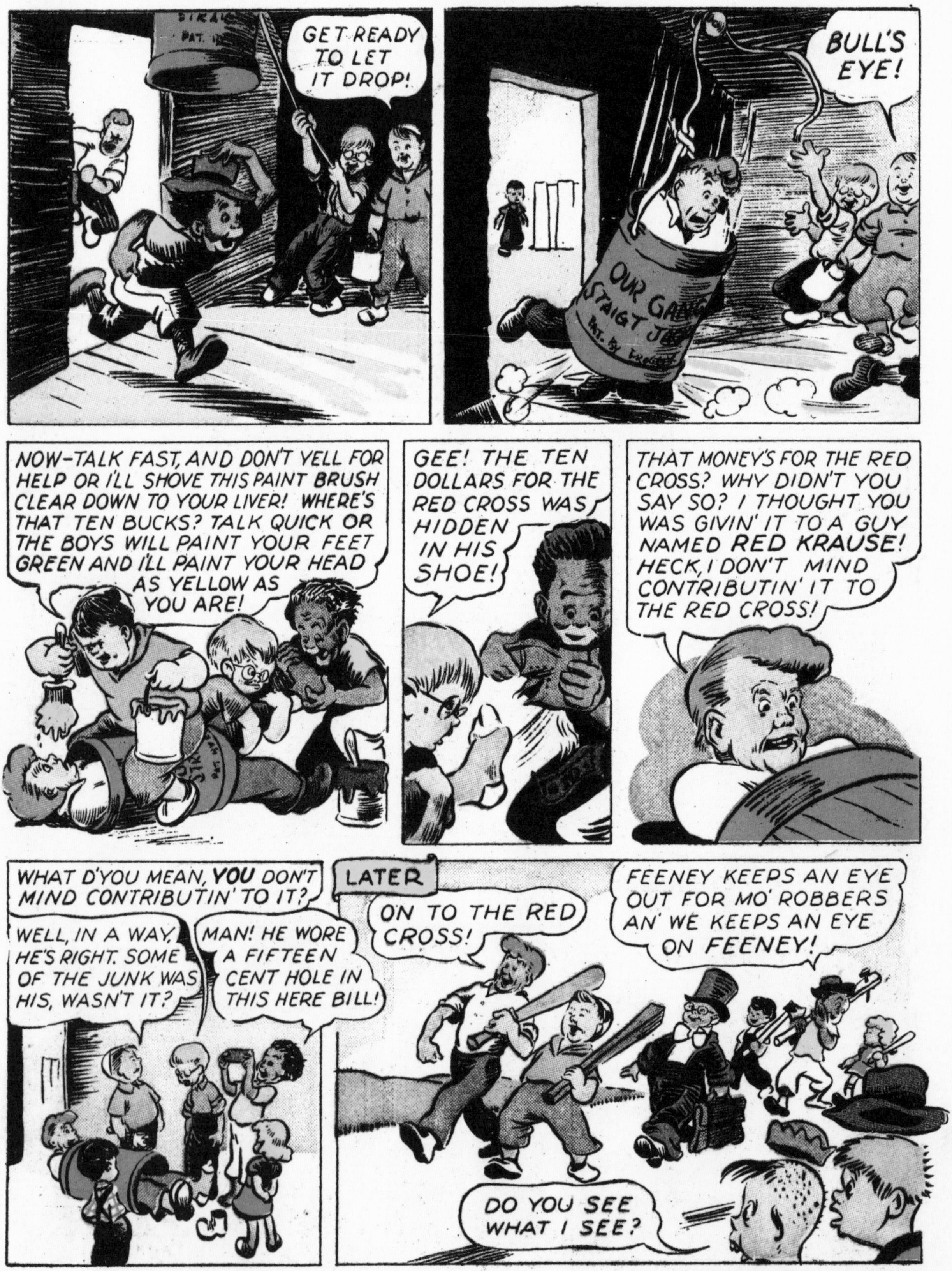
GET READY TO LET IT DROP!
BULL'S EYE!
OUR GANG STAIGT JA
NOW–TALK FAST, AND DON'T YELL FOR HELP OR I'LL SHOVE THIS PAINT BRUSH CLEAR DOWN TO YOUR LIVER! WHERE'S THAT TEN BUCKS? TALK QUICK OR THE BOYS WILL PAINT YOUR FEET GREEN AND I'LL PAINT YOUR HEAD AS YELLOW AS YOU ARE!
GEE! THE TEN DOLLARS FOR THE RED CROSS WAS HIDDEN IN HIS SHOE!
THAT MONEY'S FOR THE RED CROSS? WHY DIDN'T YOU SAY SO? I THOUGHT YOU WAS GIVIN' IT TO A GUY NAMED RED KRAUSE! HECK, I DON'T MIND CONTRIBUTIN' IT TO THE RED CROSS!
WHAT D'YOU MEAN, YOU DON'T MIND CONTRIBUTIN' TO IT?
WELL, IN A WAY, HE'S RIGHT. SOME OF THE JUNK WAS HIS, WASN'T IT?
MAN! HE WORE A FIFTEEN CENT HOLE IN THIS HERE BILL!
LATER
ON TO THE RED CROSS!
FEENEY KEEPS AN EYE OUT FOR MO' ROBBERS AN' WE KEEPS AN EYE ON FEENEY!
DO YOU SEE WHAT I SEE?

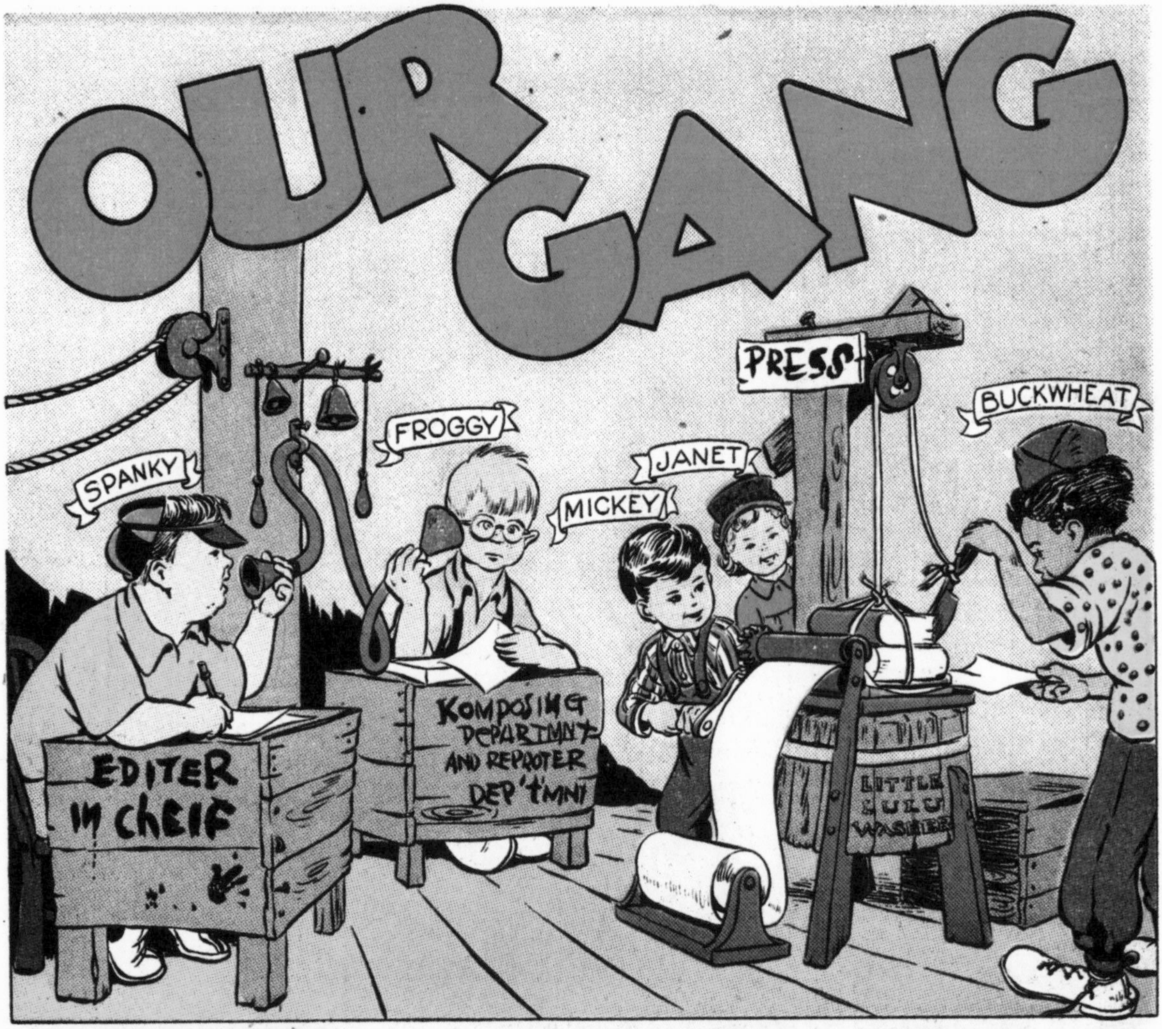
OUR GANG
PRESS
BUCKWHEAT
FROGGY
JANET
SPANKY
MICKEY
KOMPOSING DEPARTMNT AND REPROTER DEP'TMNT
EDITER IN CHEIF
LITTLE LULU WASHER

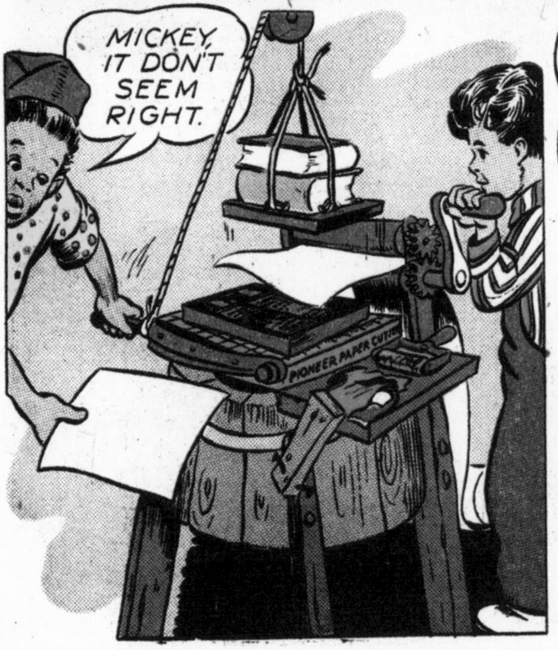
MICKEY, IT DON'T SEEM RIGHT.
PIONEER PAPER CUTTER

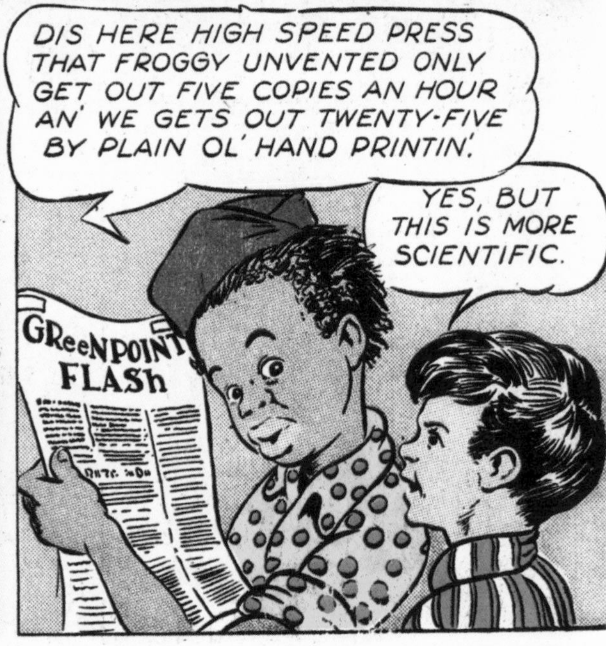
DIS HERE HIGH SPEED PRESS THAT FROGGY UNVENTED ONLY GET OUT FIVE COPIES AN HOUR AN' WE GETS OUT TWENTY-FIVE BY PLAIN OL' HAND PRINTIN'.
YES, BUT THIS IS MORE SCIENTIFIC.
GREENPOINT FLASH

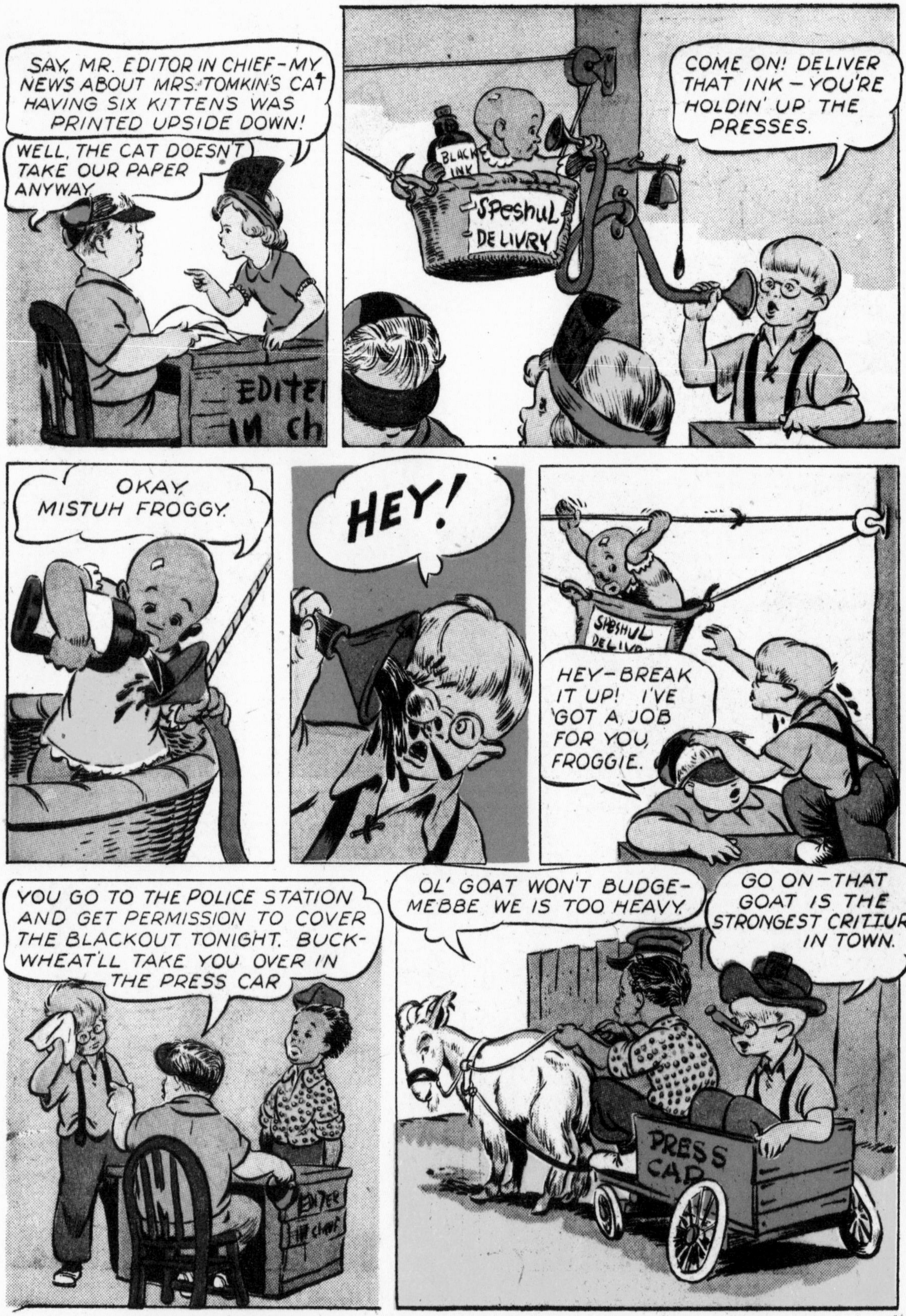

SAY, MR. EDITOR IN CHIEF—MY NEWS ABOUT MRS. TOMKIN'S CAT HAVING SIX KITTENS WAS PRINTED UPSIDE DOWN!
WELL, THE CAT DOESN'T TAKE OUR PAPER ANYWAY.
EDITER IN CH
BLACK INK
SPESHUL DELIVRY
COME ON! DELIVER THAT INK—YOU'RE HOLDIN' UP THE PRESSES.
OKAY, MISTUH FROGGY.
HEY!
SPESHUL DELIVR
HEY—BREAK IT UP! I'VE GOT A JOB FOR YOU, FROGGIE.
YOU GO TO THE POLICE STATION AND GET PERMISSION TO COVER THE BLACKOUT TONIGHT. BUCKWHEAT'LL TAKE YOU OVER IN THE PRESS CAR
EDITER IN CHIEF
OL' GOAT WON'T BUDGE—MEBBE WE IS TOO HEAVY.
GO ON—THAT GOAT IS THE STRONGEST CRITTUR IN TOWN.
PRESS CAR

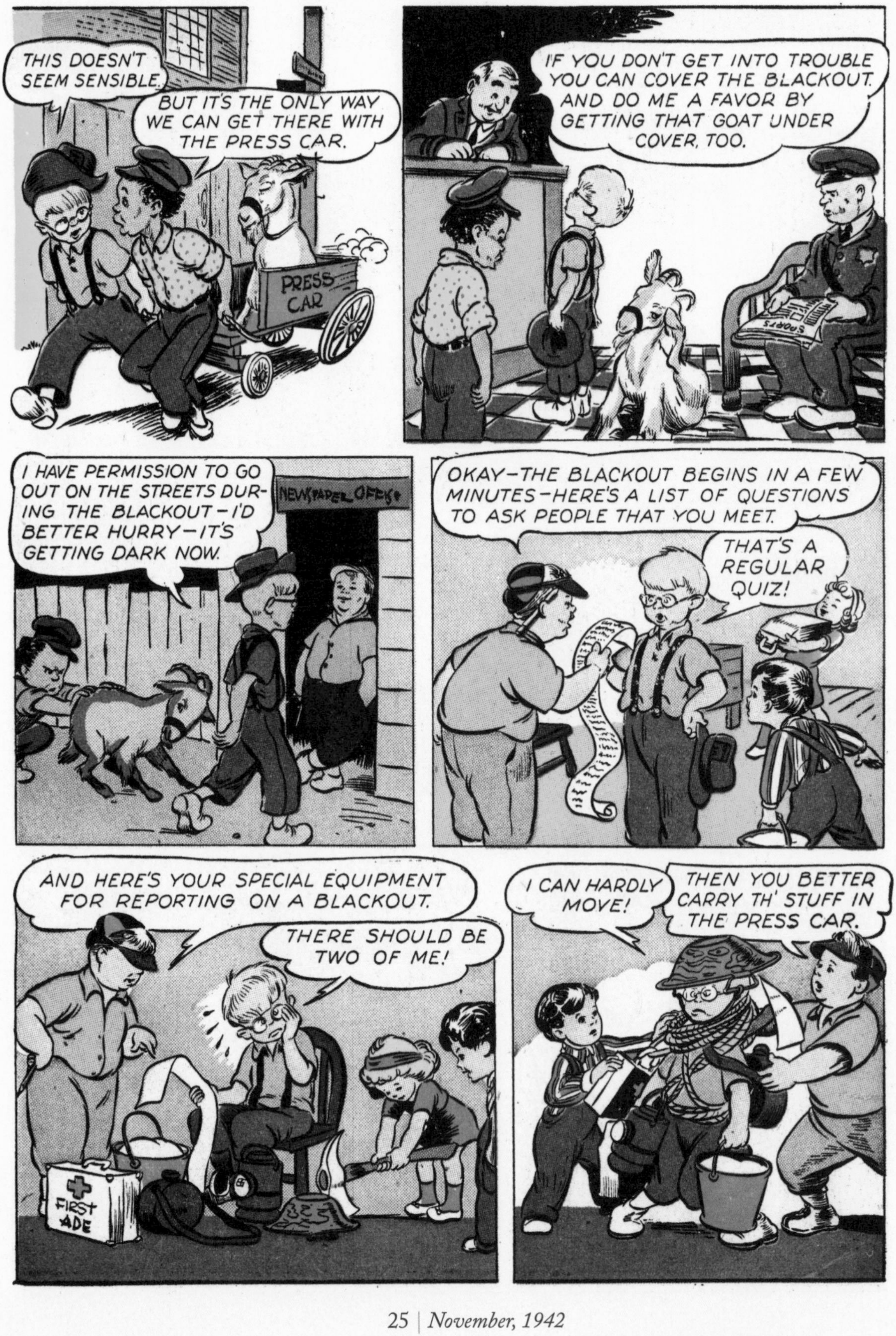

THIS DOESN'T SEEM SENSIBLE.
BUT IT'S THE ONLY WAY WE CAN GET THERE WITH THE PRESS CAR.
PRESS CAR
IF YOU DON'T GET INTO TROUBLE YOU CAN COVER THE BLACKOUT. AND DO ME A FAVOR BY GETTING THAT GOAT UNDER COVER, TOO.
SPORTS
I HAVE PERMISSION TO GO OUT ON THE STREETS DURING THE BLACKOUT—I'D BETTER HURRY—IT'S GETTING DARK NOW.
OKAY—THE BLACKOUT BEGINS IN A FEW MINUTES—HERE'S A LIST OF QUESTIONS TO ASK PEOPLE THAT YOU MEET.
THAT'S A REGULAR QUIZ!
AND HERE'S YOUR SPECIAL EQUIPMENT FOR REPORTING ON A BLACKOUT.
THERE SHOULD BE TWO OF ME!
FIRST ADE
I CAN HARDLY MOVE!
THEN YOU BETTER CARRY TH' STUFF IN THE PRESS CAR.

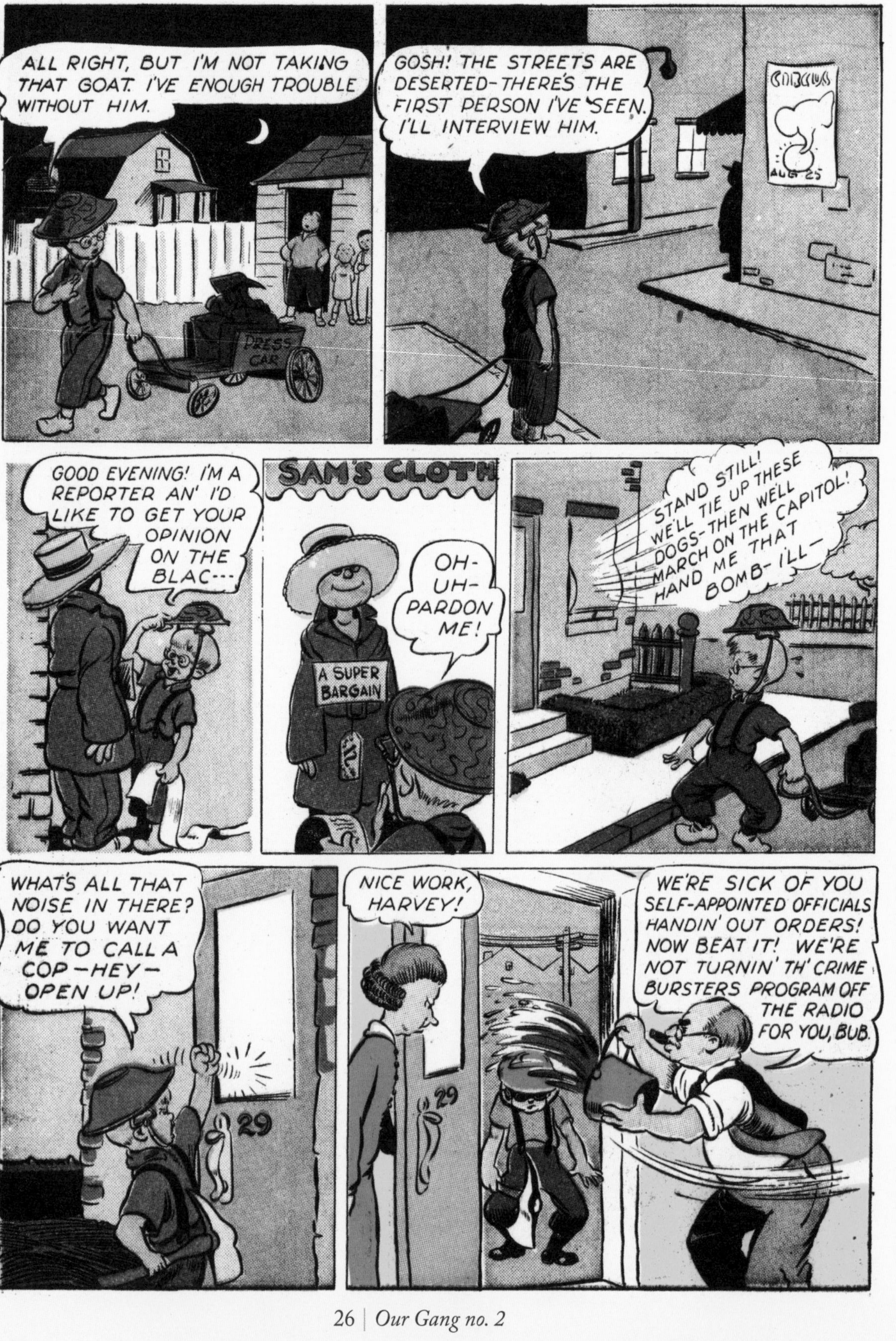
ALL RIGHT, BUT I'M NOT TAKING THAT GOAT. I'VE ENOUGH TROUBLE WITHOUT HIM.
PRESS CAR
GOSH! THE STREETS ARE DESERTED-THERE'S THE FIRST PERSON I'VE SEEN. I'LL INTERVIEW HIM.
AUG 25
GOOD EVENING! I'M A REPORTER AN' I'D LIKE TO GET YOUR OPINION ON THE BLAC---
SAM'S CLOTH
OH-UH-PARDON ME!
A SUPER BARGAIN
STAND STILL! WE'LL TIE UP THESE DOGS-THEN WE'LL MARCH ON THE CAPITOL! HAND ME THAT BOMB-I'LL-
WHAT'S ALL THAT NOISE IN THERE? DO YOU WANT ME TO CALL A COP-HEY-OPEN UP!
29
NICE WORK, HARVEY!
WE'RE SICK OF YOU SELF-APPOINTED OFFICIALS HANDIN' OUT ORDERS! NOW BEAT IT! WE'RE NOT TURNIN' TH' CRIME BUSTERS PROGRAM OFF THE RADIO FOR YOU, BUB.

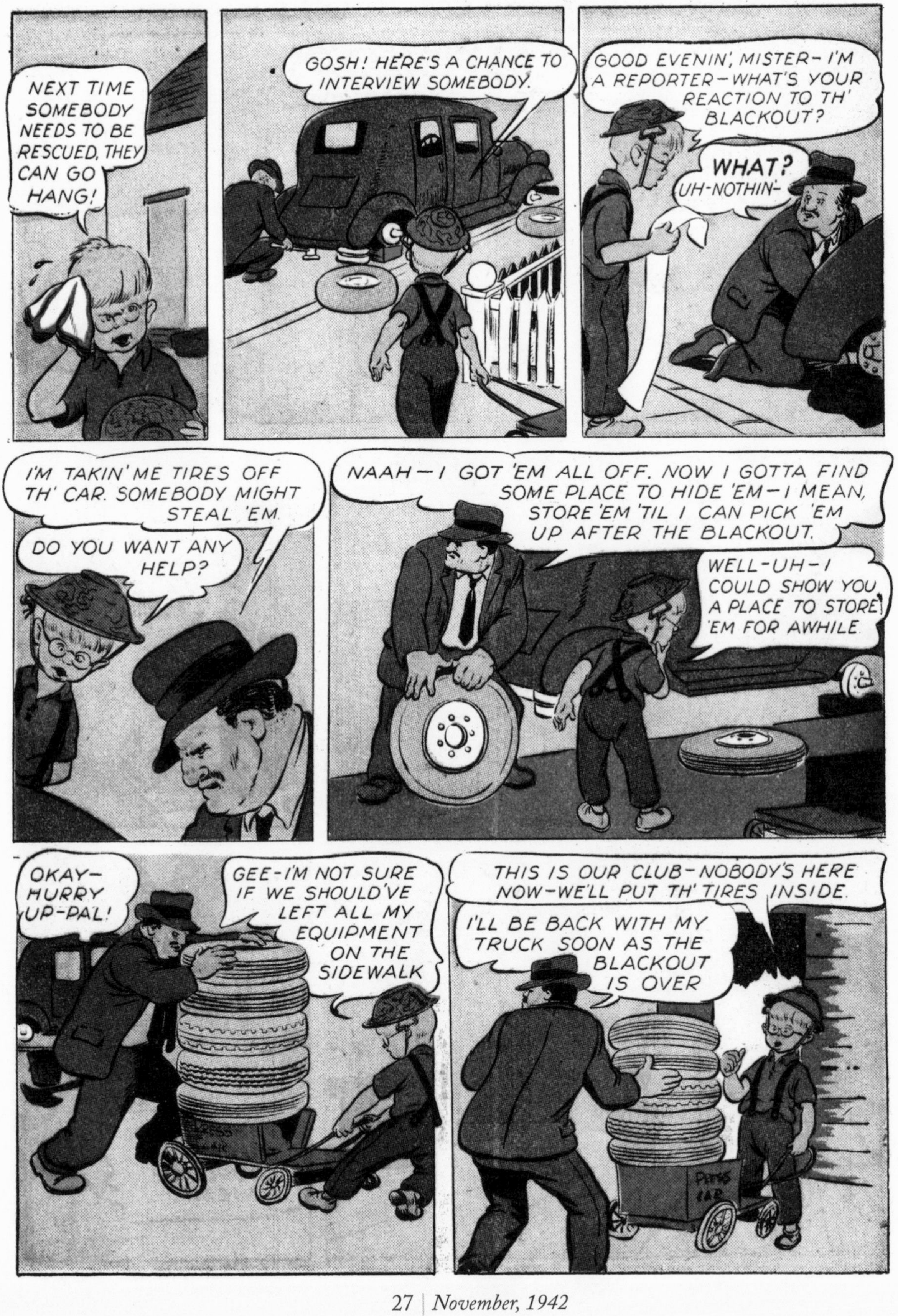

NEXT TIME SOMEBODY NEEDS TO BE RESCUED, THEY CAN GO HANG!
GOSH! HERE'S A CHANCE TO INTERVIEW SOMEBODY.
GOOD EVENIN', MISTER- I'M A REPORTER-WHAT'S YOUR REACTION TO TH' BLACKOUT?
WHAT? UH-NOTHIN-
I'M TAKIN' ME TIRES OFF TH' CAR. SOMEBODY MIGHT STEAL 'EM.
DO YOU WANT ANY HELP?
NAAH-I GOT 'EM ALL OFF. NOW I GOTTA FIND SOME PLACE TO HIDE 'EM-I MEAN, STORE 'EM 'TIL I CAN PICK 'EM UP AFTER THE BLACKOUT.
WELL-UH-I COULD SHOW YOU A PLACE TO STORE 'EM FOR AWHILE.
OKAY-HURRY UP-PAL!
GEE-I'M NOT SURE IF WE SHOULD'VE LEFT ALL MY EQUIPMENT ON THE SIDEWALK
THIS IS OUR CLUB-NOBODY'S HERE NOW-WE'LL PUT TH' TIRES INSIDE.
I'LL BE BACK WITH MY TRUCK SOON AS THE BLACKOUT IS OVER

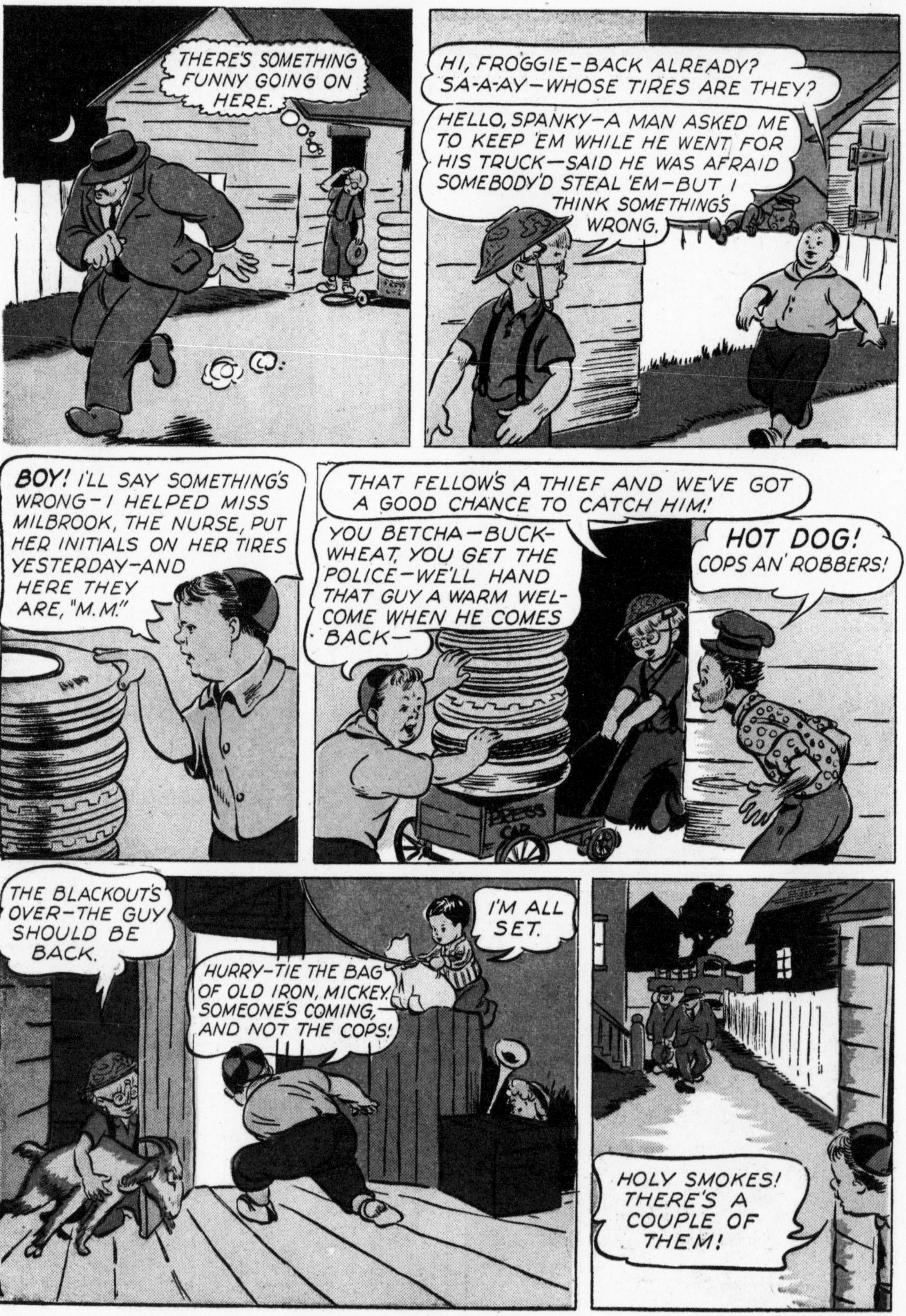
THERE'S SOMETHING FUNNY GOING ON HERE.
HI, FROGGIE-BACK ALREADY? SA-A-AY-WHOSE TIRES ARE THEY?
HELLO, SPANKY-A MAN ASKED ME TO KEEP 'EM WHILE HE WENT FOR HIS TRUCK-SAID HE WAS AFRAID SOMEBODY'D STEAL 'EM-BUT I THINK SOMETHING'S WRONG.
BOY! I'LL SAY SOMETHING'S WRONG-I HELPED MISS MILBROOK, THE NURSE, PUT HER INITIALS ON HER TIRES YESTERDAY-AND HERE THEY ARE, "M.M."
THAT FELLOW'S A THIEF AND WE'VE GOT A GOOD CHANCE TO CATCH HIM!
YOU BETCHA-BUCKWHEAT, YOU GET THE POLICE-WE'LL HAND THAT GUY A WARM WELCOME WHEN HE COMES BACK-
HOT DOG! COPS AN' ROBBERS!
THE BLACKOUT'S OVER-THE GUY SHOULD BE BACK.
I'M ALL SET.
HURRY-TIE THE BAG OF OLD IRON, MICKEY. SOMEONE'S COMING, AND NOT THE COPS!
HOLY SMOKES! THERE'S A COUPLE OF THEM!

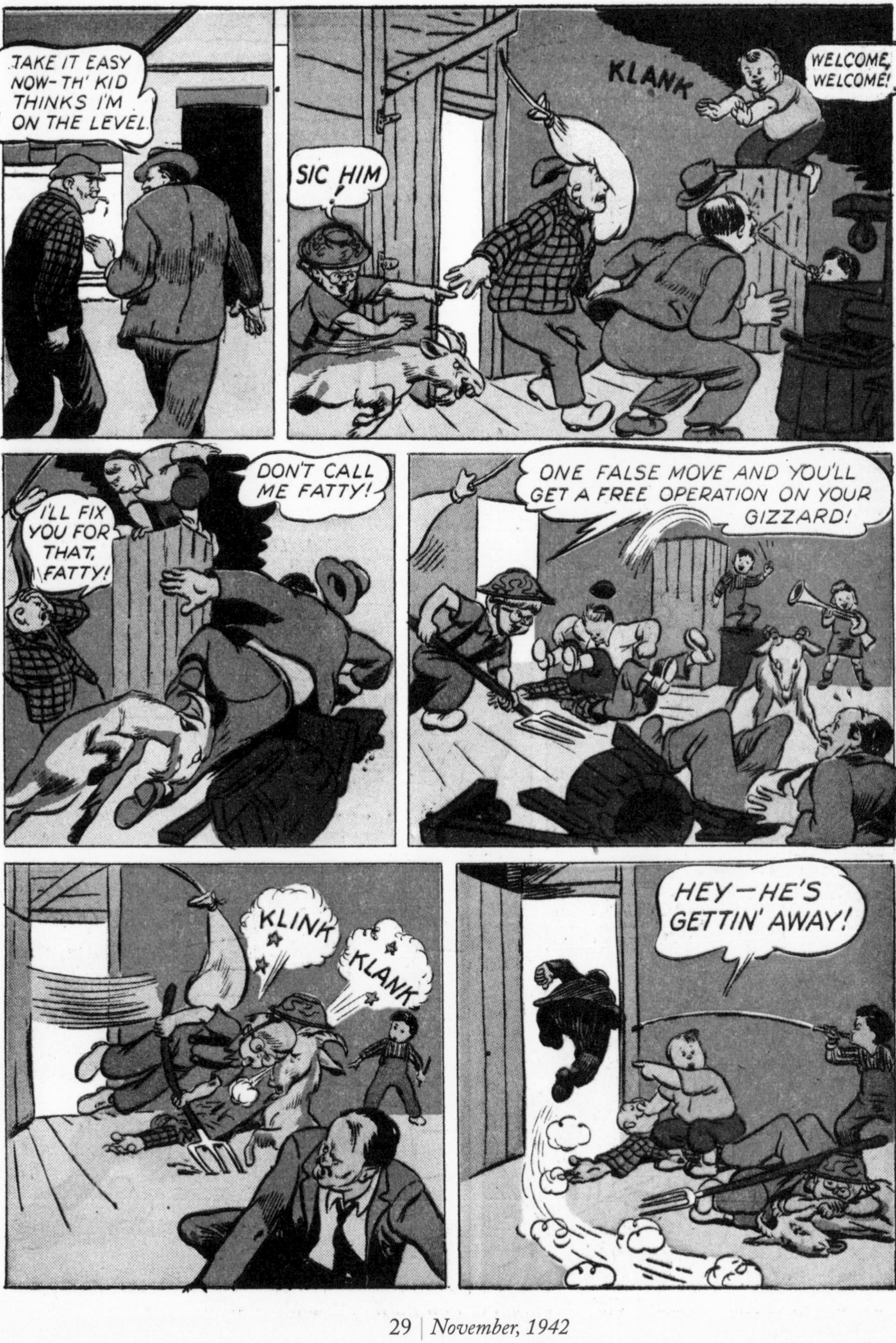
TAKE IT EASY NOW-TH' KID THINKS I'M ON THE LEVEL.
SIC HIM!
KLANK
WELCOME, WELCOME!
DON'T CALL ME FATTY!
I'LL FIX YOU FOR THAT, FATTY!
ONE FALSE MOVE AND YOU'LL GET A FREE OPERATION ON YOUR GIZZARD!
KLINK
KLANK
HEY-HE'S GETTIN' AWAY!

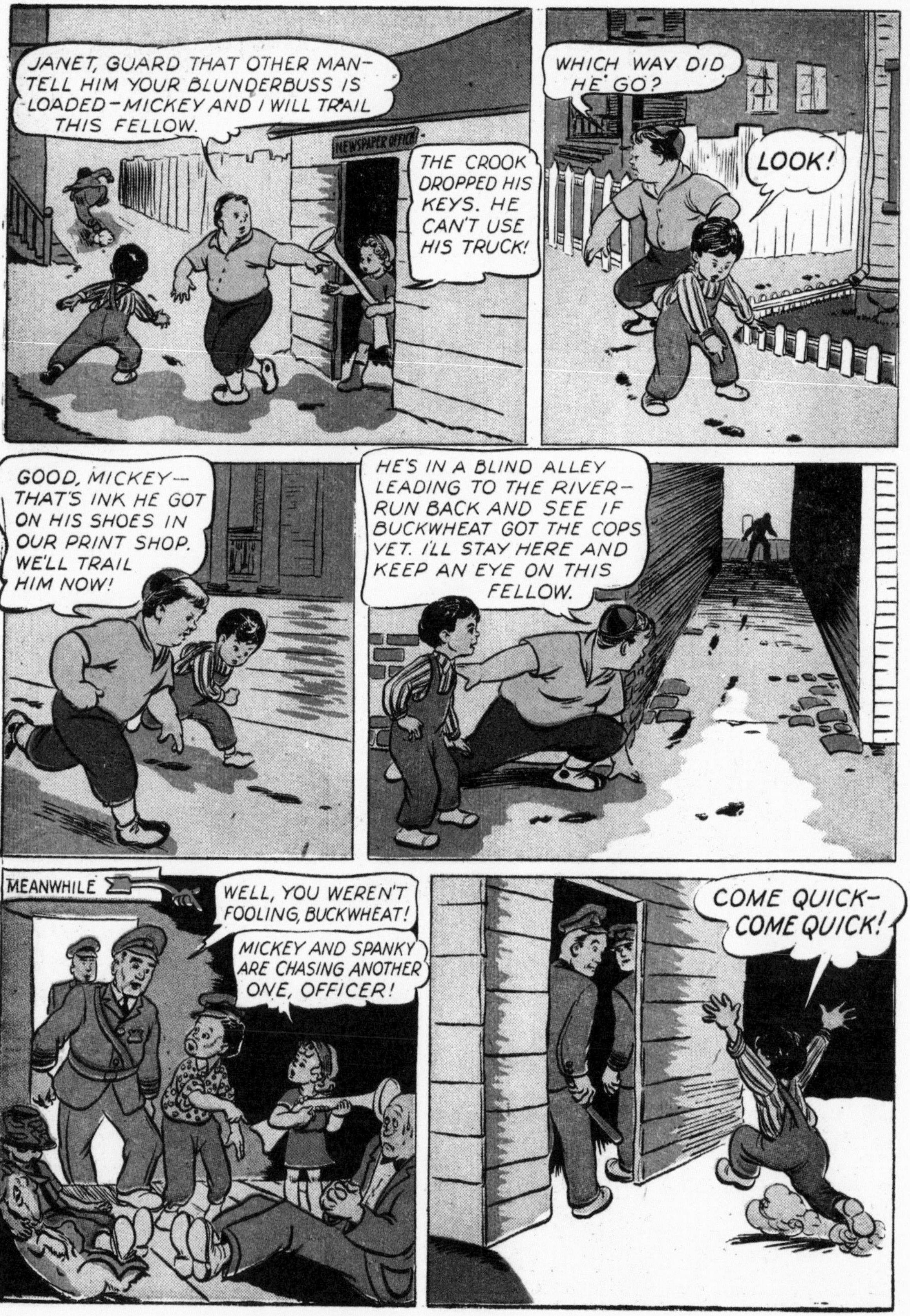
JANET, GUARD THAT OTHER MAN- TELL HIM YOUR BLUNDERBUSS IS LOADED - MICKEY AND I WILL TRAIL THIS FELLOW.
NEWSPAPER OFFICE
THE CROOK DROPPED HIS KEYS. HE CAN'T USE HIS TRUCK!
WHICH WAY DID HE GO?
LOOK!
GOOD, MICKEY— THAT'S INK HE GOT ON HIS SHOES IN OUR PRINT SHOP. WE'LL TRAIL HIM NOW!
HE'S IN A BLIND ALLEY LEADING TO THE RIVER- RUN BACK AND SEE IF BUCKWHEAT GOT THE COPS YET. I'LL STAY HERE AND KEEP AN EYE ON THIS FELLOW.
MEANWHILE
WELL, YOU WEREN'T FOOLING, BUCKWHEAT!
MICKEY AND SPANKY ARE CHASING ANOTHER ONE, OFFICER!
COME QUICK- COME QUICK!

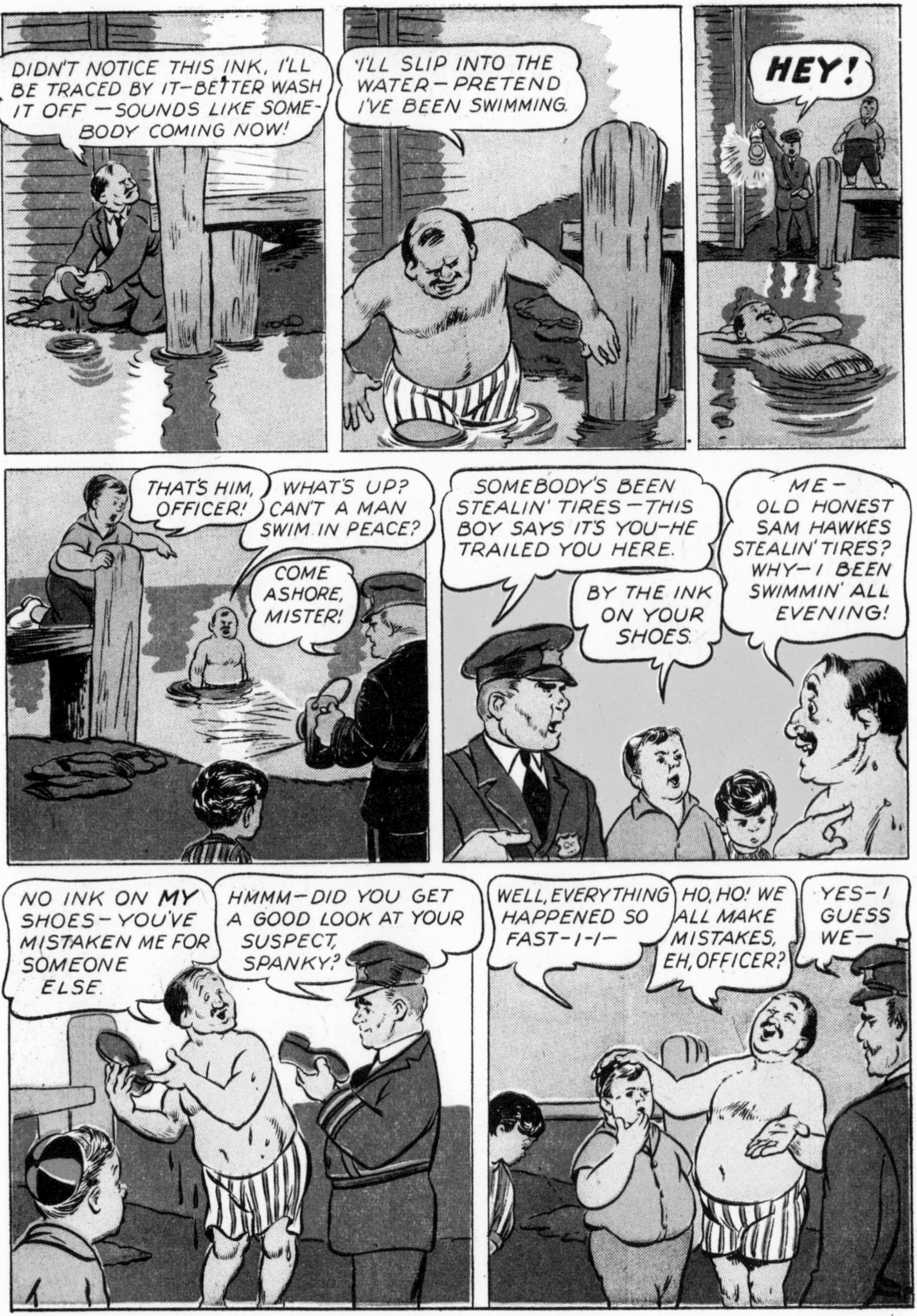
DIDN'T NOTICE THIS INK, I'LL BE TRACED BY IT—BETTER WASH IT OFF —SOUNDS LIKE SOME-BODY COMING NOW!
I'LL SLIP INTO THE WATER—PRETEND I'VE BEEN SWIMMING.
HEY!
THAT'S HIM, OFFICER!
WHAT'S UP? CAN'T A MAN SWIM IN PEACE?
COME ASHORE, MISTER!
SOMEBODY'S BEEN STEALIN' TIRES—THIS BOY SAYS IT'S YOU—HE TRAILED YOU HERE.
BY THE INK ON YOUR SHOES.
ME—OLD HONEST SAM HAWKES STEALIN' TIRES? WHY—I BEEN SWIMMIN' ALL EVENING!
NO INK ON MY SHOES—YOU'VE MISTAKEN ME FOR SOMEONE ELSE.
HMMM—DID YOU GET A GOOD LOOK AT YOUR SUSPECT, SPANKY?
WELL, EVERYTHING HAPPENED SO FAST-I-I—
HO, HO! WE ALL MAKE MISTAKES, EH, OFFICER?
YES—I GUESS WE—

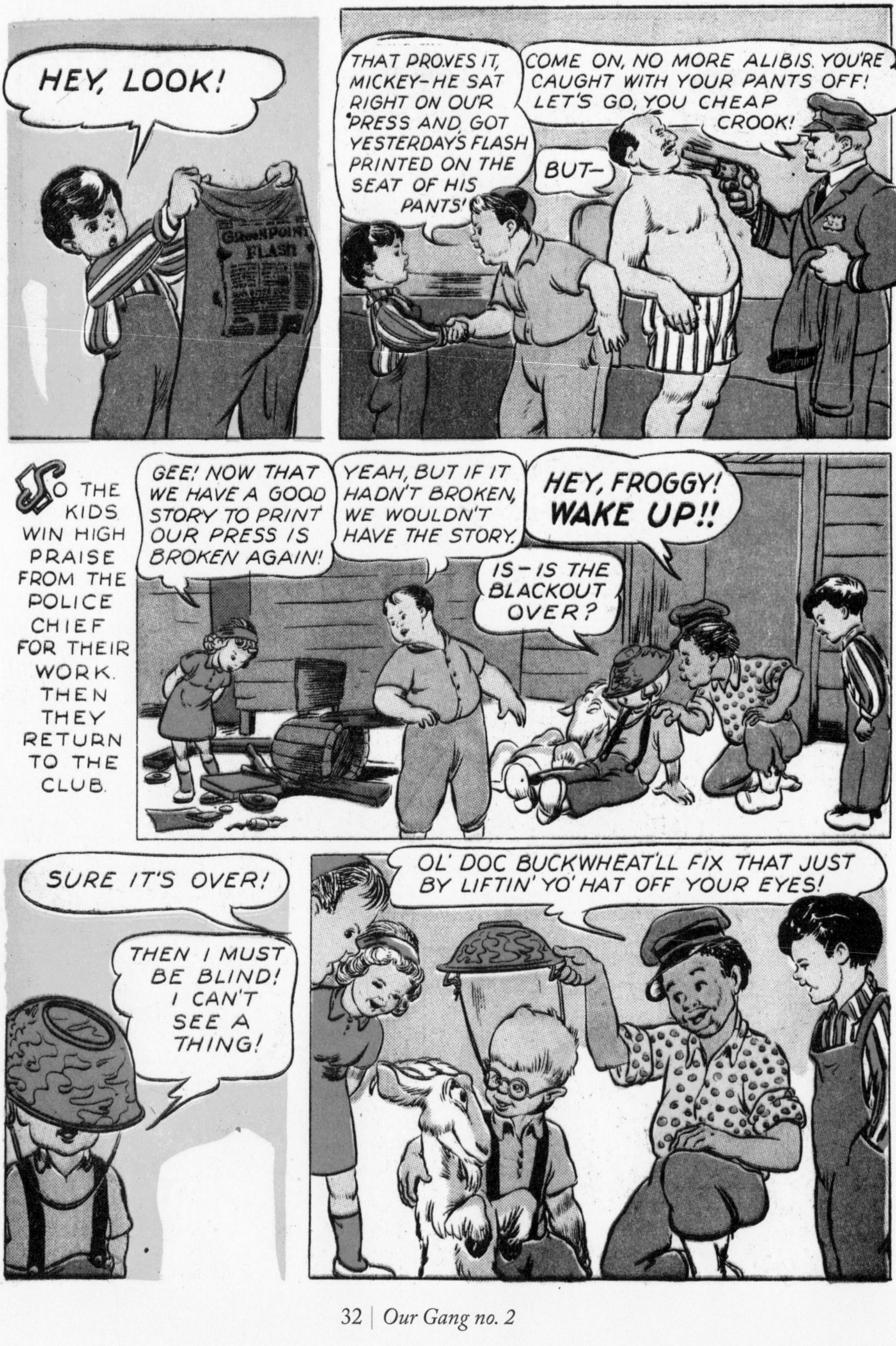
HEY, LOOK!
THAT PROVES IT, MICKEY—HE SAT RIGHT ON OUR PRESS AND GOT YESTERDAY'S FLASH PRINTED ON THE SEAT OF HIS PANTS!
COME ON, NO MORE ALIBIS. YOU'RE CAUGHT WITH YOUR PANTS OFF! LET'S GO, YOU CHEAP CROOK!
BUT—
SO THE KIDS WIN HIGH PRAISE FROM THE POLICE CHIEF FOR THEIR WORK. THEN THEY RETURN TO THE CLUB.
GEE! NOW THAT WE HAVE A GOOD STORY TO PRINT OUR PRESS IS BROKEN AGAIN!
YEAH, BUT IF IT HADN'T BROKEN, WE WOULDN'T HAVE THE STORY.
HEY, FROGGY! WAKE UP!!
IS—IS THE BLACKOUT OVER?
SURE IT'S OVER!
THEN I MUST BE BLIND! I CAN'T SEE A THING!
OL' DOC BUCKWHEAT'LL FIX THAT JUST BY LIFTIN' YO' HAT OFF YOUR EYES!

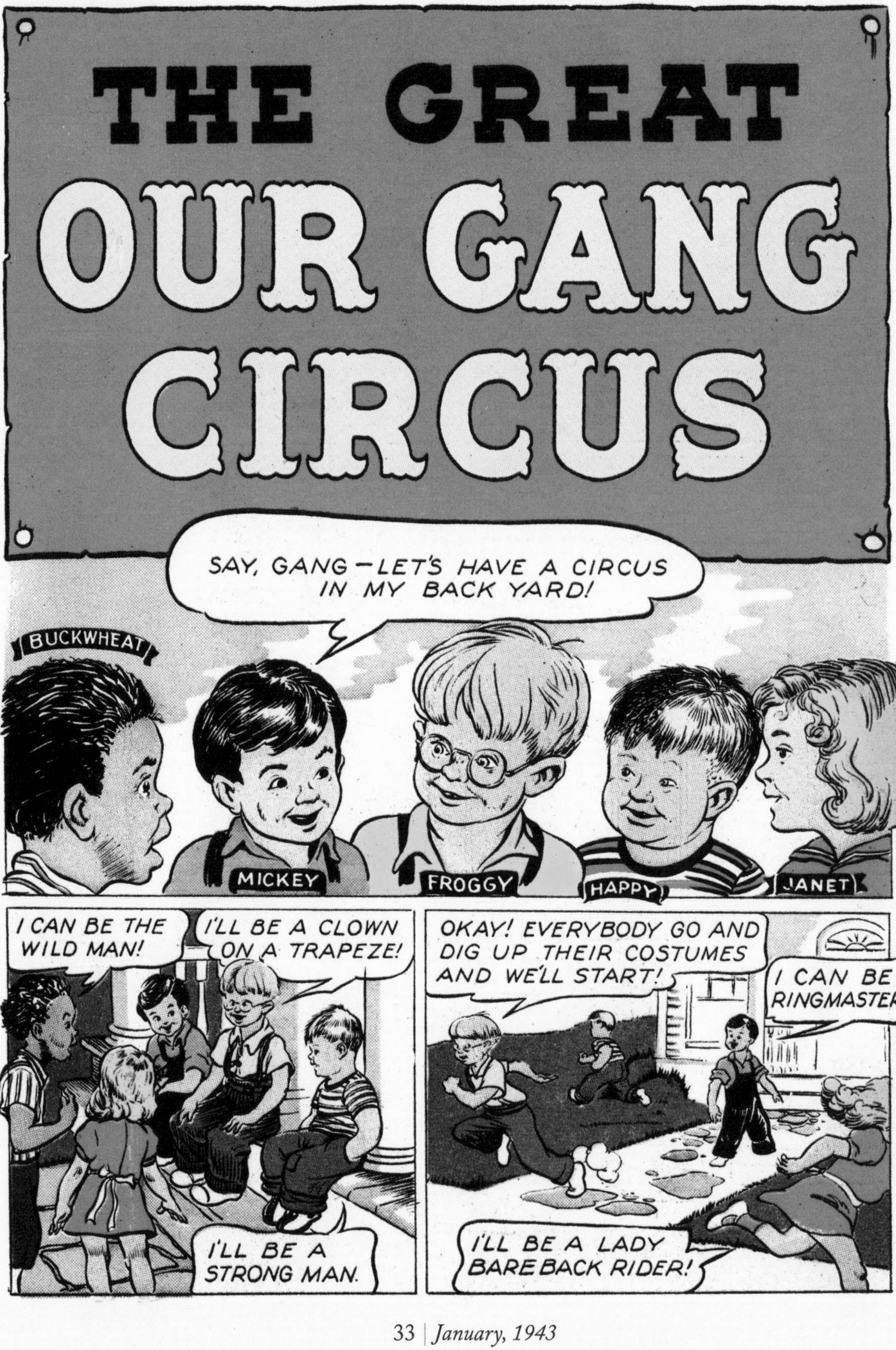
THE GREAT
OUR GANG
CIRCUS
SAY, GANG—LET'S HAVE A CIRCUS IN MY BACK YARD!
BUCKWHEAT
MICKEY
FROGGY
HAPPY
JANET
I CAN BE THE WILD MAN!
I'LL BE A CLOWN ON A TRAPEZE!
I'LL BE A STRONG MAN.
OKAY! EVERYBODY GO AND DIG UP THEIR COSTUMES AND WE'LL START!
I CAN BE RINGMASTER.
I'LL BE A LADY BAREBACK RIDER!

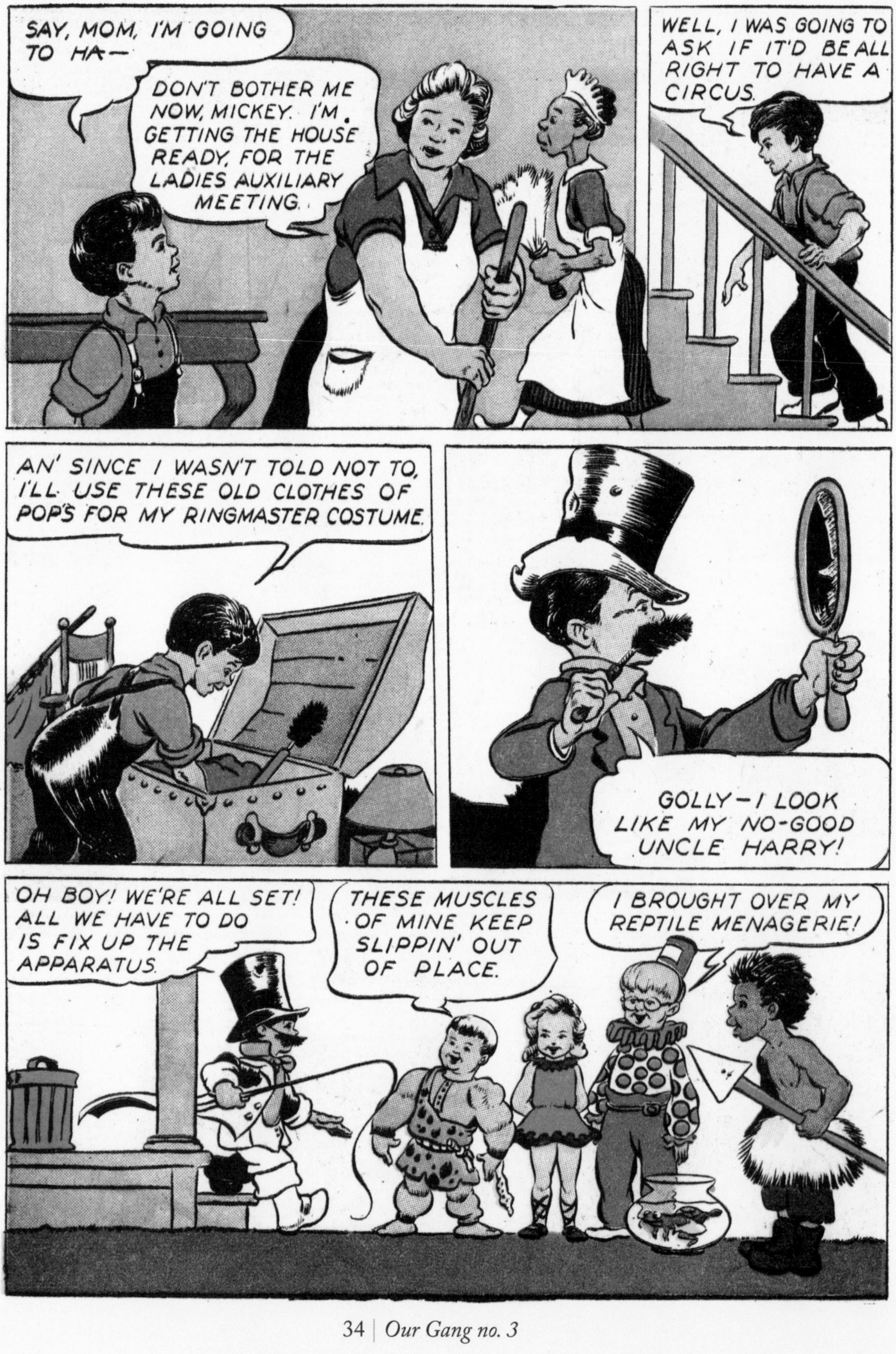
SAY, MOM, I'M GOING TO HA—
DON'T BOTHER ME NOW, MICKEY. I'M GETTING THE HOUSE READY, FOR THE LADIES AUXILIARY MEETING.
WELL, I WAS GOING TO ASK IF IT'D BE ALL RIGHT TO HAVE A CIRCUS.
AN' SINCE I WASN'T TOLD NOT TO, I'LL USE THESE OLD CLOTHES OF POP'S FOR MY RINGMASTER COSTUME.
GOLLY—I LOOK LIKE MY NO-GOOD UNCLE HARRY!
OH BOY! WE'RE ALL SET! ALL WE HAVE TO DO IS FIX UP THE APPARATUS.
THESE MUSCLES OF MINE KEEP SLIPPIN' OUT OF PLACE.
I BROUGHT OVER MY REPTILE MENAGERIE!

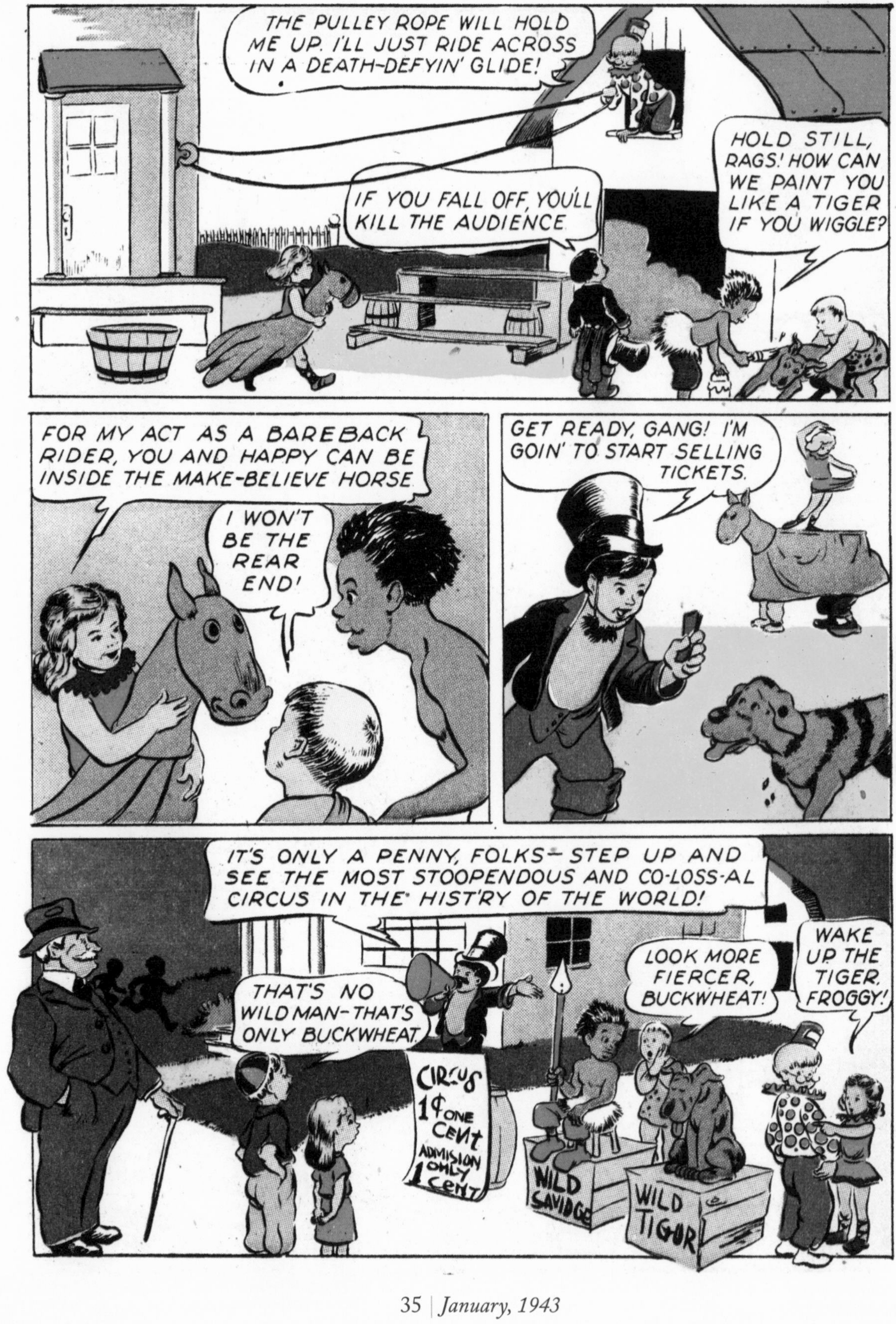
THE PULLEY ROPE WILL HOLD ME UP. I'LL JUST RIDE ACROSS IN A DEATH-DEFYIN' GLIDE!
IF YOU FALL OFF, YOU'LL KILL THE AUDIENCE.
HOLD STILL, RAGS! HOW CAN WE PAINT YOU LIKE A TIGER IF YOU WIGGLE?
FOR MY ACT AS A BAREBACK RIDER, YOU AND HAPPY CAN BE INSIDE THE MAKE-BELIEVE HORSE.
I WON'T BE THE REAR END!
GET READY, GANG! I'M GOIN' TO START SELLING TICKETS.
IT'S ONLY A PENNY, FOLKS— STEP UP AND SEE THE MOST STOOPENDOUS AND CO-LOSS-AL CIRCUS IN THE HIST'RY OF THE WORLD!
THAT'S NO WILD MAN—THAT'S ONLY BUCKWHEAT.
LOOK MORE FIERCER, BUCKWHEAT!
WAKE UP THE TIGER, FROGGY!
CIRCUS 1¢ ONE CENT ADMISION ONLY 1 CENT
WILD SAVIDGE
WILD TIGOR

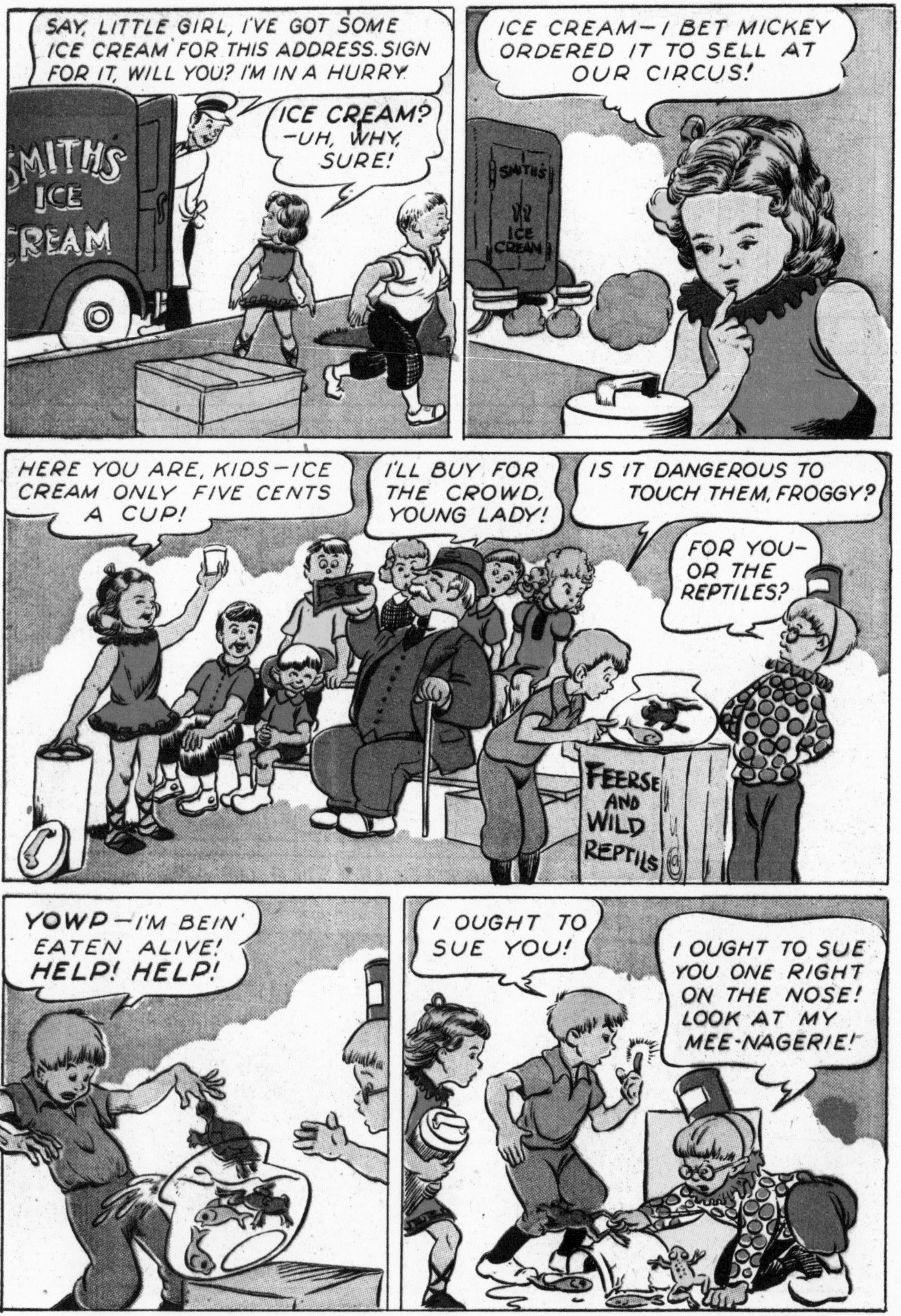
SAY, LITTLE GIRL, I'VE GOT SOME ICE CREAM FOR THIS ADDRESS. SIGN FOR IT, WILL YOU? I'M IN A HURRY.
SMITH'S ICE CREAM
ICE CREAM? -UH, WHY, SURE!
ICE CREAM—I BET MICKEY ORDERED IT TO SELL AT OUR CIRCUS!
SMITH'S ICE CREAM
HERE YOU ARE, KIDS—ICE CREAM ONLY FIVE CENTS A CUP!
I'LL BUY FOR THE CROWD, YOUNG LADY!
IS IT DANGEROUS TO TOUCH THEM, FROGGY?
FOR YOU— OR THE REPTILES?
FEERSE AND WILD REPTILS
YOWP—I'M BEIN' EATEN ALIVE! HELP! HELP!
I OUGHT TO SUE YOU!
I OUGHT TO SUE YOU ONE RIGHT ON THE NOSE! LOOK AT MY MEE-NAGERIE!

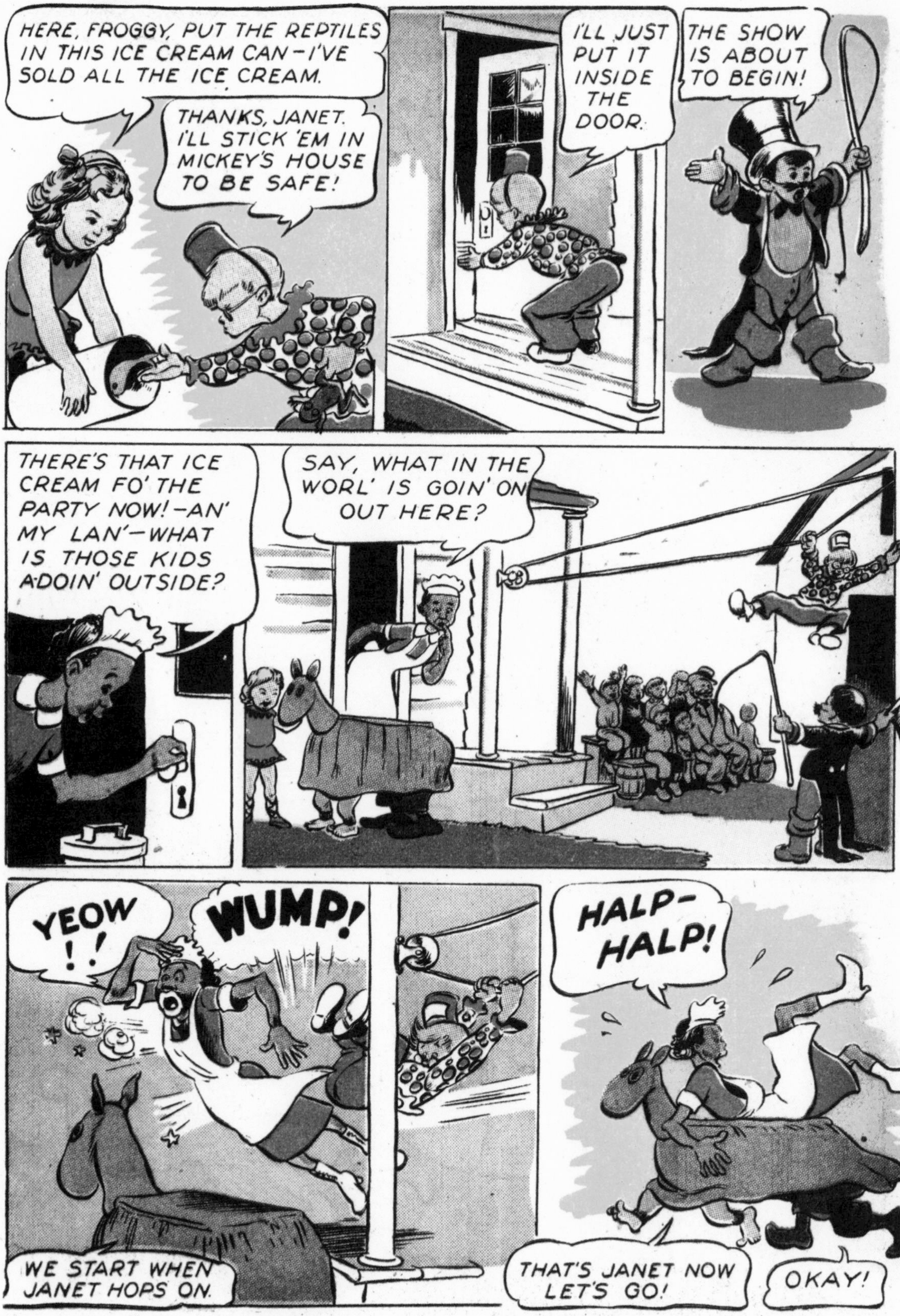
HERE, FROGGY, PUT THE REPTILES IN THIS ICE CREAM CAN—I'VE SOLD ALL THE ICE CREAM.
THANKS, JANET. I'LL STICK 'EM IN MICKEY'S HOUSE TO BE SAFE!
I'LL JUST PUT IT INSIDE THE DOOR.
THE SHOW IS ABOUT TO BEGIN!
THERE'S THAT ICE CREAM FO' THE PARTY NOW!—AN' MY LAN'—WHAT IS THOSE KIDS A-DOIN' OUTSIDE?
SAY, WHAT IN THE WORL' IS GOIN' ON OUT HERE?
YEOW !!
WUMP!
WE START WHEN JANET HOPS ON.
HALP-HALP!
THAT'S JANET NOW LET'S GO!
OKAY!

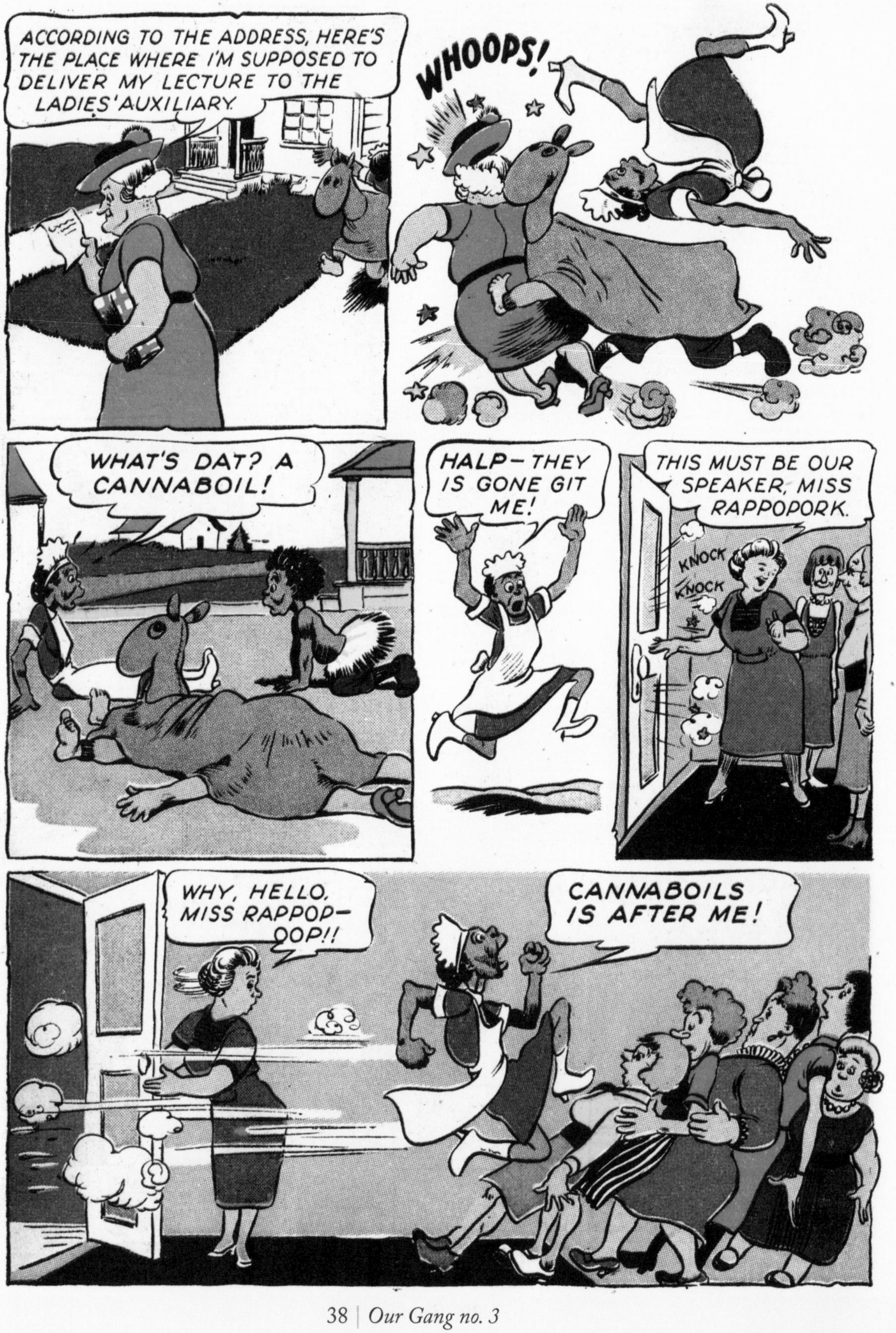

ACCORDING TO THE ADDRESS, HERE'S THE PLACE WHERE I'M SUPPOSED TO DELIVER MY LECTURE TO THE LADIES' AUXILIARY.
WHOOPS!
WHAT'S DAT? A CANNABOIL!
HALP—THEY IS GONE GIT ME!
THIS MUST BE OUR SPEAKER, MISS RAPPOPORK.
KNOCK
KNOCK
WHY, HELLO, MISS RAPPOP-OOP!!
CANNABOILS IS AFTER ME!

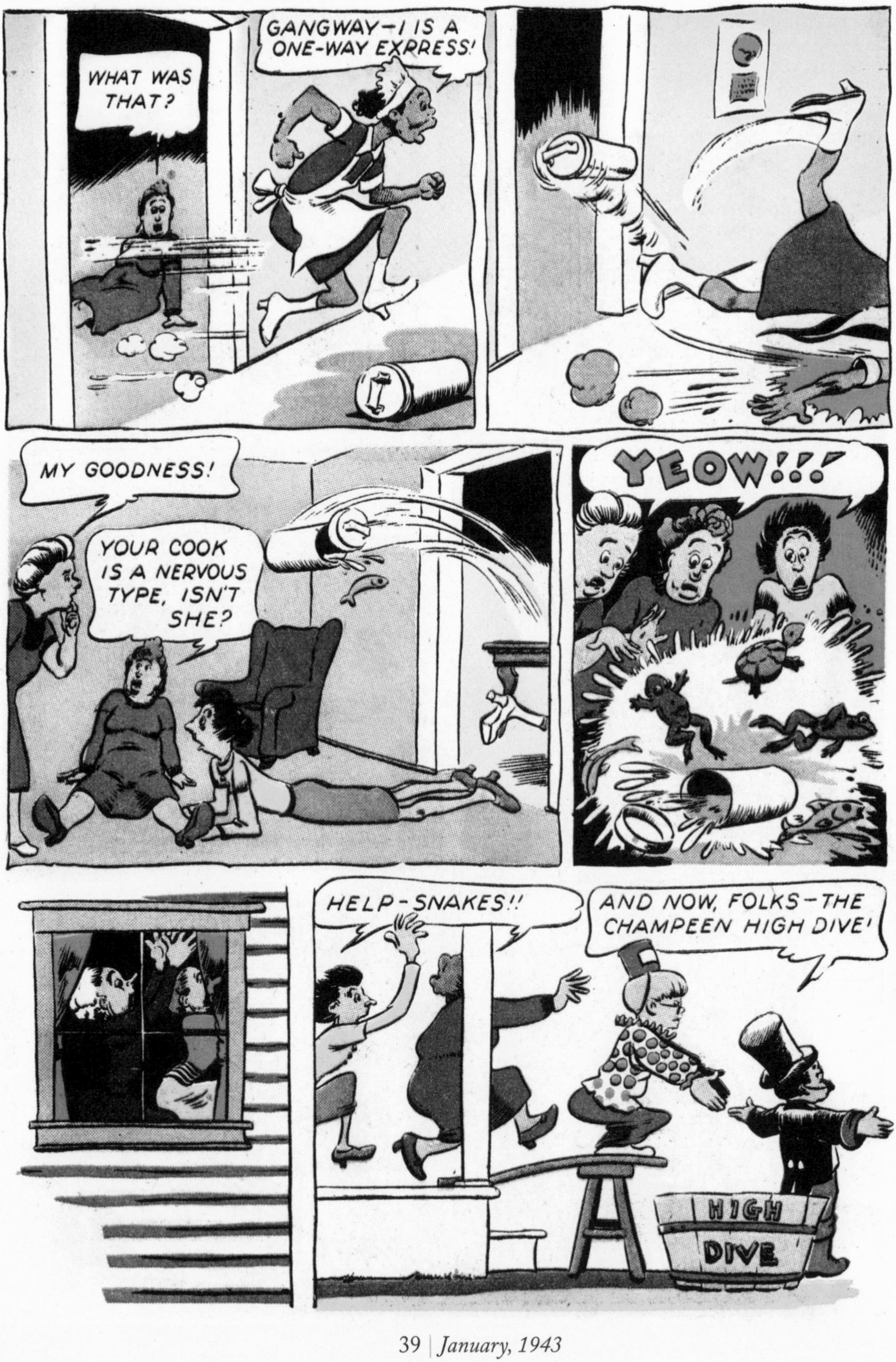
WHAT WAS THAT?
GANGWAY—I IS A ONE-WAY EXPRESS!
MY GOODNESS!
YOUR COOK IS A NERVOUS TYPE, ISN'T SHE?
YEOW!!!
HELP-SNAKES!!
AND NOW, FOLKS—THE CHAMPEEN HIGH DIVE!
HIGH DIVE

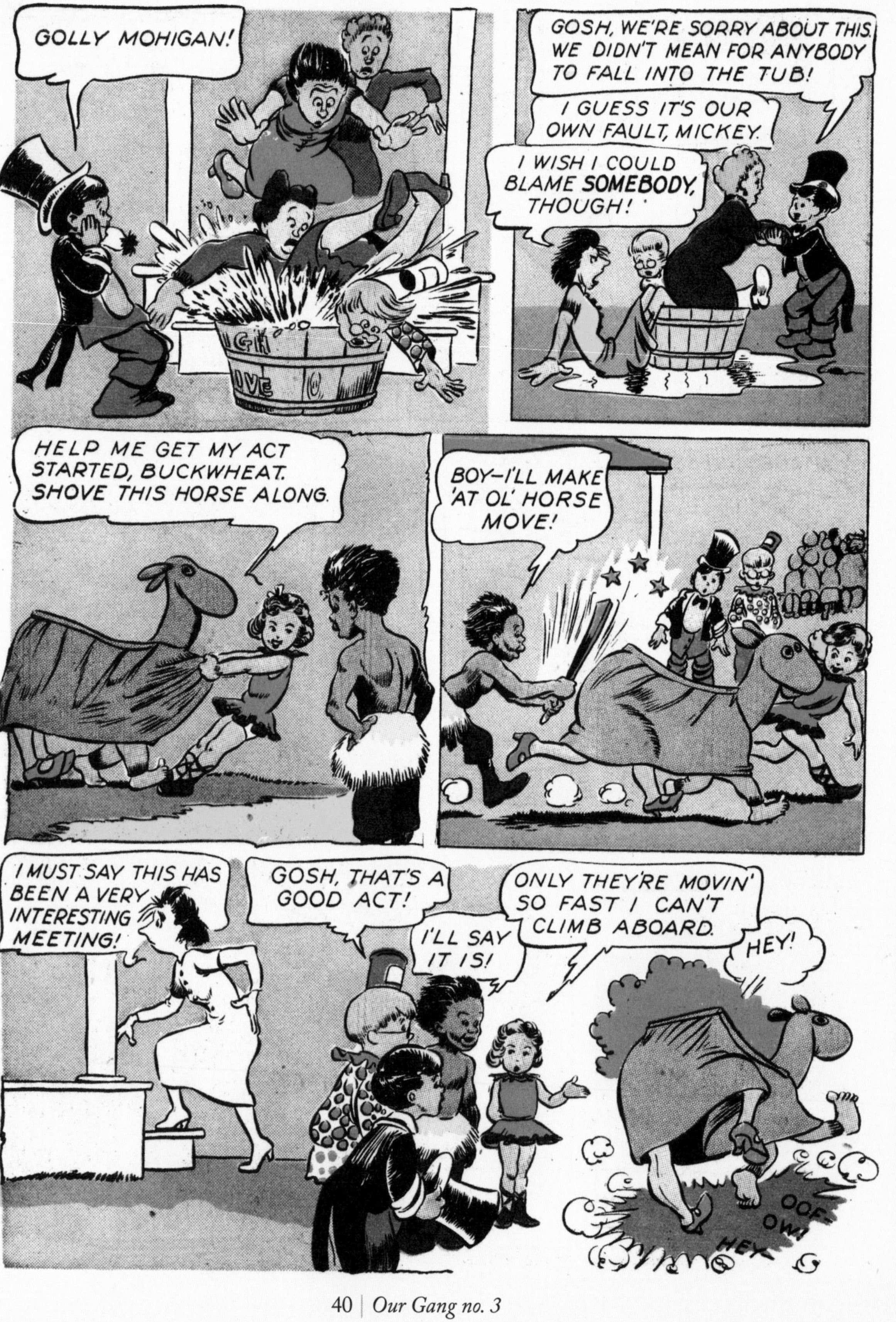
GOLLY MOHIGAN!
GOSH, WE'RE SORRY ABOUT THIS. WE DIDN'T MEAN FOR ANYBODY TO FALL INTO THE TUB!
I GUESS IT'S OUR OWN FAULT, MICKEY.
I WISH I COULD BLAME **SOMEBODY**, THOUGH!
HELP ME GET MY ACT STARTED, BUCKWHEAT. SHOVE THIS HORSE ALONG.
BOY—I'LL MAKE 'AT OL' HORSE MOVE!
I MUST SAY THIS HAS BEEN A VERY INTERESTING MEETING!
GOSH, THAT'S A GOOD ACT!
ONLY THEY'RE MOVIN' SO FAST I CAN'T CLIMB ABOARD.
I'LL SAY IT IS!
HEY!
OOF-
OW!

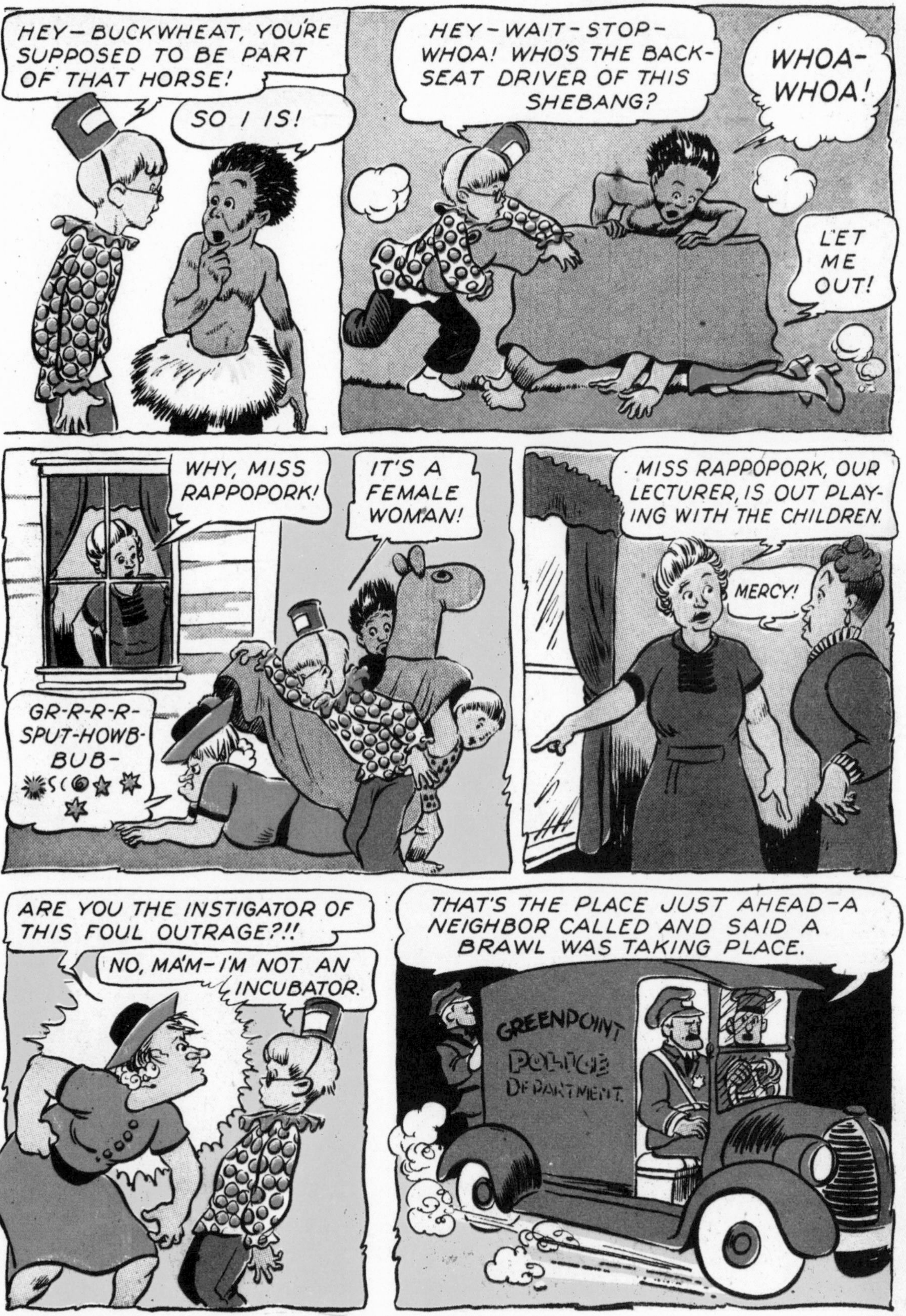
HEY—BUCKWHEAT, YOU'RE SUPPOSED TO BE PART OF THAT HORSE!
SO I IS!
HEY—WAIT—STOP—WHOA! WHO'S THE BACK-SEAT DRIVER OF THIS SHEBANG?
WHOA-WHOA!
LET ME OUT!
WHY, MISS RAPPOPORK!
IT'S A FEMALE WOMAN!
GR-R-R-R-SPUT-HOWB-BUB-
MISS RAPPOPORK, OUR LECTURER, IS OUT PLAYING WITH THE CHILDREN.
MERCY!
ARE YOU THE INSTIGATOR OF THIS FOUL OUTRAGE?!!
NO, MA'M—I'M NOT AN INCUBATOR.
THAT'S THE PLACE JUST AHEAD—A NEIGHBOR CALLED AND SAID A BRAWL WAS TAKING PLACE.
GREENPOINT POLICE DEPARTMENT.

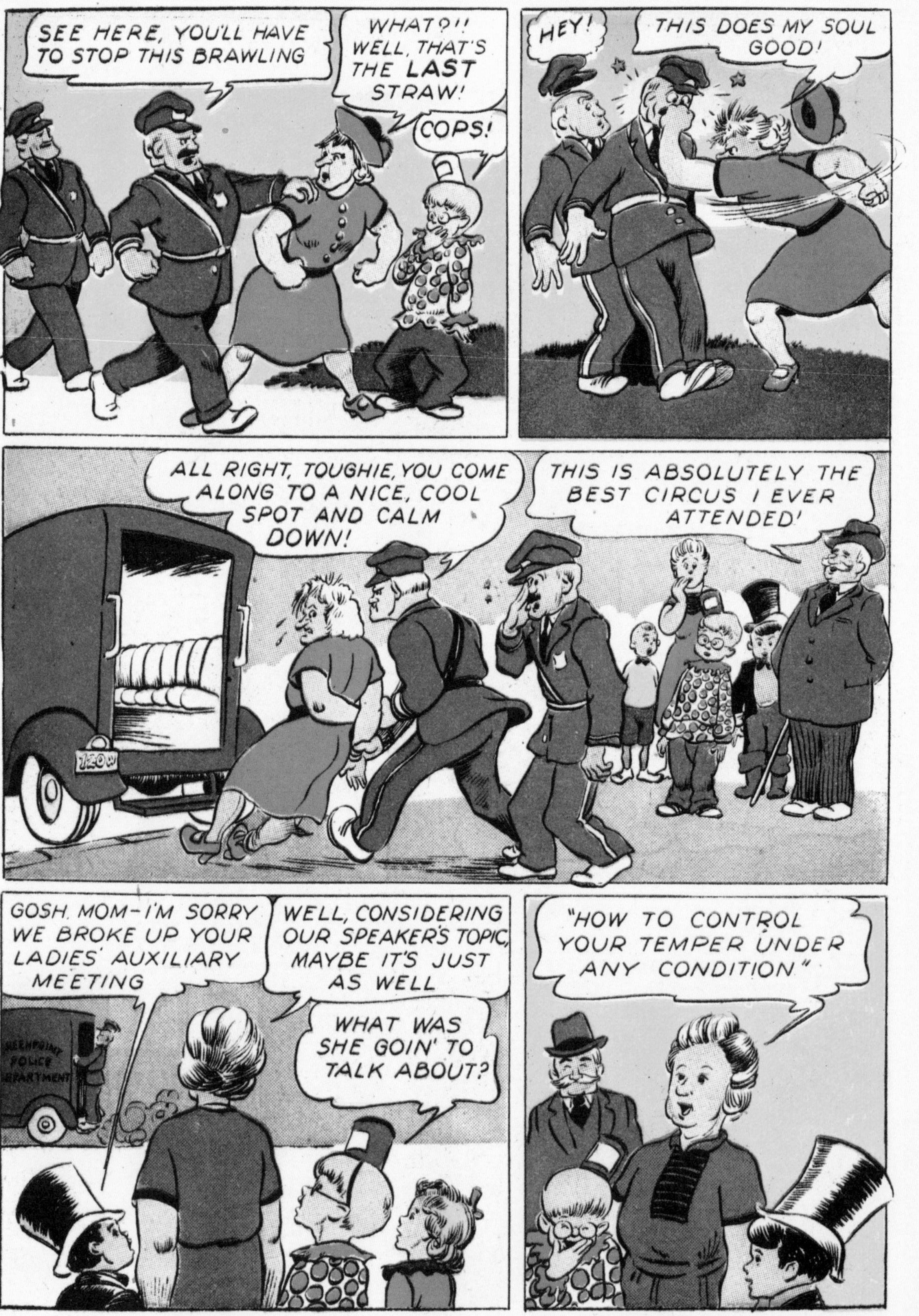
SEE HERE, YOU'LL HAVE TO STOP THIS BRAWLING
WHAT?!! WELL, THAT'S THE LAST STRAW!
COPS!
HEY!
THIS DOES MY SOUL GOOD!
ALL RIGHT, TOUGHIE, YOU COME ALONG TO A NICE, COOL SPOT AND CALM DOWN!
THIS IS ABSOLUTELY THE BEST CIRCUS I EVER ATTENDED!
GOSH, MOM–I'M SORRY WE BROKE UP YOUR LADIES' AUXILIARY MEETING
WELL, CONSIDERING OUR SPEAKER'S TOPIC, MAYBE IT'S JUST AS WELL
WHAT WAS SHE GOIN' TO TALK ABOUT?
"HOW TO CONTROL YOUR TEMPER UNDER ANY CONDITION"

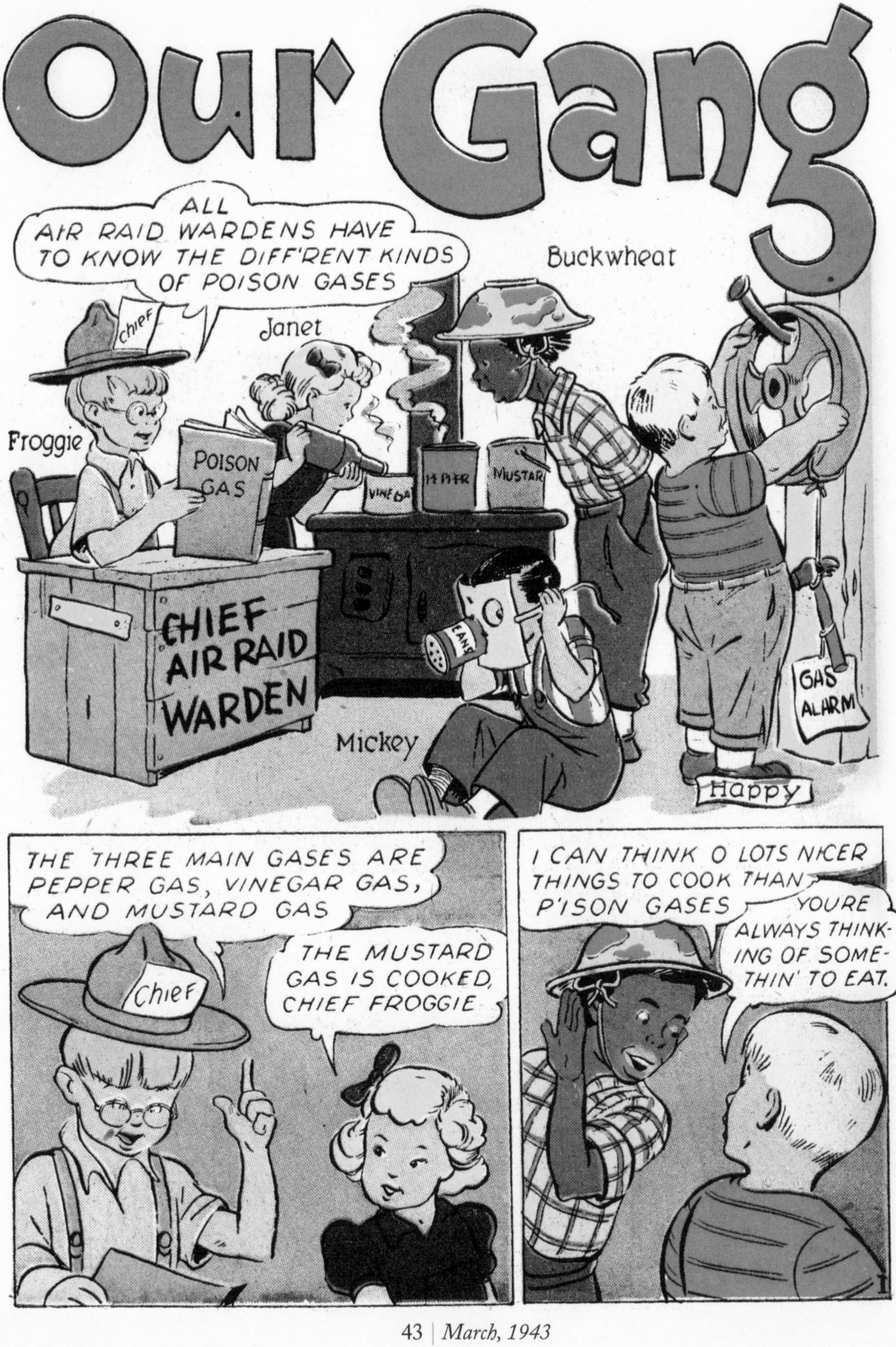
Our Gang
ALL AIR RAID WARDENS HAVE TO KNOW THE DIFF'RENT KINDS OF POISON GASES
Buckwheat
Janet
Froggie
CHIEF
POISON GAS
VINEGAR
PEPPER
MUSTARD
CHIEF AIR RAID WARDEN
CANS
GAS ALARM
Mickey
Happy
THE THREE MAIN GASES ARE PEPPER GAS, VINEGAR GAS, AND MUSTARD GAS
THE MUSTARD GAS IS COOKED, CHIEF FROGGIE
Chief
I CAN THINK O LOTS NICER THINGS TO COOK THAN P'ISON GASES
YOURE ALWAYS THINKING OF SOMETHIN' TO EAT.

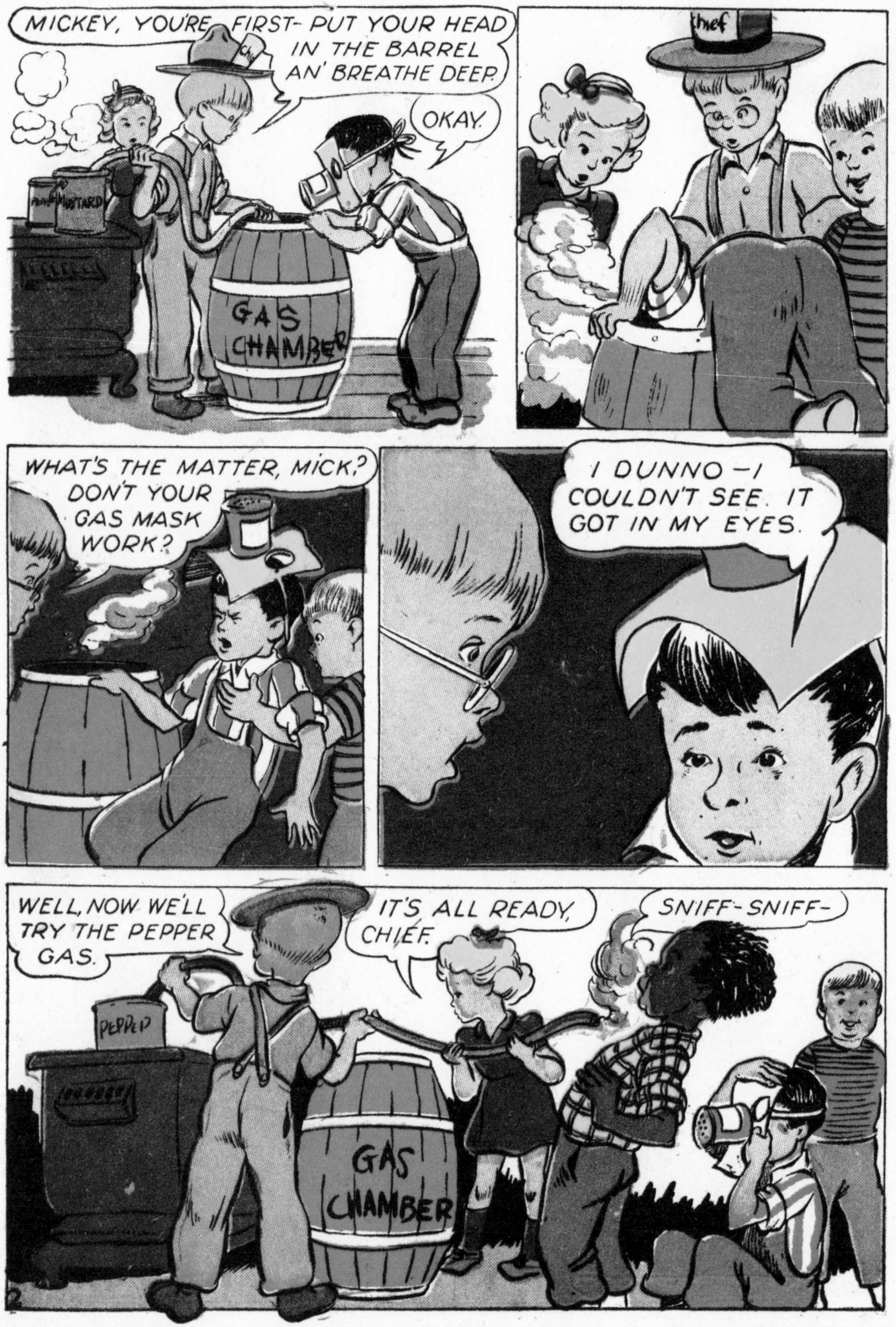
MICKEY, YOU'RE FIRST- PUT YOUR HEAD IN THE BARREL AN' BREATHE DEEP.
OKAY.
MUSTARD
GAS CHAMBER
thief
WHAT'S THE MATTER, MICK? DON'T YOUR GAS MASK WORK?
I DUNNO -I COULDN'T SEE. IT GOT IN MY EYES.
WELL, NOW WE'LL TRY THE PEPPER GAS.
IT'S ALL READY, CHIEF.
SNIFF-SNIFF-
PEPPER
GAS CHAMBER

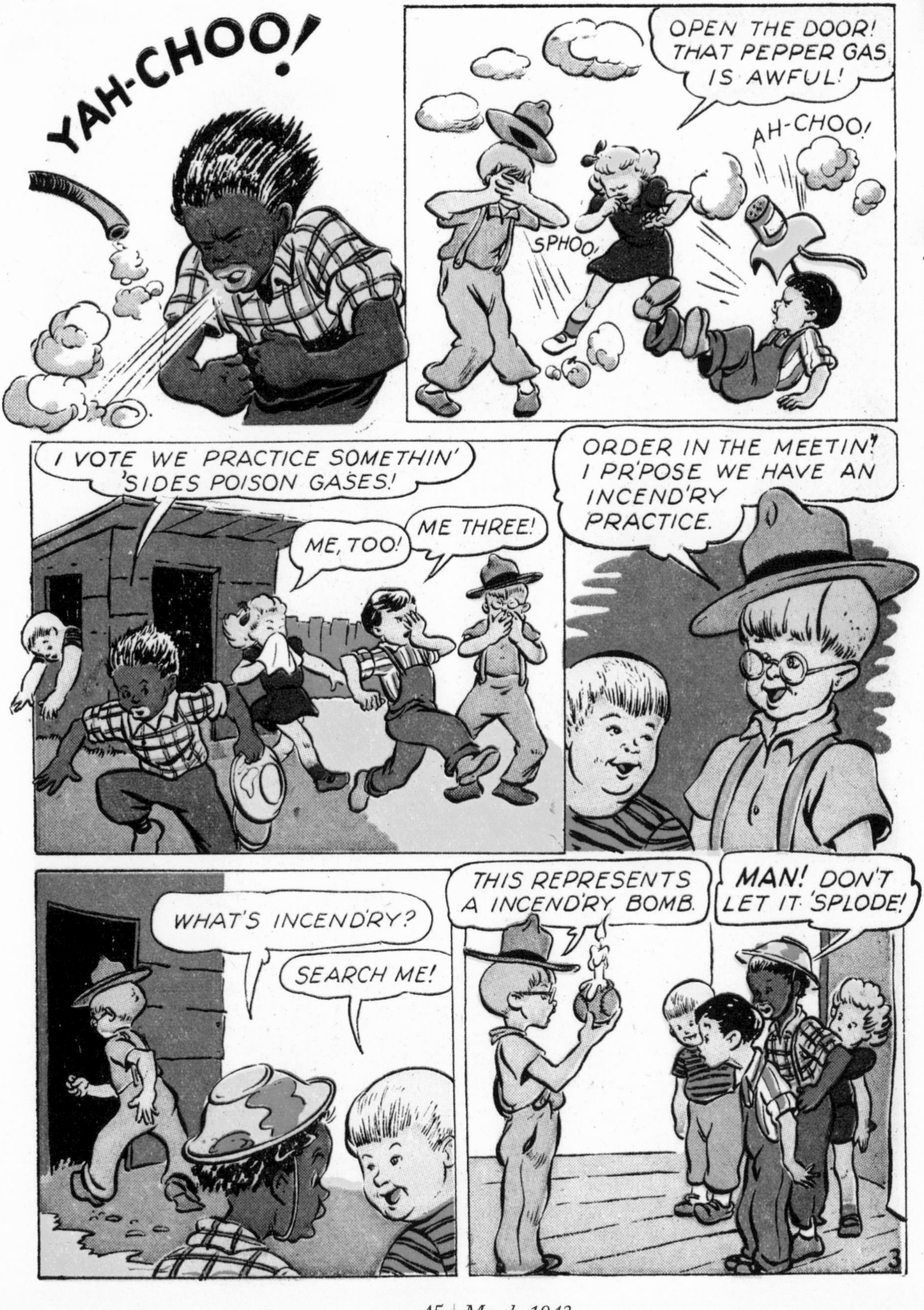
YAH-CHOO!
OPEN THE DOOR! THAT PEPPER GAS IS AWFUL!
AH-CHOO!
SPHOO!
I VOTE WE PRACTICE SOMETHIN' 'SIDES POISON GASES!
ME, TOO!
ME THREE!
ORDER IN THE MEETIN'! I PR'POSE WE HAVE AN INCEND'RY PRACTICE.
WHAT'S INCEND'RY?
SEARCH ME!
THIS REPRESENTS A INCEND'RY BOMB.
MAN! DON'T LET IT 'SPLODE!
3

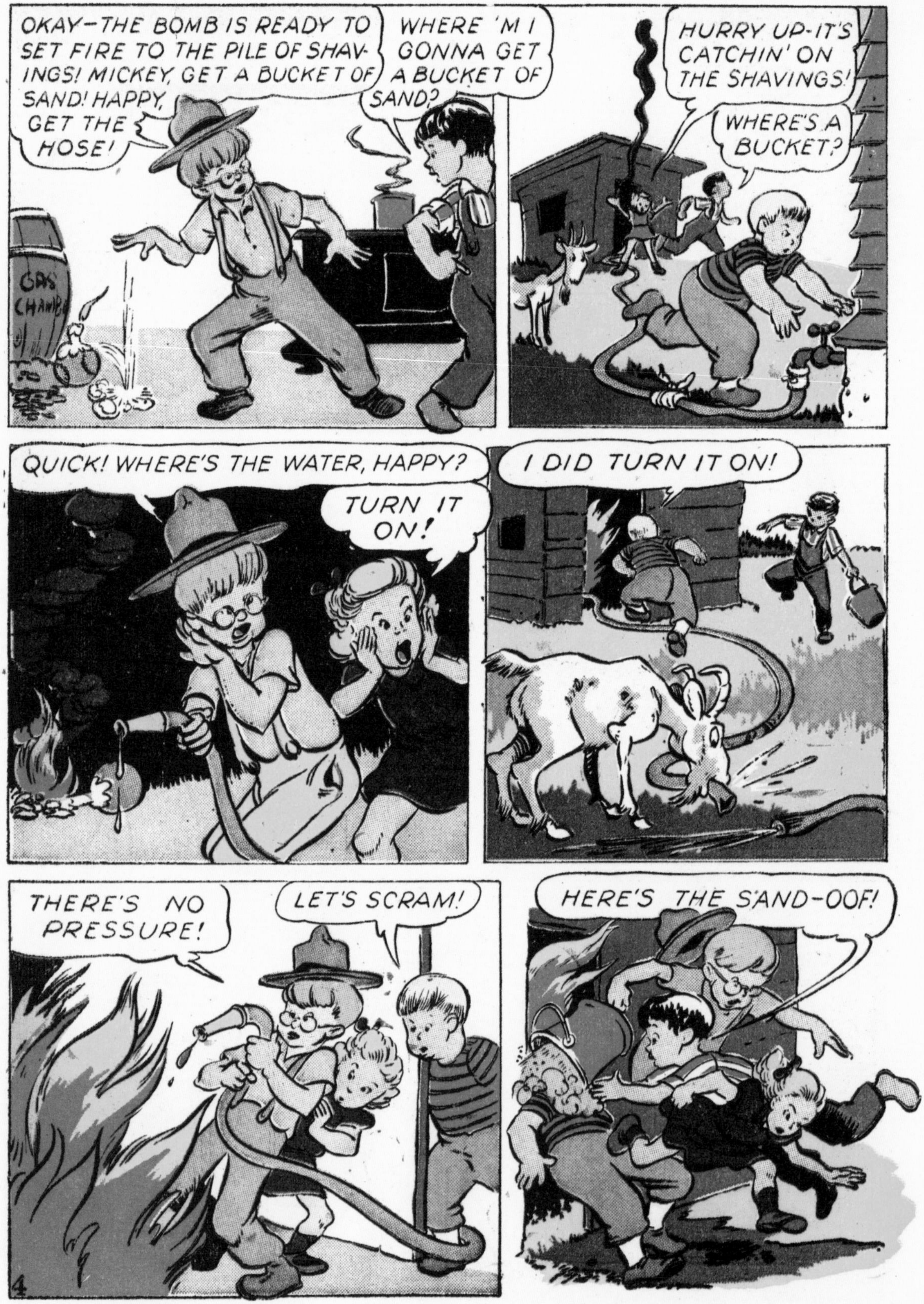
OKAY—THE BOMB IS READY TO SET FIRE TO THE PILE OF SHAVINGS! MICKEY, GET A BUCKET OF SAND! HAPPY, GET THE HOSE!
WHERE 'M I GONNA GET A BUCKET OF SAND?
HURRY UP-IT'S CATCHIN' ON THE SHAVINGS!
WHERE'S A BUCKET?
QUICK! WHERE'S THE WATER, HAPPY?
TURN IT ON!
I DID TURN IT ON!
THERE'S NO PRESSURE!
LET'S SCRAM!
HERE'S THE SAND-OOF!
4

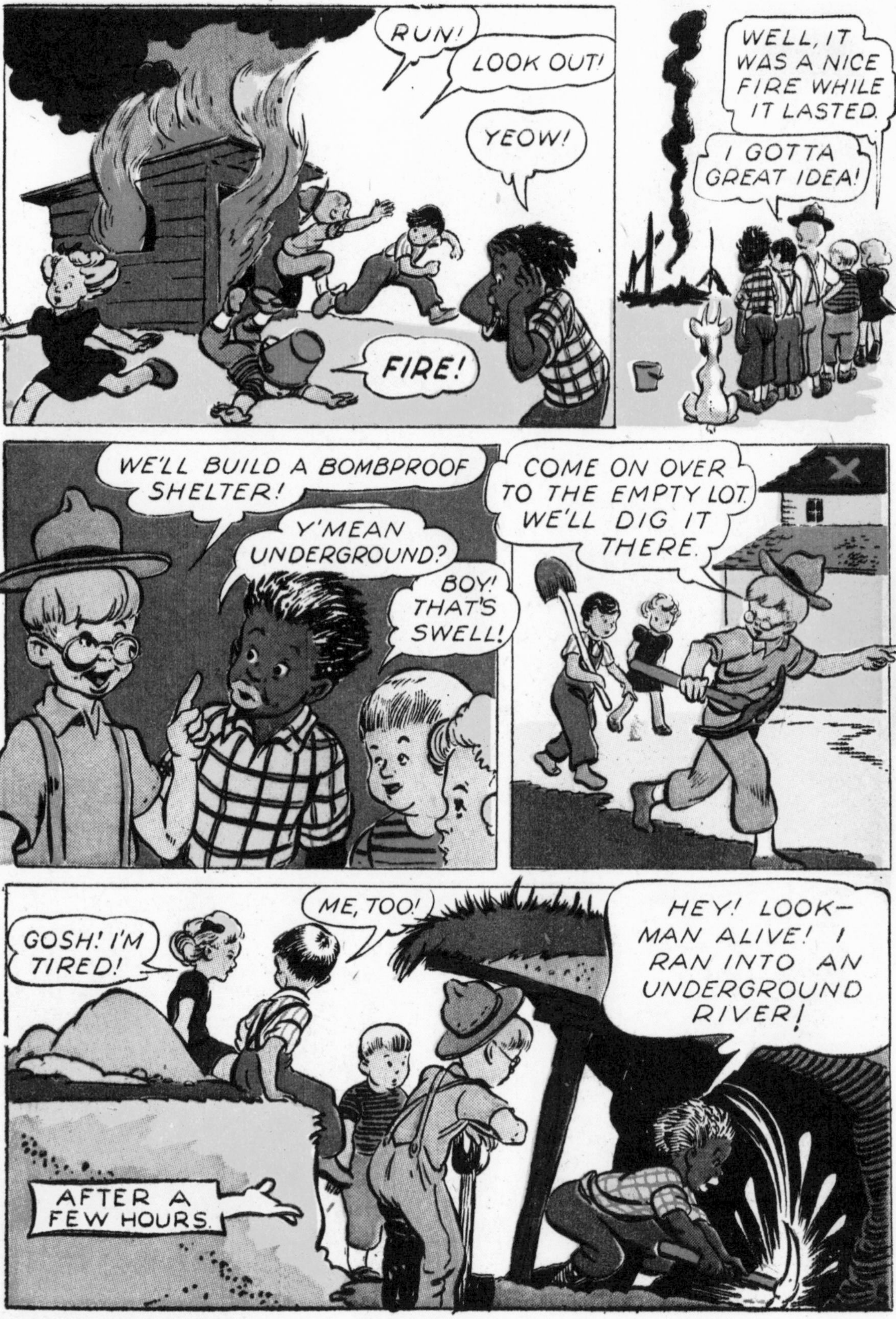
RUN!
LOOK OUT!
YEOW!
FIRE!
WELL, IT WAS A NICE FIRE WHILE IT LASTED.
I GOTTA GREAT IDEA!
WE'LL BUILD A BOMBPROOF SHELTER!
Y'MEAN UNDERGROUND?
BOY! THAT'S SWELL!
COME ON OVER TO THE EMPTY LOT. WE'LL DIG IT THERE.
AFTER A FEW HOURS.
GOSH! I'M TIRED!
ME, TOO!
HEY! LOOK— MAN ALIVE! I RAN INTO AN UNDERGROUND RIVER!

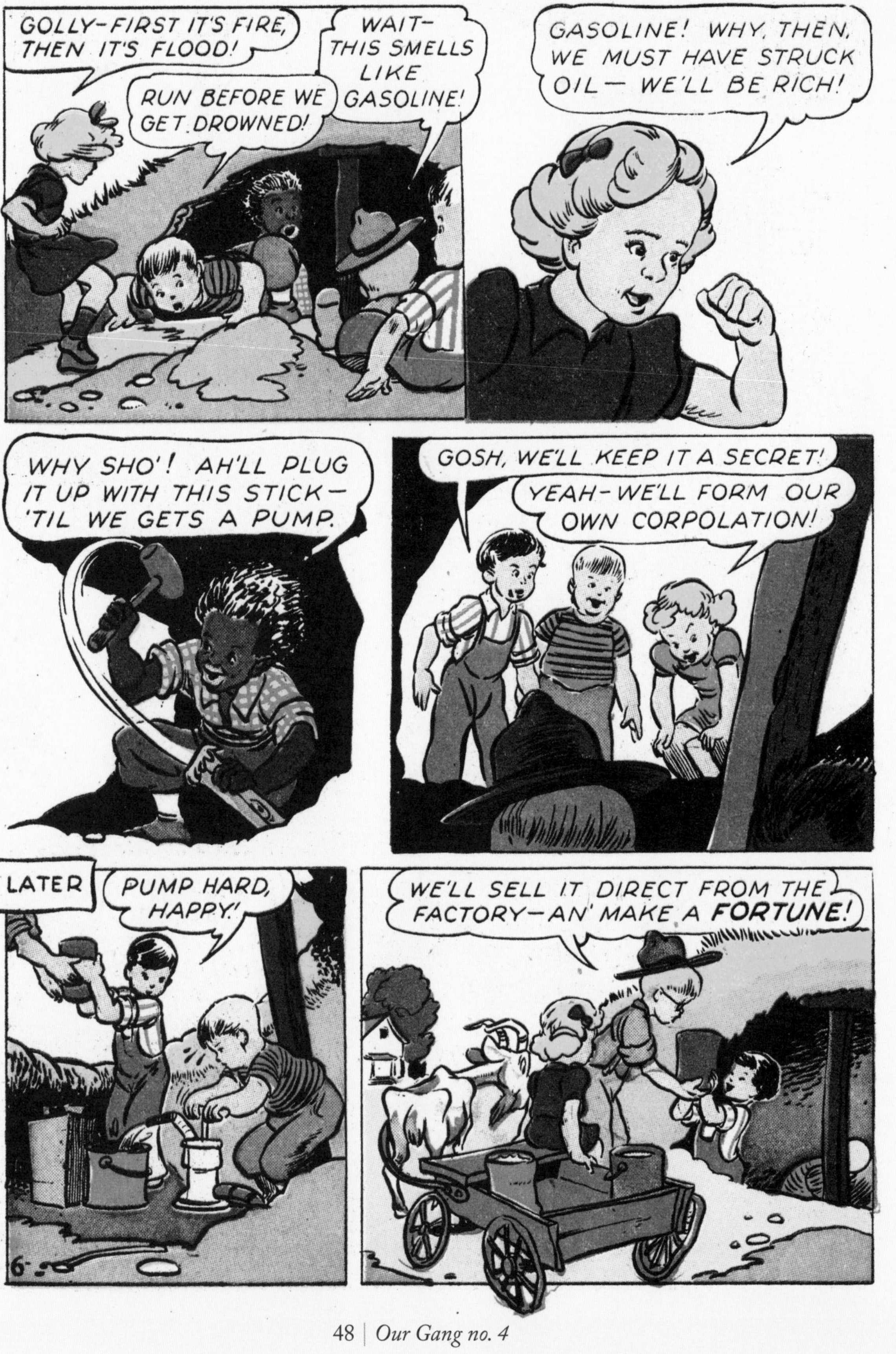
GOLLY-FIRST IT'S FIRE, THEN IT'S FLOOD!
RUN BEFORE WE GET DROWNED!
WAIT- THIS SMELLS LIKE GASOLINE!
GASOLINE! WHY, THEN, WE MUST HAVE STRUCK OIL— WE'LL BE RICH!
WHY SHO'! AH'LL PLUG IT UP WITH THIS STICK— 'TIL WE GETS A PUMP.
GOSH, WE'LL KEEP IT A SECRET!
YEAH-WE'LL FORM OUR OWN CORPOLATION!
LATER
PUMP HARD, HAPPY!
6
WE'LL SELL IT DIRECT FROM THE FACTORY—AN' MAKE A FORTUNE!

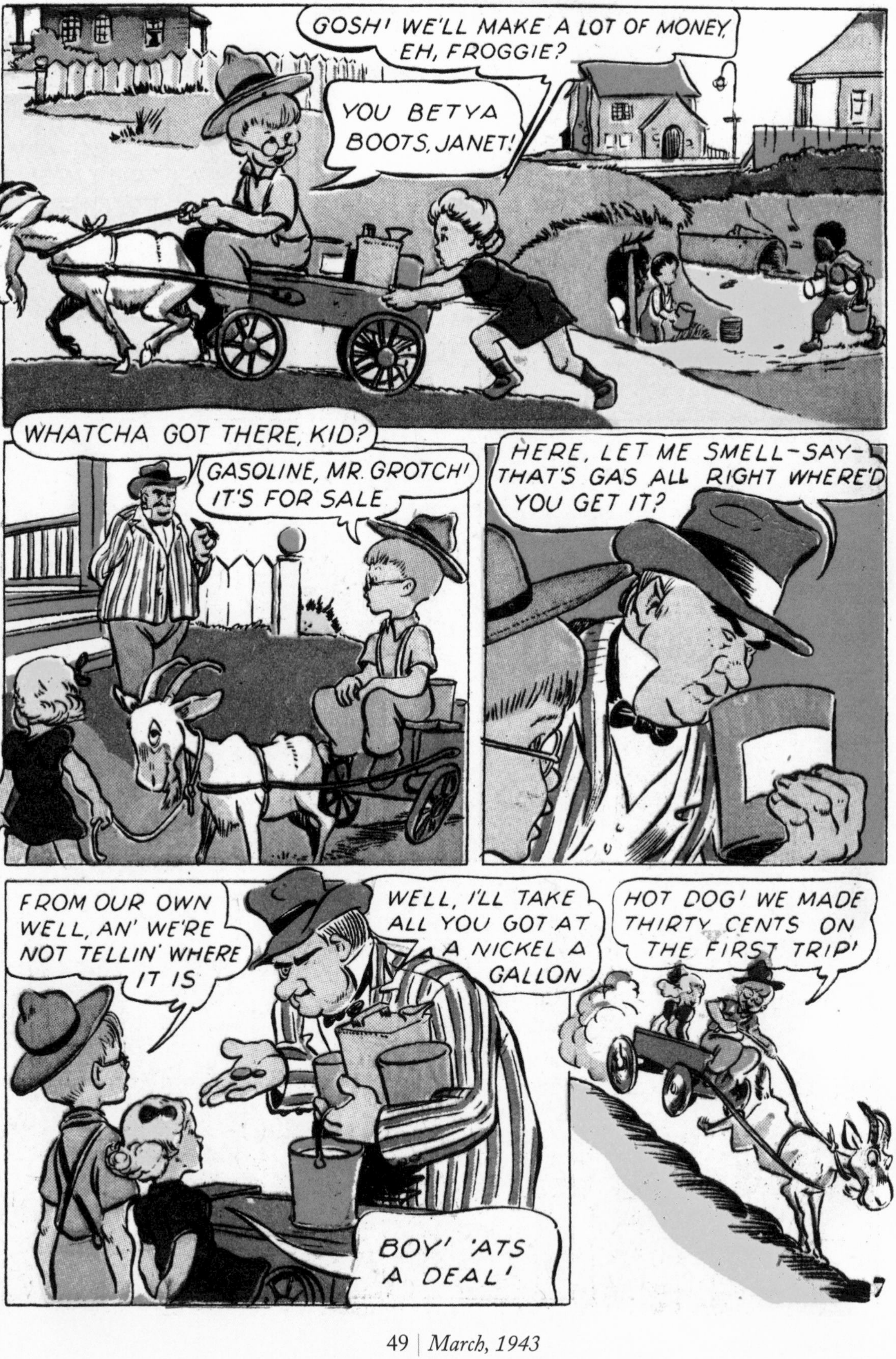
GOSH! WE'LL MAKE A LOT OF MONEY, EH, FROGGIE?
YOU BETYA BOOTS, JANET!
WHATCHA GOT THERE, KID?
GASOLINE, MR. GROTCH! IT'S FOR SALE
HERE, LET ME SMELL—SAY—THAT'S GAS ALL RIGHT WHERE'D YOU GET IT?
FROM OUR OWN WELL, AN' WE'RE NOT TELLIN' WHERE IT IS
WELL, I'LL TAKE ALL YOU GOT AT A NICKEL A GALLON
BOY! 'ATS A DEAL!
HOT DOG! WE MADE THIRTY CENTS ON THE FIRST TRIP!
7

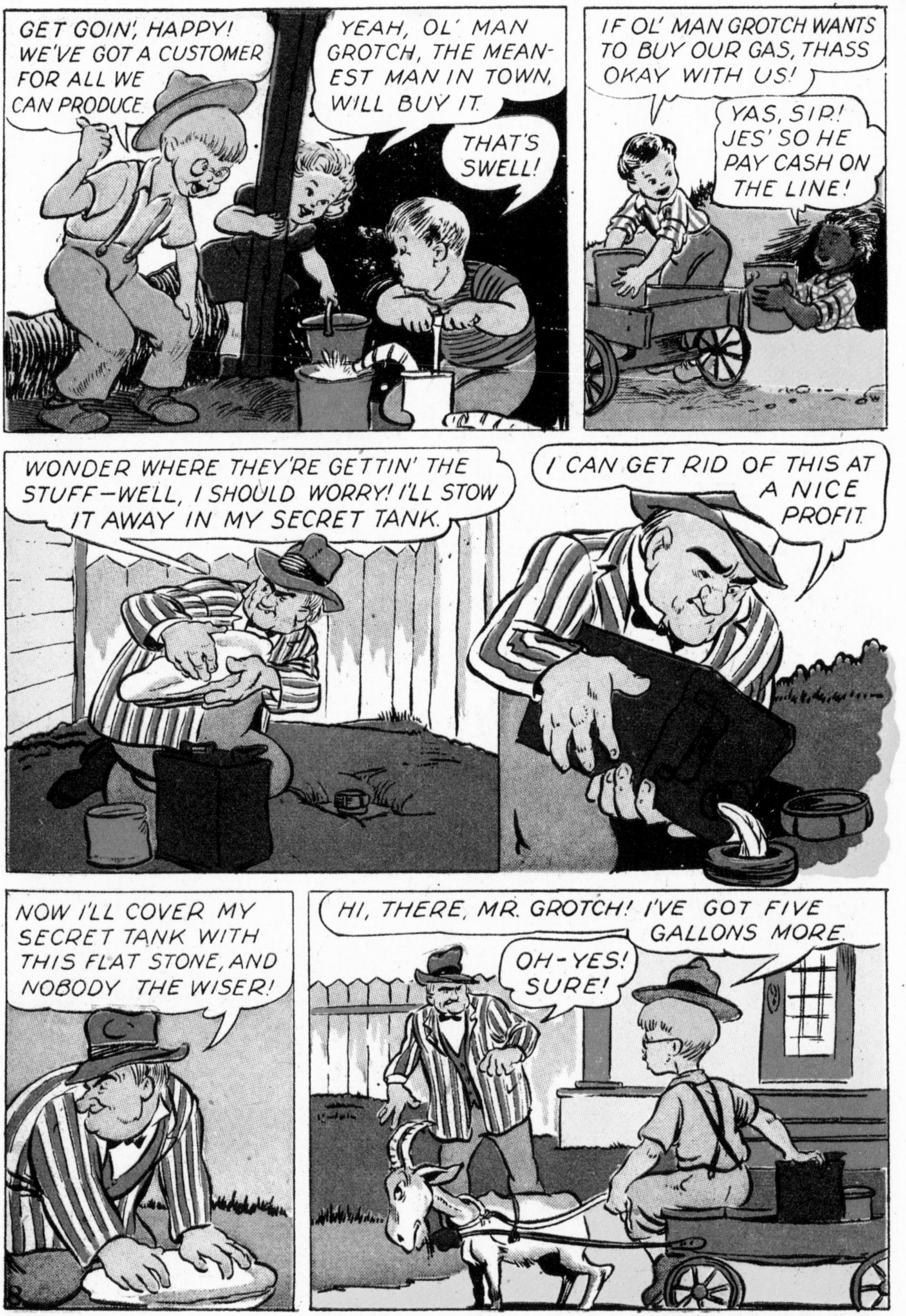
GET GOIN', HAPPY! WE'VE GOT A CUSTOMER FOR ALL WE CAN PRODUCE.
YEAH, OL' MAN GROTCH, THE MEAN-EST MAN IN TOWN, WILL BUY IT.
THAT'S SWELL!
IF OL' MAN GROTCH WANTS TO BUY OUR GAS, THASS OKAY WITH US!
YAS, SIR! JES' SO HE PAY CASH ON THE LINE!
WONDER WHERE THEY'RE GETTIN' THE STUFF—WELL, I SHOULD WORRY! I'LL STOW IT AWAY IN MY SECRET TANK.
I CAN GET RID OF THIS AT A NICE PROFIT.
NOW I'LL COVER MY SECRET TANK WITH THIS FLAT STONE, AND NOBODY THE WISER!
HI, THERE, MR. GROTCH! I'VE GOT FIVE GALLONS MORE.
OH-YES! SURE!

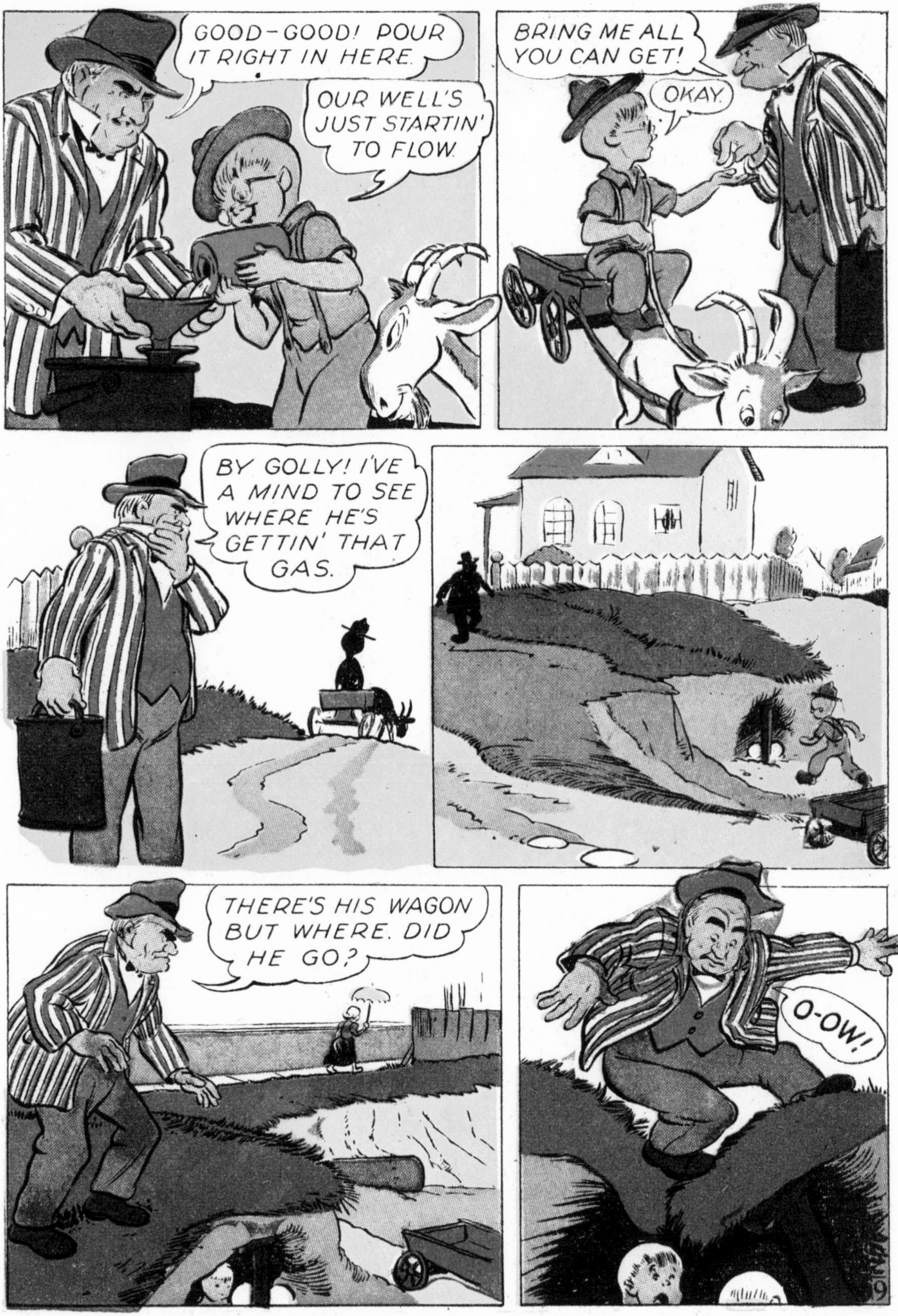
GOOD-GOOD! POUR IT RIGHT IN HERE.
OUR WELL'S JUST STARTIN' TO FLOW.
BRING ME ALL YOU CAN GET!
OKAY.
BY GOLLY! I'VE A MIND TO SEE WHERE HE'S GETTIN' THAT GAS.
THERE'S HIS WAGON BUT WHERE. DID HE GO?
O-OW!

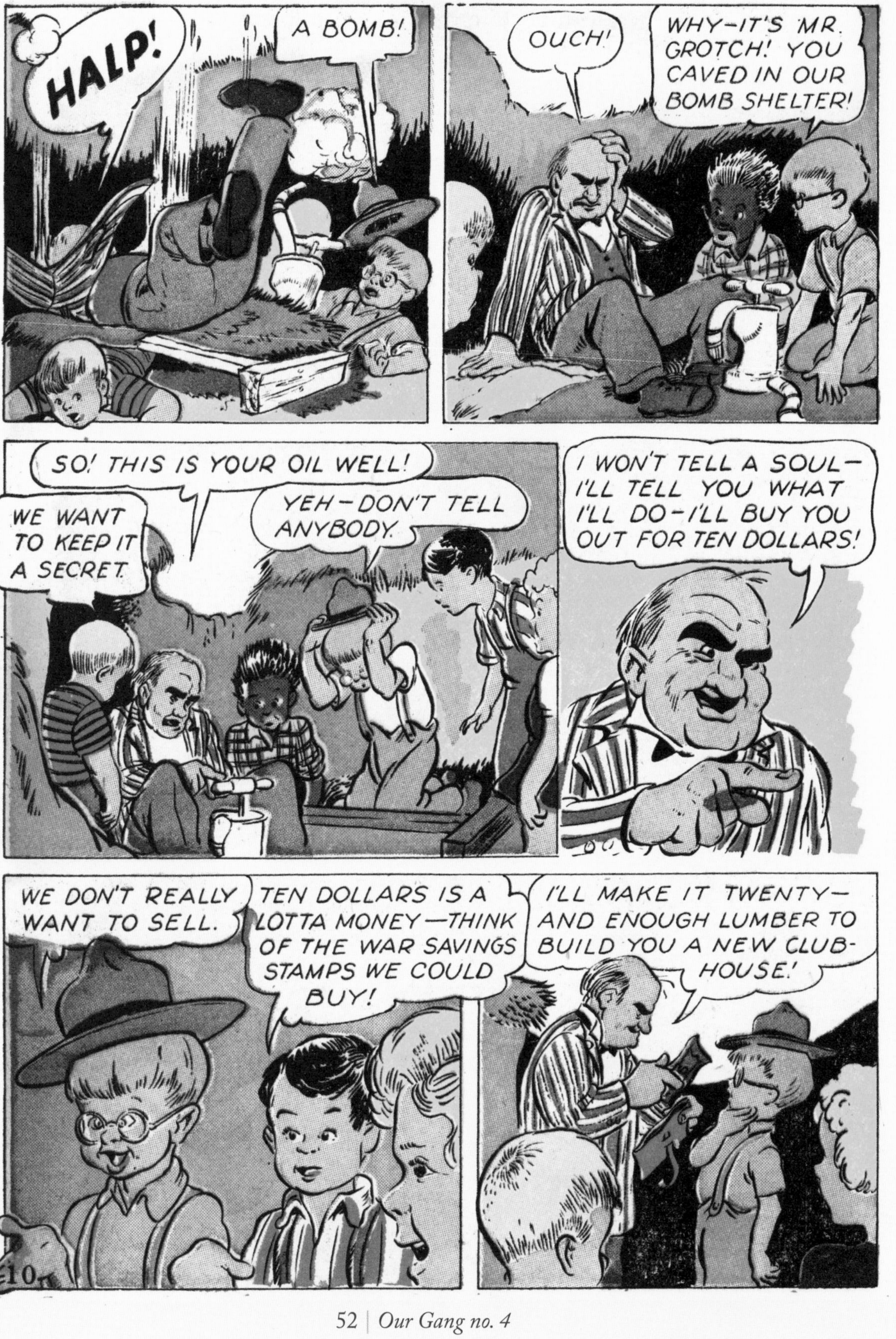
HALP!
A BOMB!
OUCH!
WHY—IT'S MR. GROTCH! YOU CAVED IN OUR BOMB SHELTER!
SO! THIS IS YOUR OIL WELL!
WE WANT TO KEEP IT A SECRET.
YEH—DON'T TELL ANYBODY.
I WON'T TELL A SOUL—I'LL TELL YOU WHAT I'LL DO—I'LL BUY YOU OUT FOR TEN DOLLARS!
WE DON'T REALLY WANT TO SELL.
TEN DOLLARS IS A LOTTA MONEY—THINK OF THE WAR SAVINGS STAMPS WE COULD BUY!
I'LL MAKE IT TWENTY—AND ENOUGH LUMBER TO BUILD YOU A NEW CLUB-HOUSE!
10

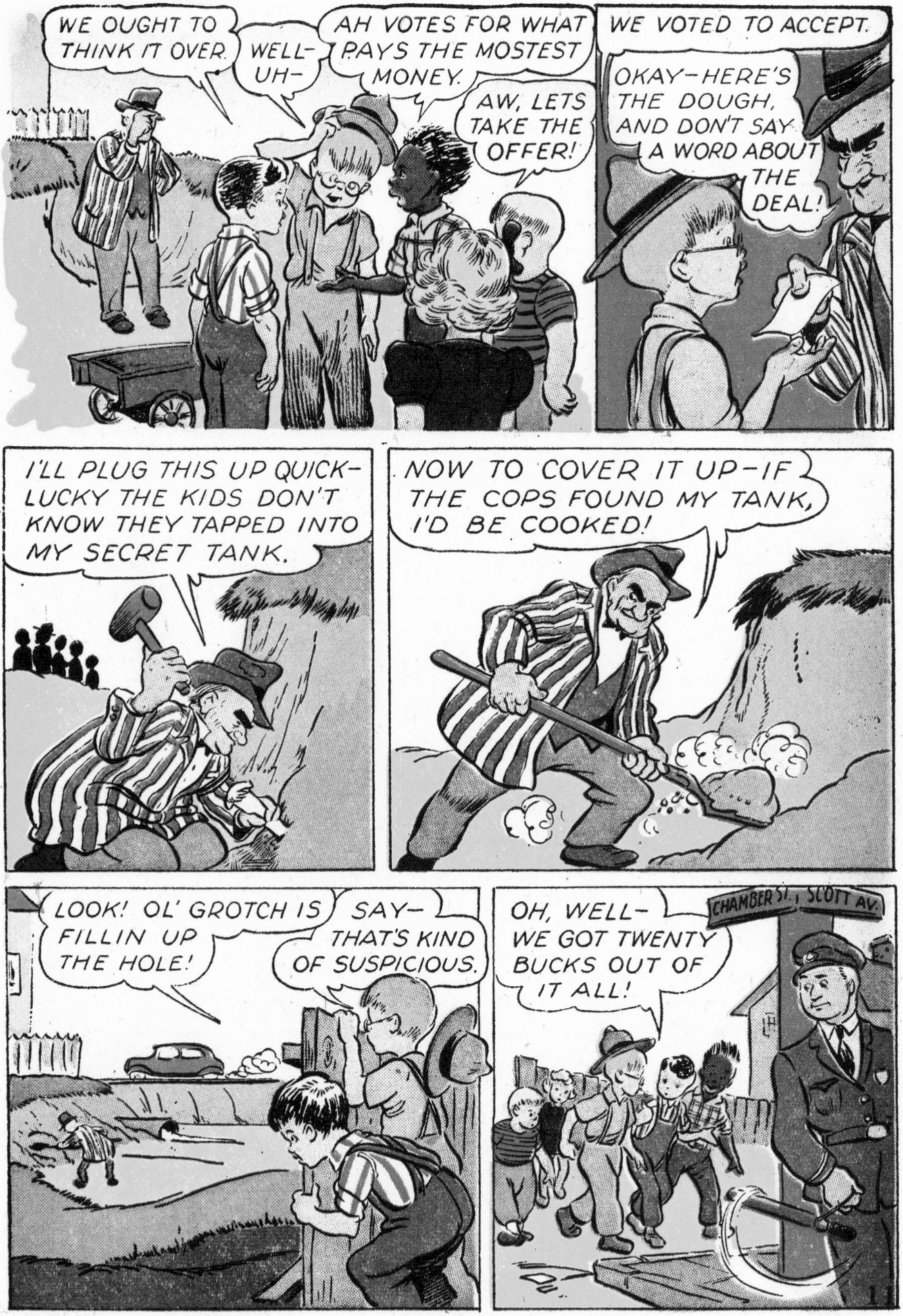
WE OUGHT TO THINK IT OVER.
WELL-UH-
AH VOTES FOR WHAT PAYS THE MOSTEST MONEY.
AW, LETS TAKE THE OFFER!
WE VOTED TO ACCEPT.
OKAY-HERE'S THE DOUGH, AND DON'T SAY A WORD ABOUT THE DEAL!
I'LL PLUG THIS UP QUICK-LUCKY THE KIDS DON'T KNOW THEY TAPPED INTO MY SECRET TANK.
NOW TO COVER IT UP-IF THE COPS FOUND MY TANK, I'D BE COOKED!
LOOK! OL' GROTCH IS FILLIN UP THE HOLE!
SAY-THAT'S KIND OF SUSPICIOUS.
CHAMBER ST.
SCOTT AV.
OH, WELL-WE GOT TWENTY BUCKS OUT OF IT ALL!

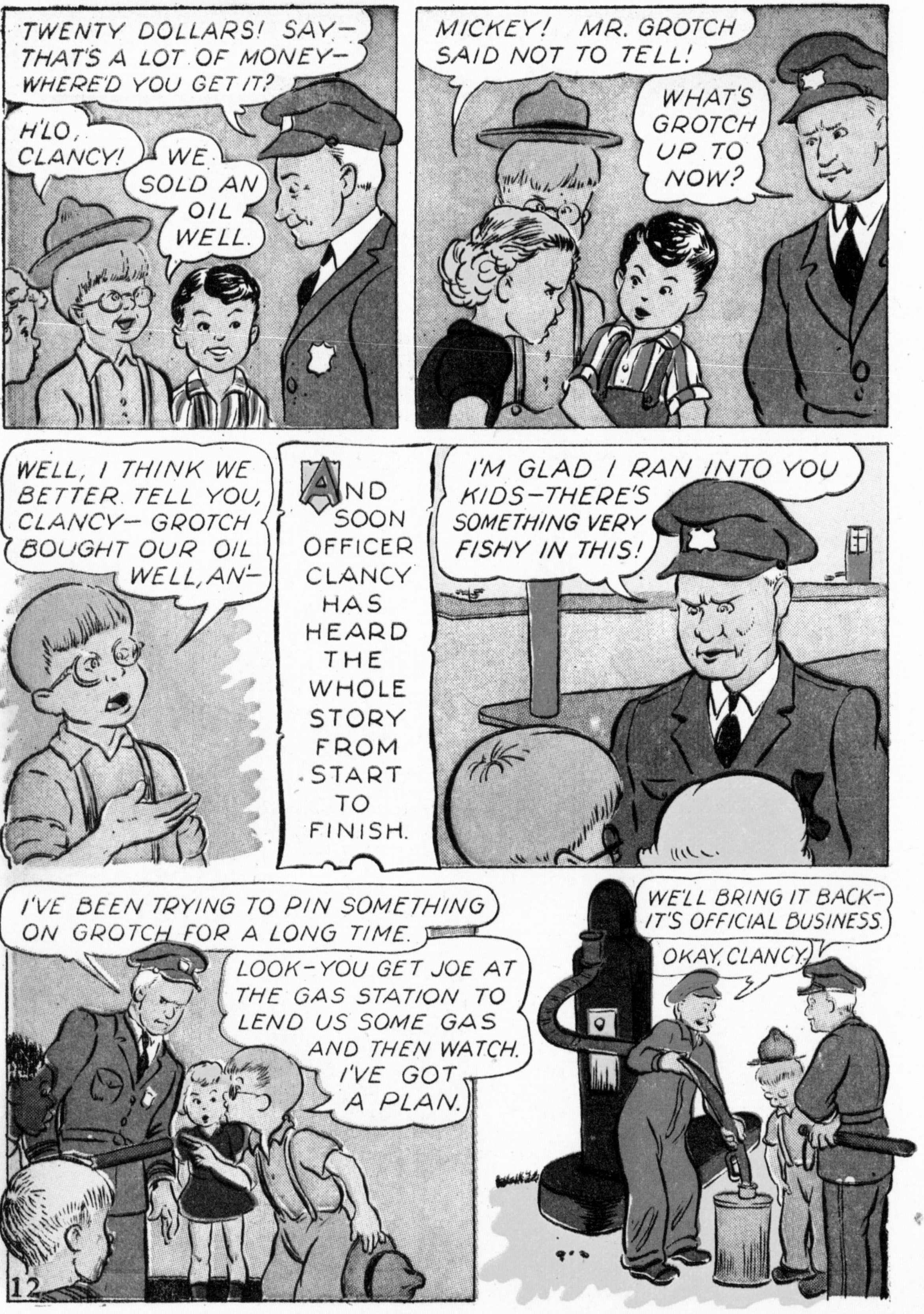
TWENTY DOLLARS! SAY— THAT'S A LOT OF MONEY— WHERE'D YOU GET IT?
H'LO, CLANCY!
WE SOLD AN OIL WELL.
MICKEY! MR. GROTCH SAID NOT TO TELL!
WHAT'S GROTCH UP TO NOW?
WELL, I THINK WE BETTER TELL YOU, CLANCY— GROTCH BOUGHT OUR OIL WELL, AN'—
AND SOON OFFICER CLANCY HAS HEARD THE WHOLE STORY FROM START TO FINISH.
I'M GLAD I RAN INTO YOU KIDS—THERE'S SOMETHING VERY FISHY IN THIS!
I'VE BEEN TRYING TO PIN SOMETHING ON GROTCH FOR A LONG TIME.
LOOK—YOU GET JOE AT THE GAS STATION TO LEND US SOME GAS AND THEN WATCH. I'VE GOT A PLAN.
12
WE'LL BRING IT BACK— IT'S OFFICIAL BUSINESS.
OKAY, CLANCY.

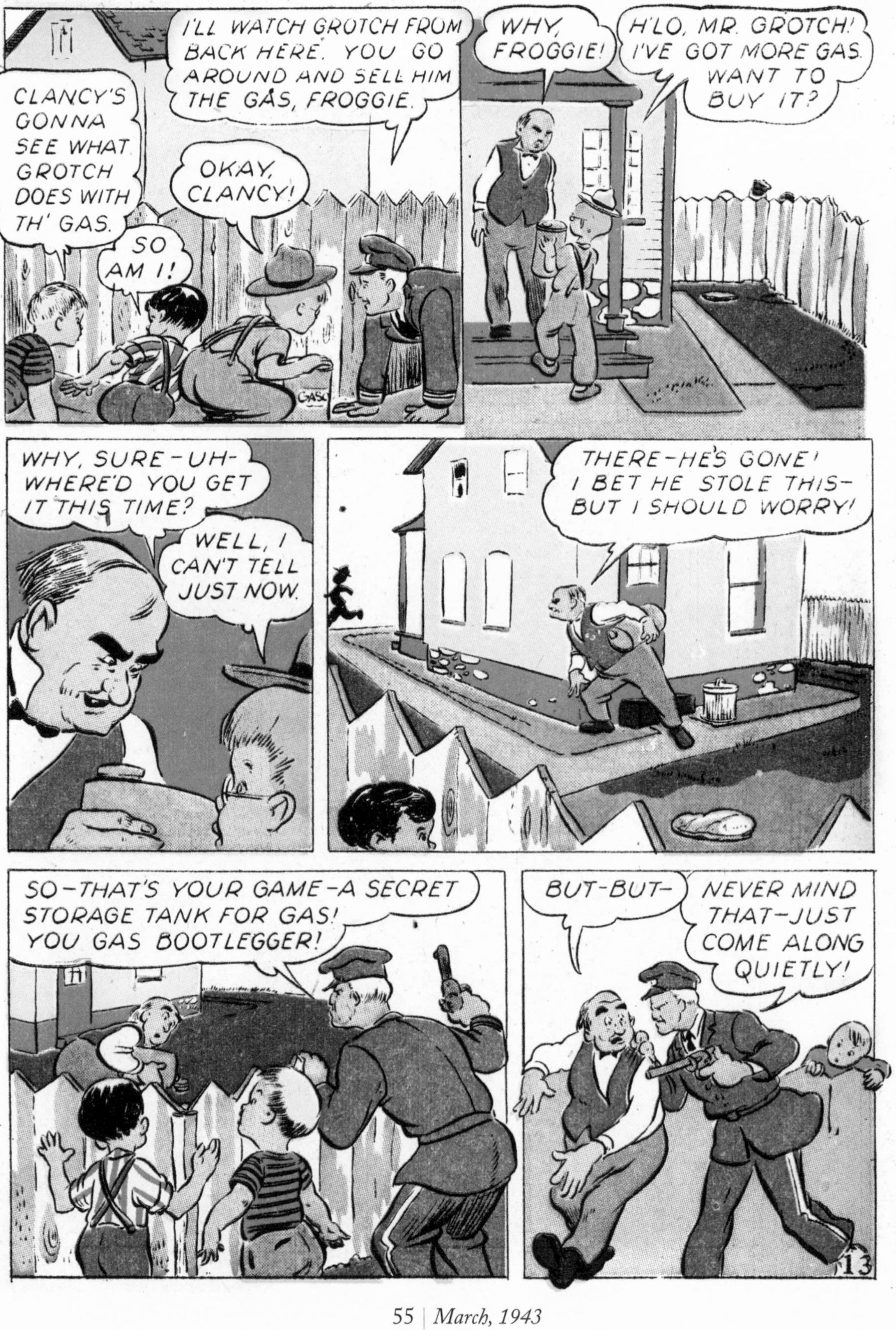
CLANCY'S GONNA SEE WHAT GROTCH DOES WITH TH' GAS.
SO AM I!
I'LL WATCH GROTCH FROM BACK HERE. YOU GO AROUND AND SELL HIM THE GAS, FROGGIE.
OKAY, CLANCY!
GASO
WHY, FROGGIE!
H'LO, MR. GROTCH! I'VE GOT MORE GAS. WANT TO BUY IT?
WHY, SURE-UH-WHERE'D YOU GET IT THIS TIME?
WELL, I CAN'T TELL JUST NOW.
THERE-HE'S GONE! I BET HE STOLE THIS-BUT I SHOULD WORRY!
SO-THAT'S YOUR GAME-A SECRET STORAGE TANK FOR GAS! YOU GAS BOOTLEGGER!
BUT-BUT-
NEVER MIND THAT-JUST COME ALONG QUIETLY!
13

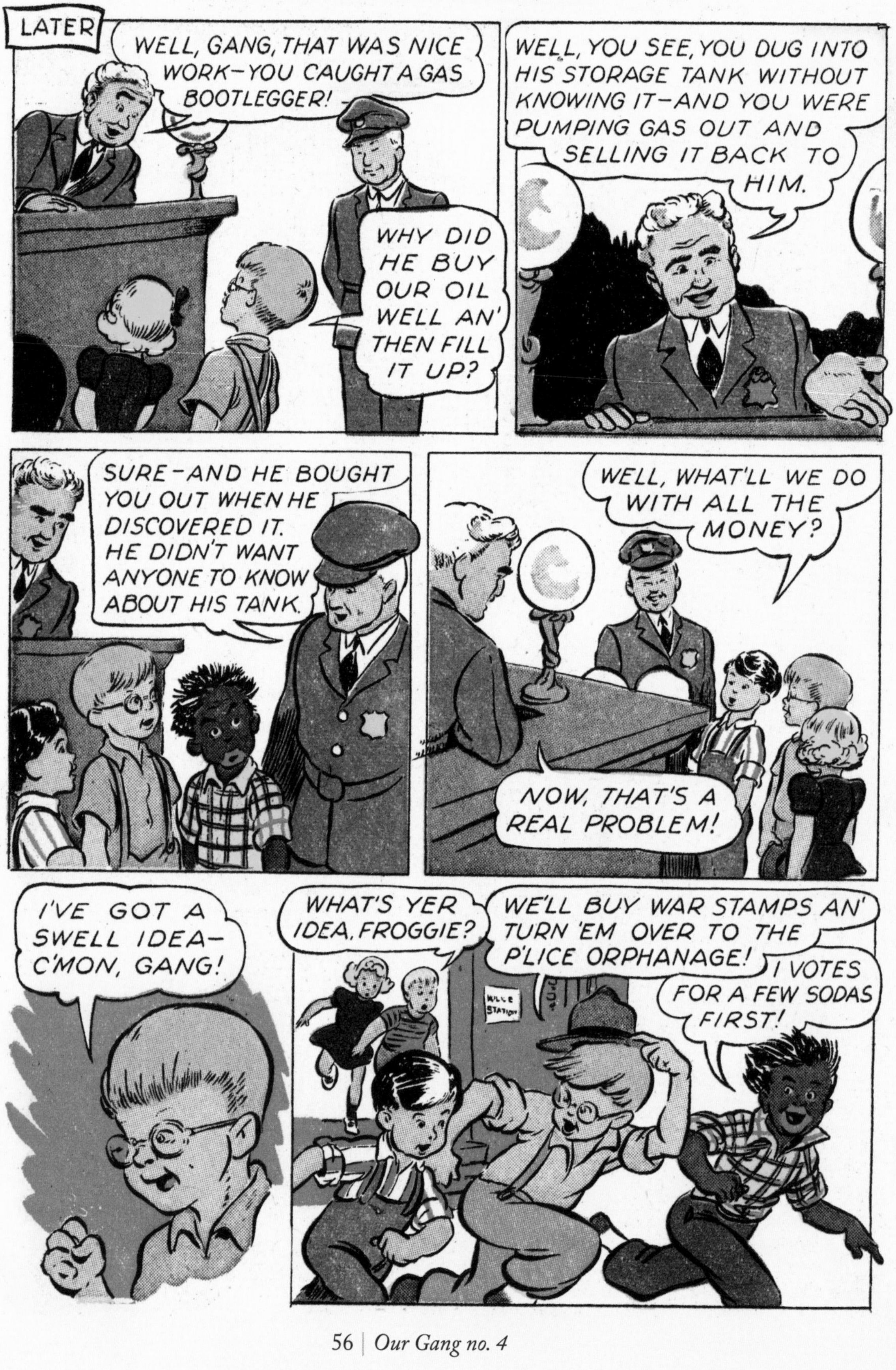
LATER
WELL, GANG, THAT WAS NICE WORK—YOU CAUGHT A GAS BOOTLEGGER!
WHY DID HE BUY OUR OIL WELL AN' THEN FILL IT UP?
WELL, YOU SEE, YOU DUG INTO HIS STORAGE TANK WITHOUT KNOWING IT—AND YOU WERE PUMPING GAS OUT AND SELLING IT BACK TO HIM.
SURE—AND HE BOUGHT YOU OUT WHEN HE DISCOVERED IT. HE DIDN'T WANT ANYONE TO KNOW ABOUT HIS TANK.
WELL, WHAT'LL WE DO WITH ALL THE MONEY?
NOW, THAT'S A REAL PROBLEM!
I'VE GOT A SWELL IDEA—C'MON, GANG!
WHAT'S YER IDEA, FROGGIE?
WE'LL BUY WAR STAMPS AN' TURN 'EM OVER TO THE P'LICE ORPHANAGE!
I VOTES FOR A FEW SODAS FIRST!

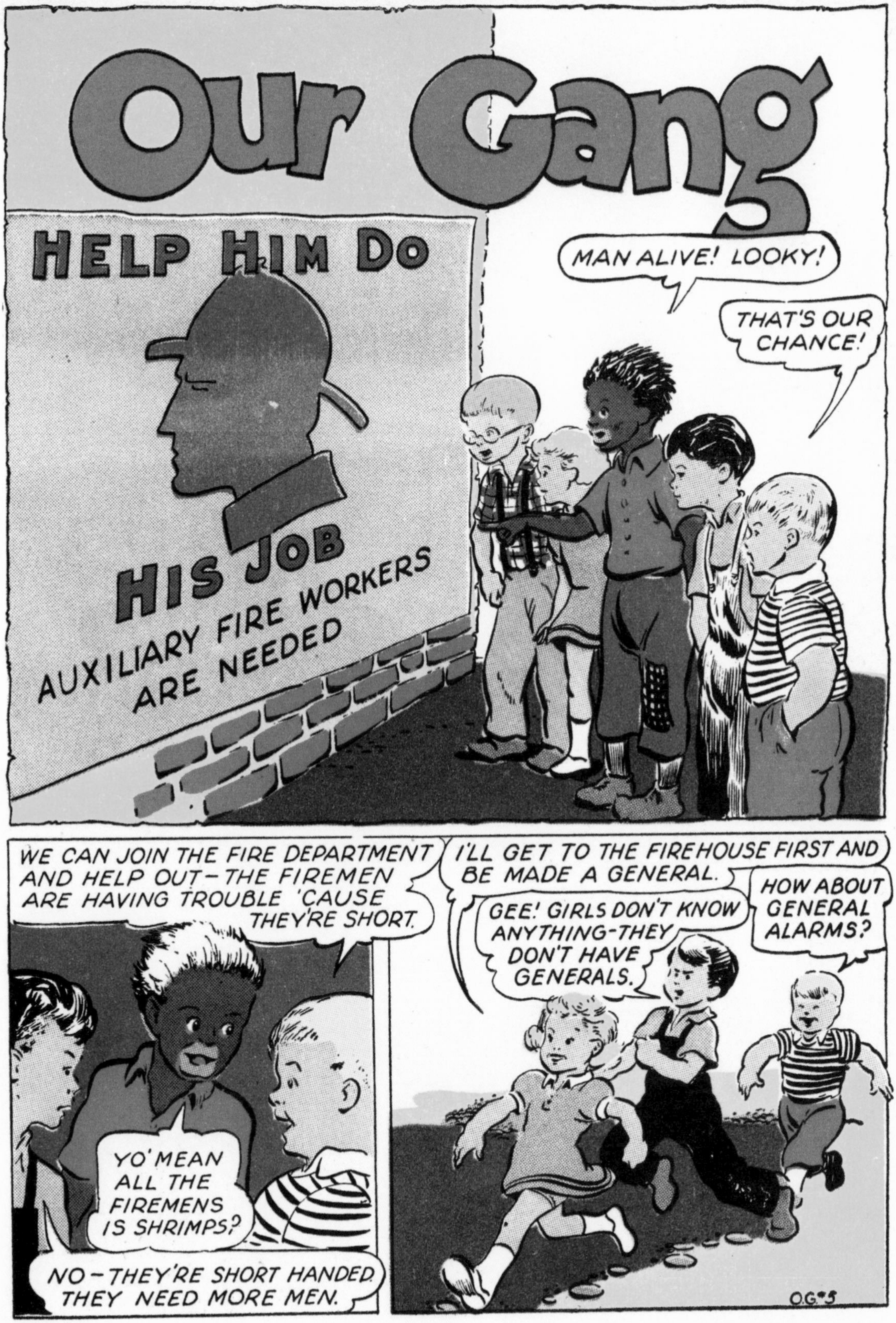
Our Gang
HELP HIM DO HIS JOB
AUXILIARY FIRE WORKERS ARE NEEDED
MAN ALIVE! LOOKY!
THAT'S OUR CHANCE!
WE CAN JOIN THE FIRE DEPARTMENT AND HELP OUT – THE FIREMEN ARE HAVING TROUBLE 'CAUSE THEY'RE SHORT.
YO' MEAN ALL THE FIREMENS IS SHRIMPS?
NO – THEY'RE SHORT HANDED. THEY NEED MORE MEN.
I'LL GET TO THE FIREHOUSE FIRST AND BE MADE A GENERAL.
GEE! GIRLS DON'T KNOW ANYTHING – THEY DON'T HAVE GENERALS.
HOW ABOUT GENERAL ALARMS?
O.G.*5

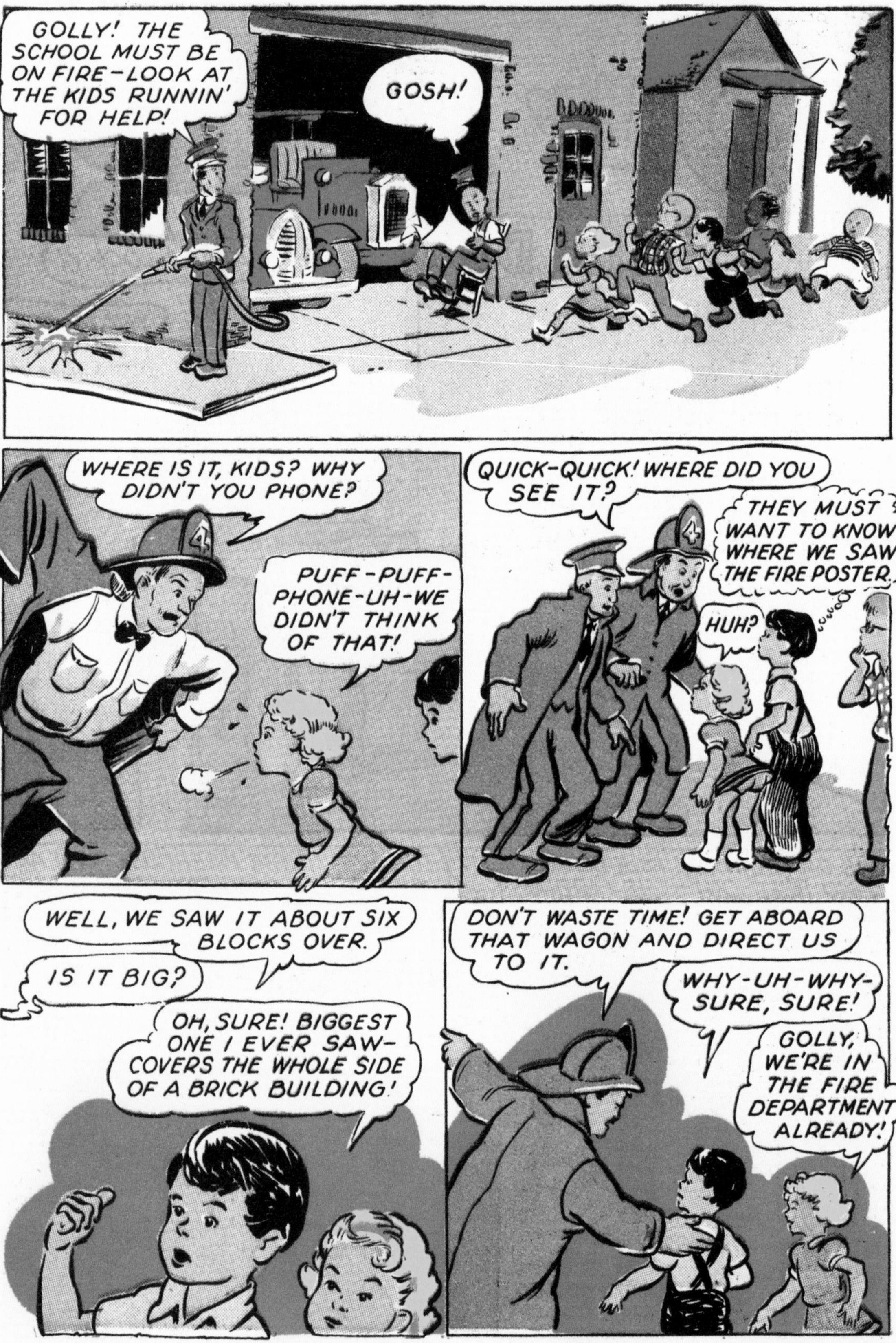

GOLLY! THE SCHOOL MUST BE ON FIRE—LOOK AT THE KIDS RUNNIN' FOR HELP!
GOSH!
WHERE IS IT, KIDS? WHY DIDN'T YOU PHONE?
PUFF-PUFF-PHONE-UH-WE DIDN'T THINK OF THAT!
QUICK-QUICK! WHERE DID YOU SEE IT?
THEY MUST WANT TO KNOW WHERE WE SAW THE FIRE POSTER.
HUH?
WELL, WE SAW IT ABOUT SIX BLOCKS OVER.
IS IT BIG?
OH, SURE! BIGGEST ONE I EVER SAW—COVERS THE WHOLE SIDE OF A BRICK BUILDING!
DON'T WASTE TIME! GET ABOARD THAT WAGON AND DIRECT US TO IT.
WHY-UH-WHY-SURE, SURE!
GOLLY, WE'RE IN THE FIRE DEPARTMENT ALREADY!

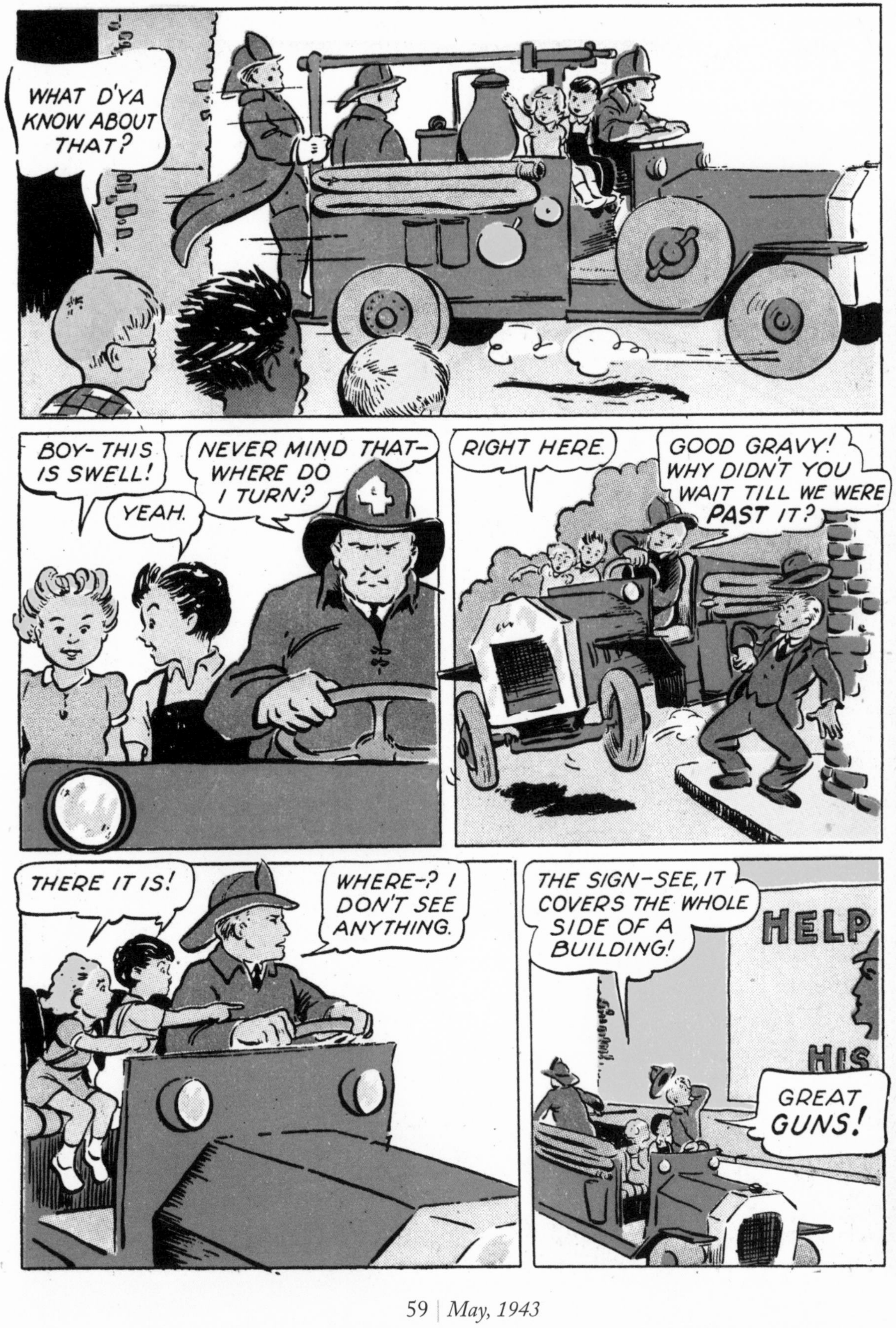
WHAT D'YA KNOW ABOUT THAT?
BOY- THIS IS SWELL!
YEAH.
NEVER MIND THAT- WHERE DO I TURN?
RIGHT HERE.
GOOD GRAVY! WHY DIDN'T YOU WAIT TILL WE WERE PAST IT?
THERE IT IS!
WHERE-? I DON'T SEE ANYTHING.
THE SIGN-SEE, IT COVERS THE WHOLE SIDE OF A BUILDING!
HELP
HIS
GREAT GUNS!

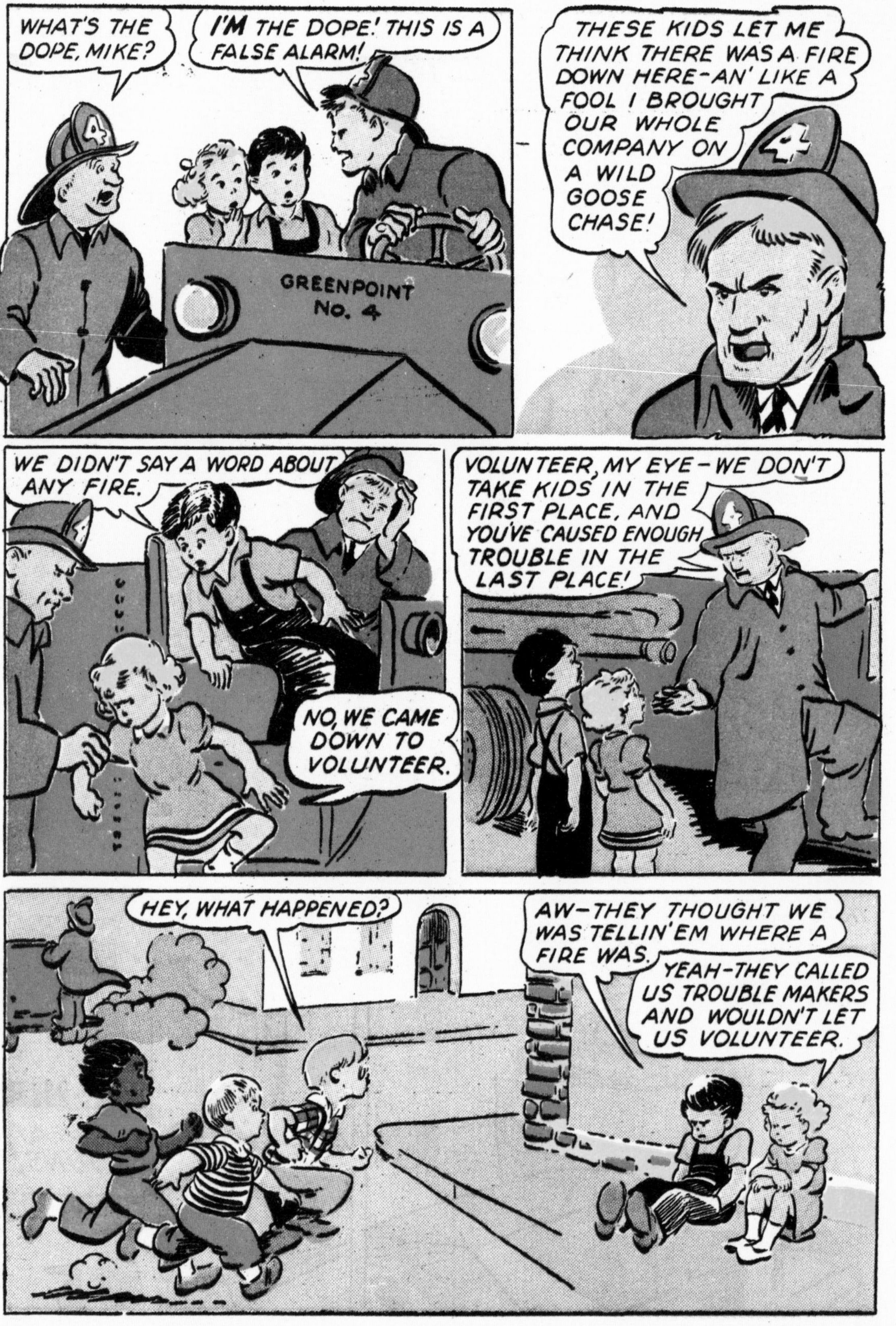
WHAT'S THE DOPE, MIKE?
I'M THE DOPE! THIS IS A FALSE ALARM!
GREENPOINT No. 4
THESE KIDS LET ME THINK THERE WAS A FIRE DOWN HERE-AN' LIKE A FOOL I BROUGHT OUR WHOLE COMPANY ON A WILD GOOSE CHASE!
WE DIDN'T SAY A WORD ABOUT ANY FIRE.
NO, WE CAME DOWN TO VOLUNTEER.
VOLUNTEER, MY EYE-WE DON'T TAKE KIDS IN THE FIRST PLACE, AND YOU'VE CAUSED ENOUGH TROUBLE IN THE LAST PLACE!
HEY, WHAT HAPPENED?
AW-THEY THOUGHT WE WAS TELLIN'EM WHERE A FIRE WAS.
YEAH-THEY CALLED US TROUBLE MAKERS AND WOULDN'T LET US VOLUNTEER.

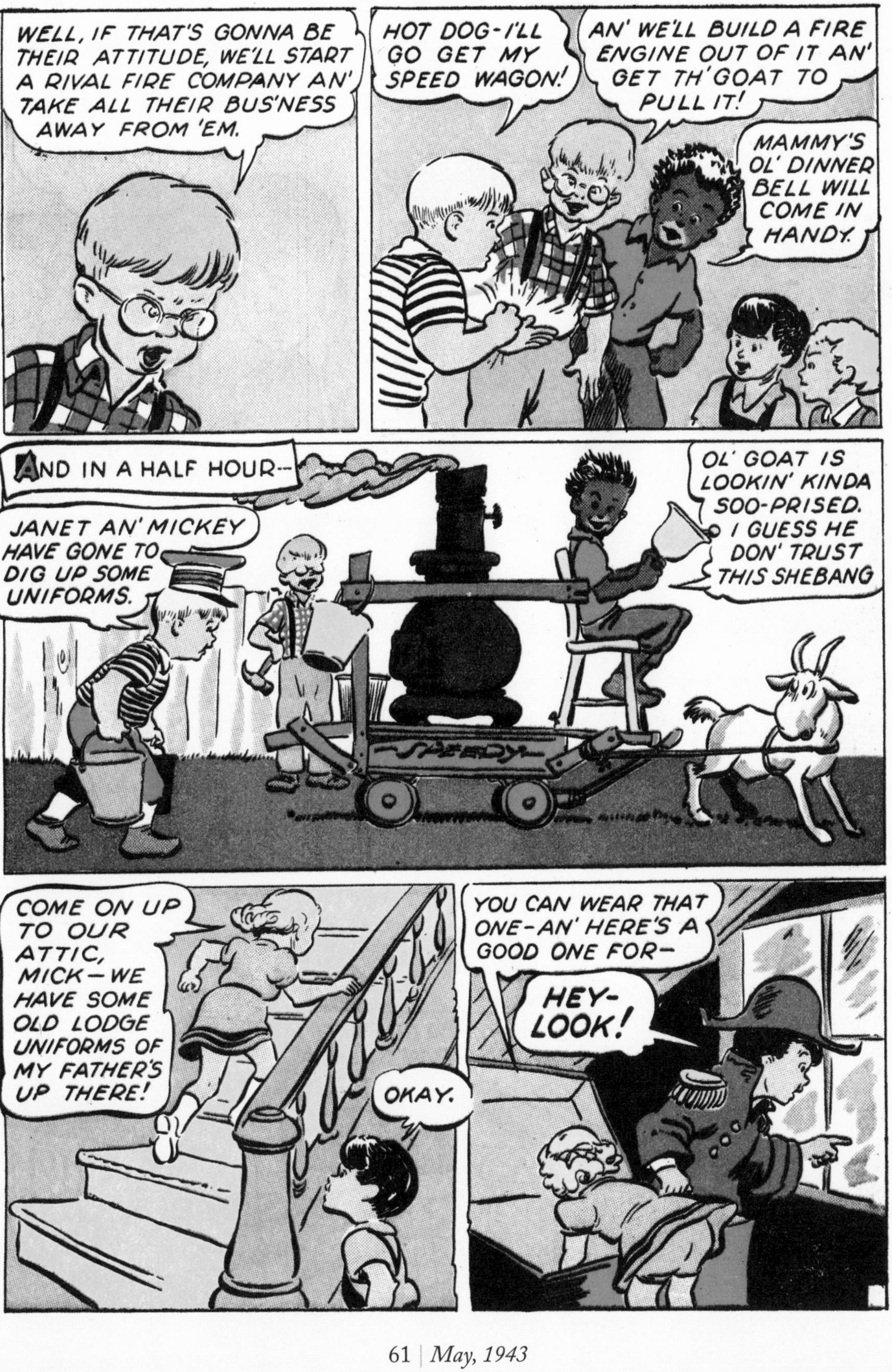
WELL, IF THAT'S GONNA BE THEIR ATTITUDE, WE'LL START A RIVAL FIRE COMPANY AN' TAKE ALL THEIR BUS'NESS AWAY FROM 'EM.
HOT DOG-I'LL GO GET MY SPEED WAGON!
AN' WE'LL BUILD A FIRE ENGINE OUT OF IT AN' GET TH' GOAT TO PULL IT!
MAMMY'S OL' DINNER BELL WILL COME IN HANDY.
AND IN A HALF HOUR--
JANET AN' MICKEY HAVE GONE TO DIG UP SOME UNIFORMS.
OL' GOAT IS LOOKIN' KINDA SOO-PRISED. I GUESS HE DON' TRUST THIS SHEBANG
SPEEDY
COME ON UP TO OUR ATTIC, MICK—WE HAVE SOME OLD LODGE UNIFORMS OF MY FATHER'S UP THERE!
OKAY.
YOU CAN WEAR THAT ONE-AN' HERE'S A GOOD ONE FOR—
HEY-LOOK!

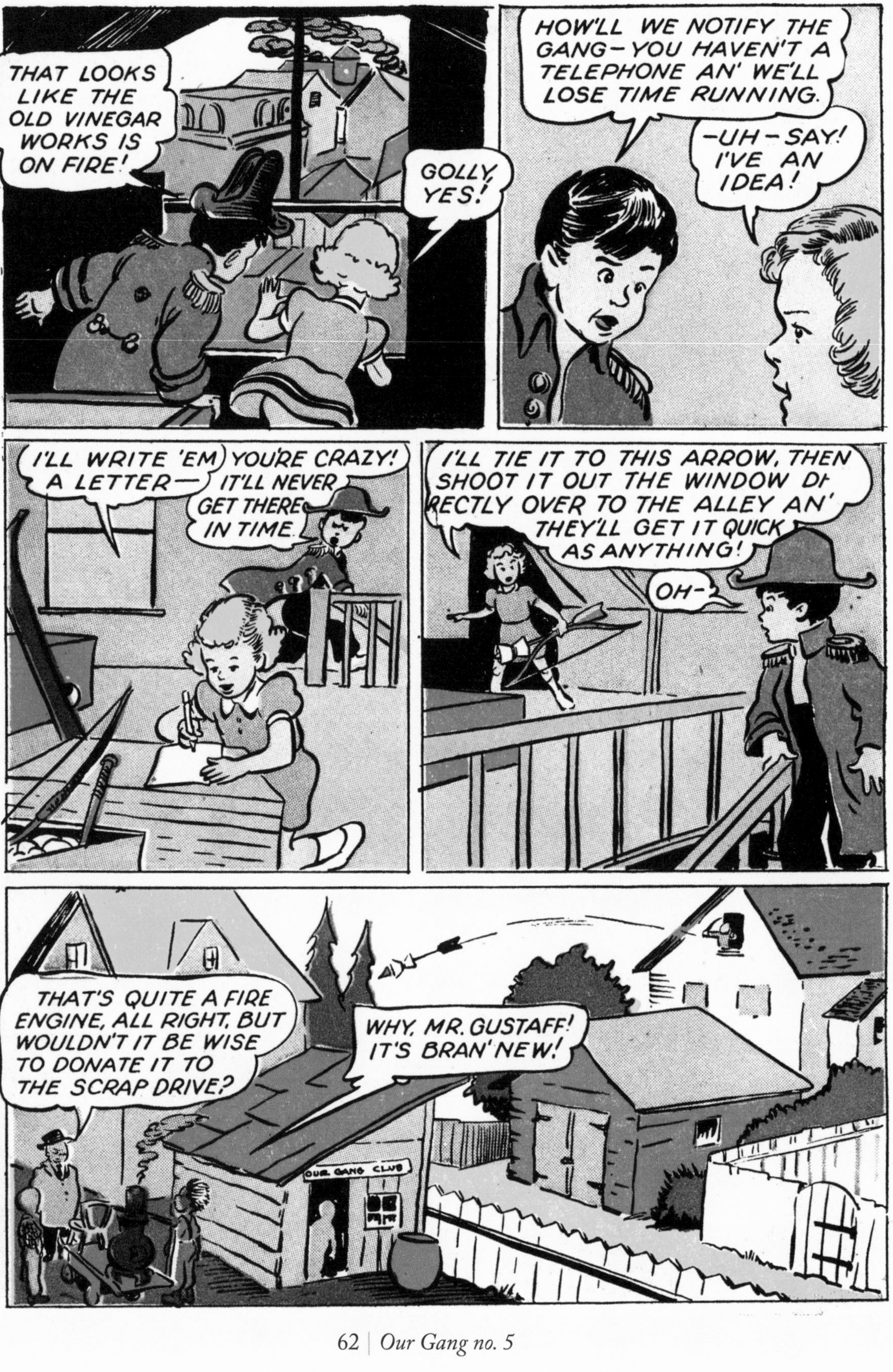
THAT LOOKS LIKE THE OLD VINEGAR WORKS IS ON FIRE!
GOLLY, YES!
HOW'LL WE NOTIFY THE GANG—YOU HAVEN'T A TELEPHONE AN' WE'LL LOSE TIME RUNNING.
—UH—SAY! I'VE AN IDEA!
I'LL WRITE 'EM A LETTER—
YOU'RE CRAZY! IT'LL NEVER GET THERE IN TIME.
I'LL TIE IT TO THIS ARROW, THEN SHOOT IT OUT THE WINDOW DIRECTLY OVER TO THE ALLEY AN' THEY'LL GET IT QUICK AS ANYTHING!
OH—
THAT'S QUITE A FIRE ENGINE, ALL RIGHT, BUT WOULDN'T IT BE WISE TO DONATE IT TO THE SCRAP DRIVE?
WHY, MR. GUSTAFF! IT'S BRAN' NEW!
OUR GANG CLUB

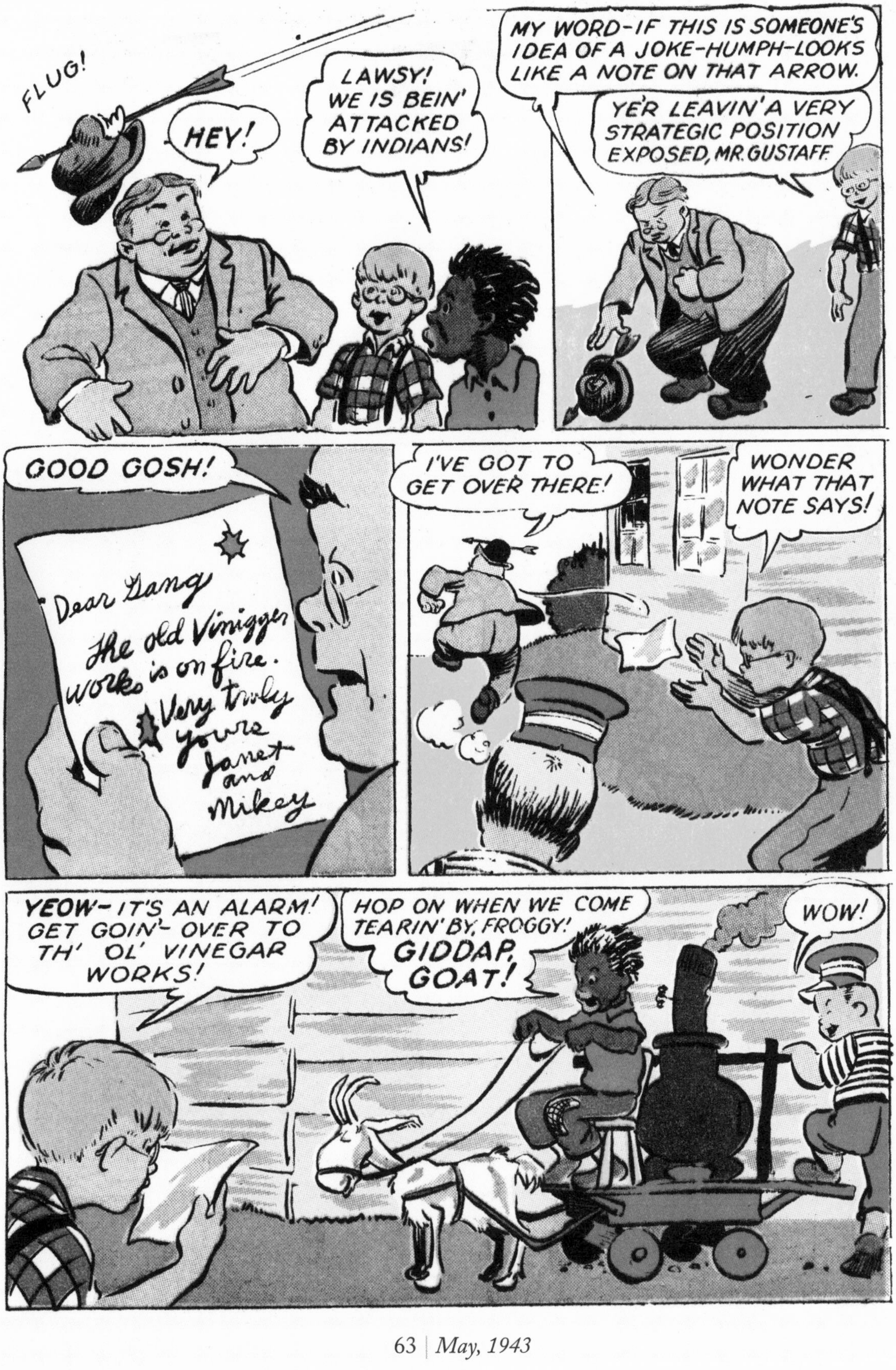
FLUG!
HEY!
LAWSY! WE IS BEIN' ATTACKED BY INDIANS!
MY WORD-IF THIS IS SOMEONE'S IDEA OF A JOKE-HUMPH-LOOKS LIKE A NOTE ON THAT ARROW.
YE'R LEAVIN' A VERY STRATEGIC POSITION EXPOSED, MR. GUSTAFF
GOOD GOSH!
Dear Gang
The old Viniggar works is on fire.
Very truly youre Janet and Mikey
I'VE GOT TO GET OVER THERE!
WONDER WHAT THAT NOTE SAYS!
YEOW- IT'S AN ALARM! GET GOIN'- OVER TO TH' OL' VINEGAR WORKS!
HOP ON WHEN WE COME TEARIN' BY, FROGGY! GIDDAP, GOAT!
WOW!

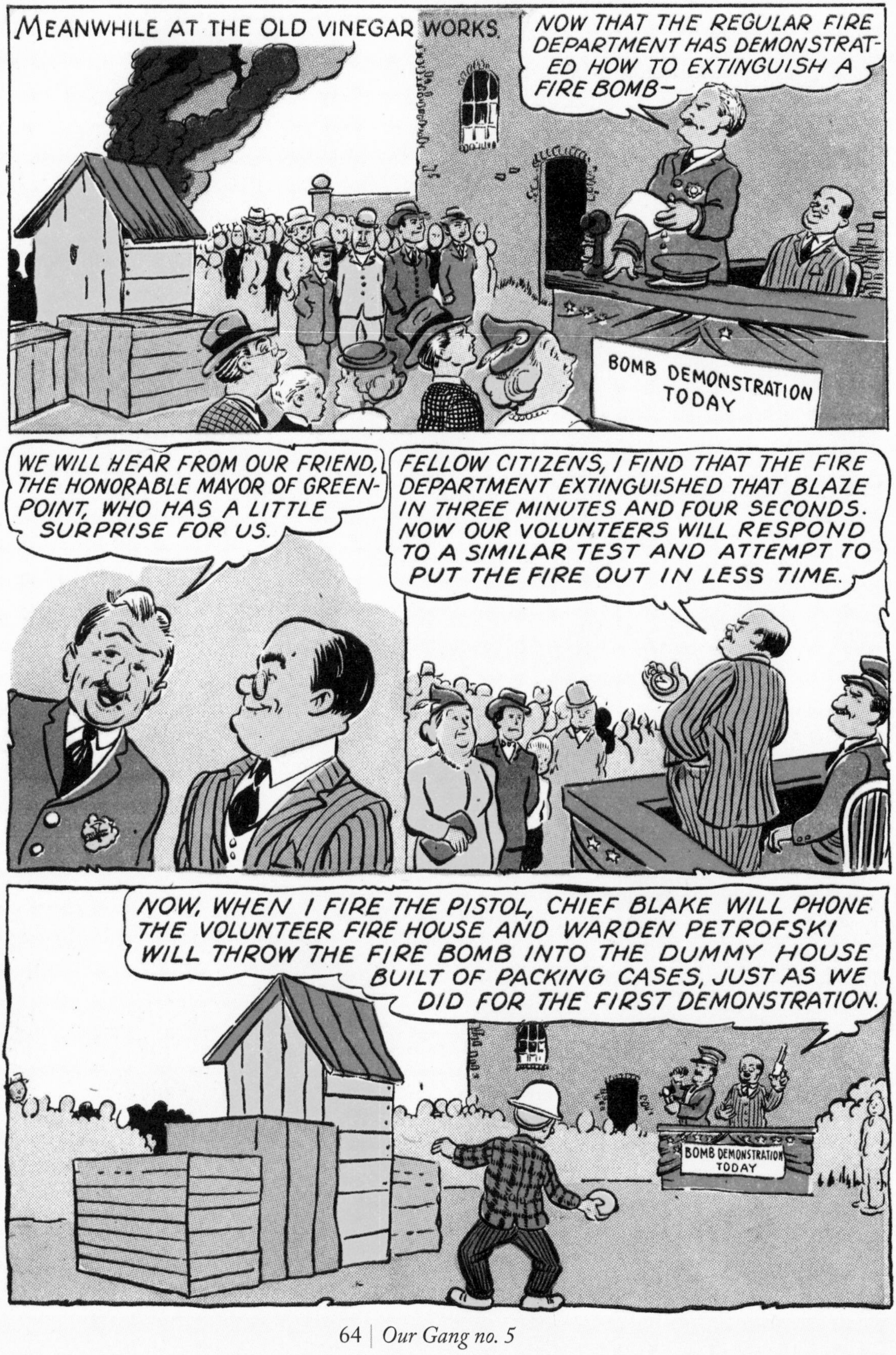
MEANWHILE AT THE OLD VINEGAR WORKS.
NOW THAT THE REGULAR FIRE DEPARTMENT HAS DEMONSTRATED HOW TO EXTINGUISH A FIRE BOMB—
BOMB DEMONSTRATION TODAY
WE WILL HEAR FROM OUR FRIEND, THE HONORABLE MAYOR OF GREENPOINT, WHO HAS A LITTLE SURPRISE FOR US.
FELLOW CITIZENS, I FIND THAT THE FIRE DEPARTMENT EXTINGUISHED THAT BLAZE IN THREE MINUTES AND FOUR SECONDS. NOW OUR VOLUNTEERS WILL RESPOND TO A SIMILAR TEST AND ATTEMPT TO PUT THE FIRE OUT IN LESS TIME.
NOW, WHEN I FIRE THE PISTOL, CHIEF BLAKE WILL PHONE THE VOLUNTEER FIRE HOUSE AND WARDEN PETROFSKI WILL THROW THE FIRE BOMB INTO THE DUMMY HOUSE BUILT OF PACKING CASES, JUST AS WE DID FOR THE FIRST DEMONSTRATION.
BOMB DEMONSTRATION TODAY

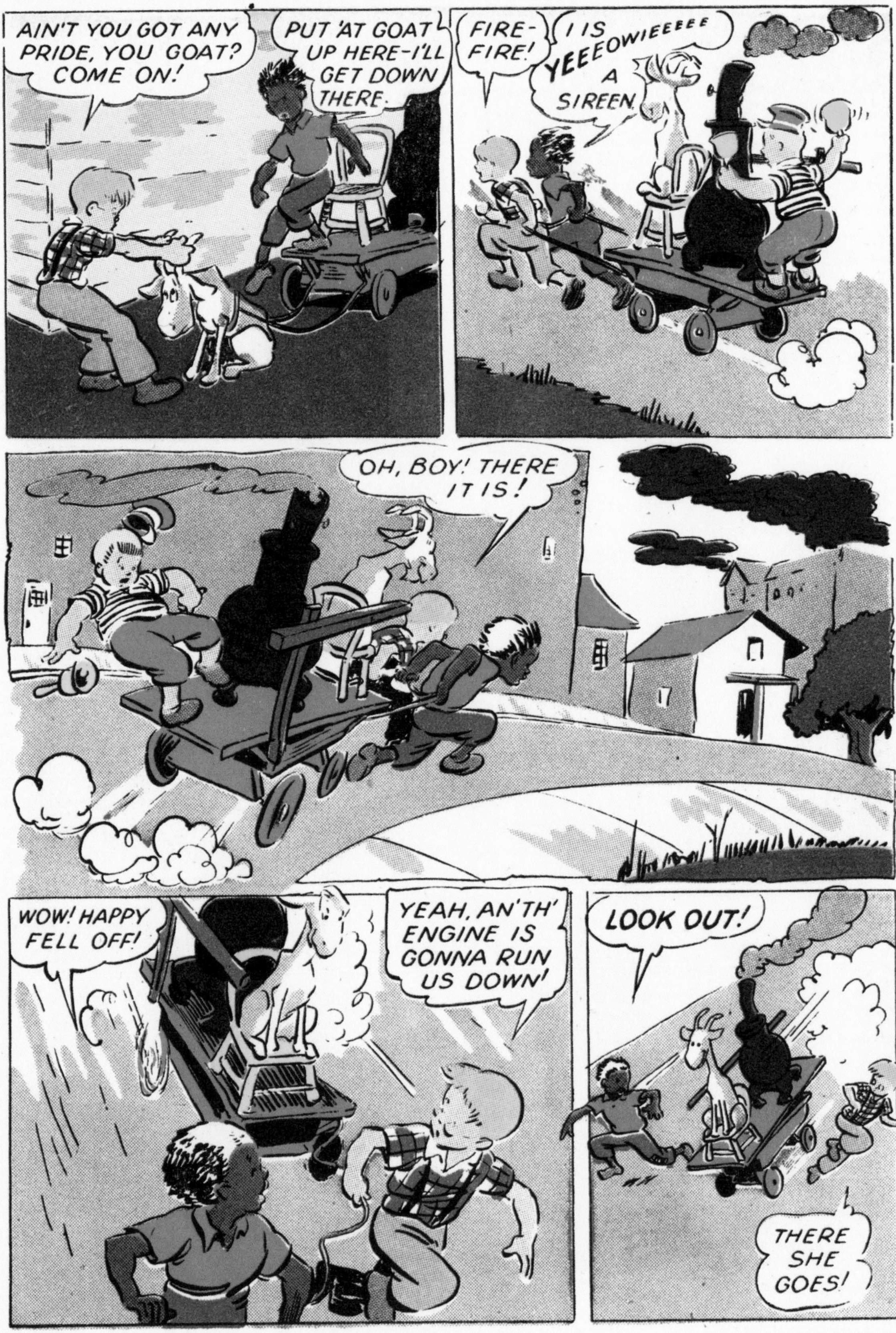
AIN'T YOU GOT ANY PRIDE, YOU GOAT? COME ON!
PUT 'AT GOAT UP HERE-I'LL GET DOWN THERE.
FIRE-FIRE!
I IS YEEEOWIEEEEE A SIREEN.
OH, BOY! THERE IT IS!
WOW! HAPPY FELL OFF!
YEAH, AN'TH' ENGINE IS GONNA RUN US DOWN!
LOOK OUT!
THERE SHE GOES!

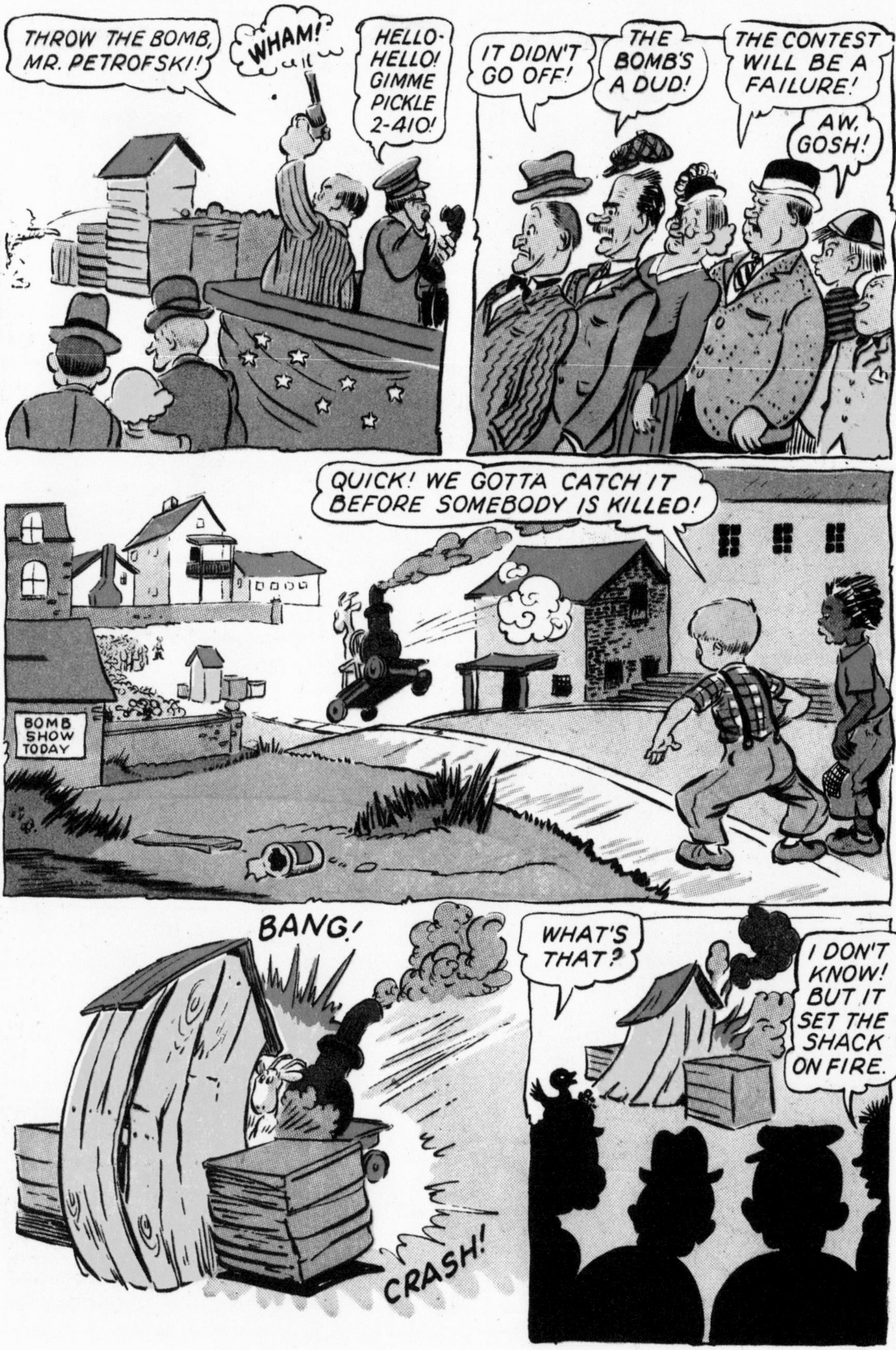
THROW THE BOMB, MR. PETROFSKI!
WHAM!
HELLO-HELLO! GIMME PICKLE 2-410!
IT DIDN'T GO OFF!
THE BOMB'S A DUD!
THE CONTEST WILL BE A FAILURE!
AW, GOSH!
QUICK! WE GOTTA CATCH IT BEFORE SOMEBODY IS KILLED!
BOMB SHOW TODAY
BANG!
CRASH!
WHAT'S THAT?
I DON'T KNOW! BUT IT SET THE SHACK ON FIRE.

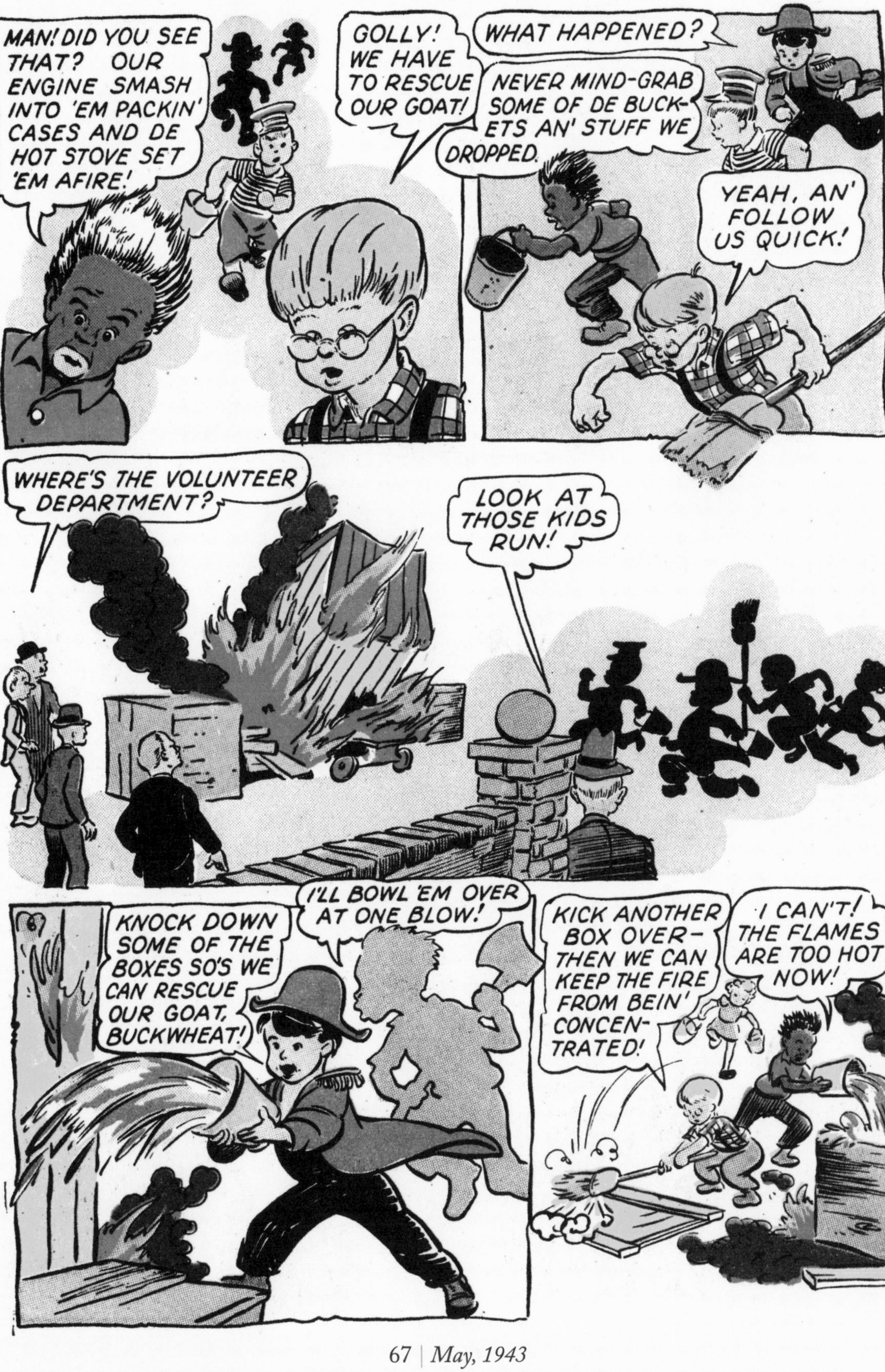

MAN! DID YOU SEE THAT? OUR ENGINE SMASH INTO 'EM PACKIN' CASES AND DE HOT STOVE SET 'EM AFIRE!
GOLLY! WE HAVE TO RESCUE OUR GOAT!
WHAT HAPPENED?
NEVER MIND-GRAB SOME OF DE BUCK-ETS AN' STUFF WE DROPPED.
YEAH, AN' FOLLOW US QUICK!
WHERE'S THE VOLUNTEER DEPARTMENT?
LOOK AT THOSE KIDS RUN!
KNOCK DOWN SOME OF THE BOXES SO'S WE CAN RESCUE OUR GOAT, BUCKWHEAT!
I'LL BOWL 'EM OVER AT ONE BLOW!
KICK ANOTHER BOX OVER—THEN WE CAN KEEP THE FIRE FROM BEIN' CONCEN-TRATED!
I CAN'T! THE FLAMES ARE TOO HOT NOW!

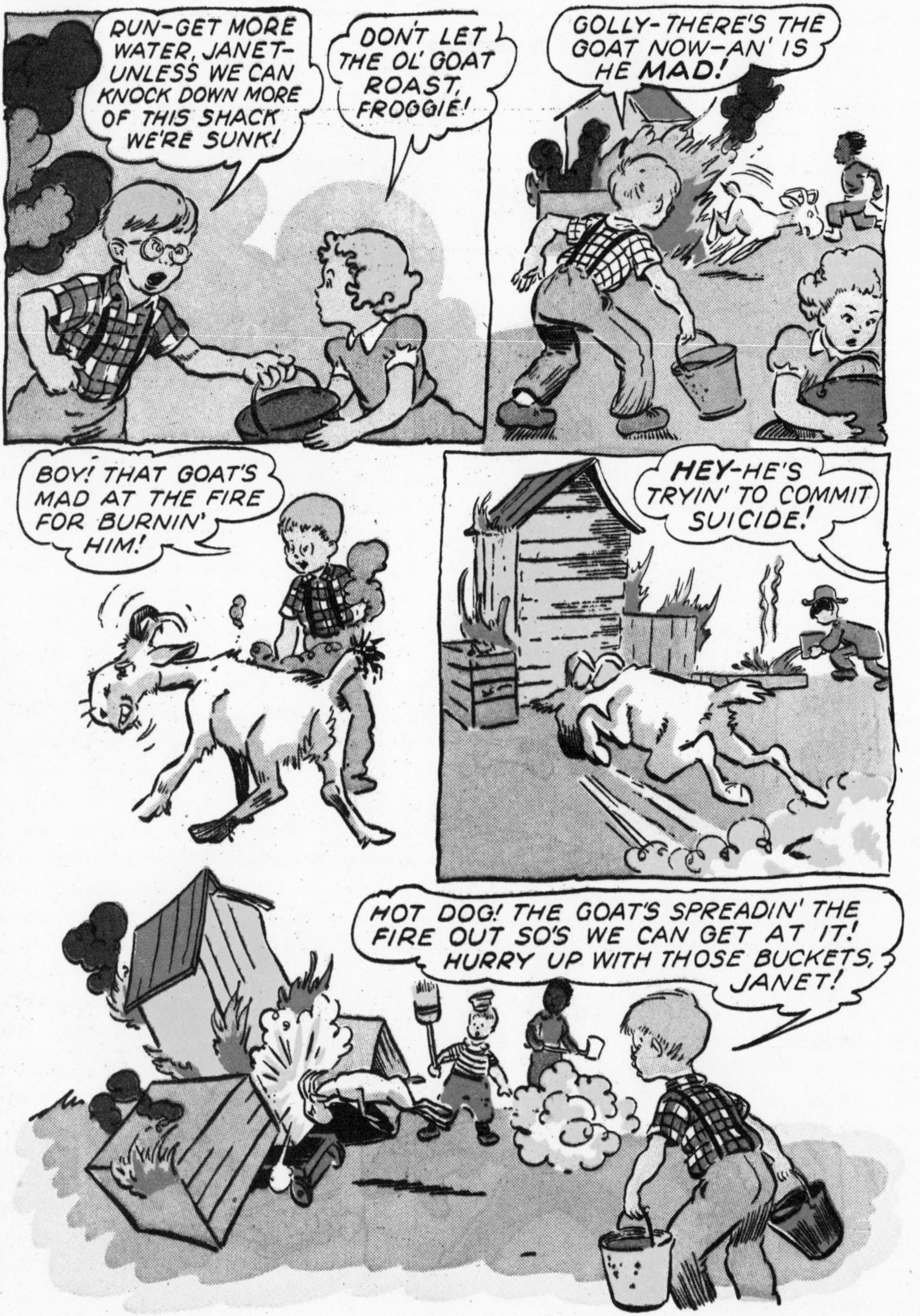
RUN-GET MORE WATER, JANET-UNLESS WE CAN KNOCK DOWN MORE OF THIS SHACK WE'RE SUNK!
DON'T LET THE OL' GOAT ROAST, FROGGIE!
GOLLY-THERE'S THE GOAT NOW-AN' IS HE **MAD!**
BOY! THAT GOAT'S MAD AT THE FIRE FOR BURNIN' HIM!
HEY-HE'S TRYIN' TO COMMIT SUICIDE!
HOT DOG! THE GOAT'S SPREADIN' THE FIRE OUT SO'S WE CAN GET AT IT! HURRY UP WITH THOSE BUCKETS, JANET!

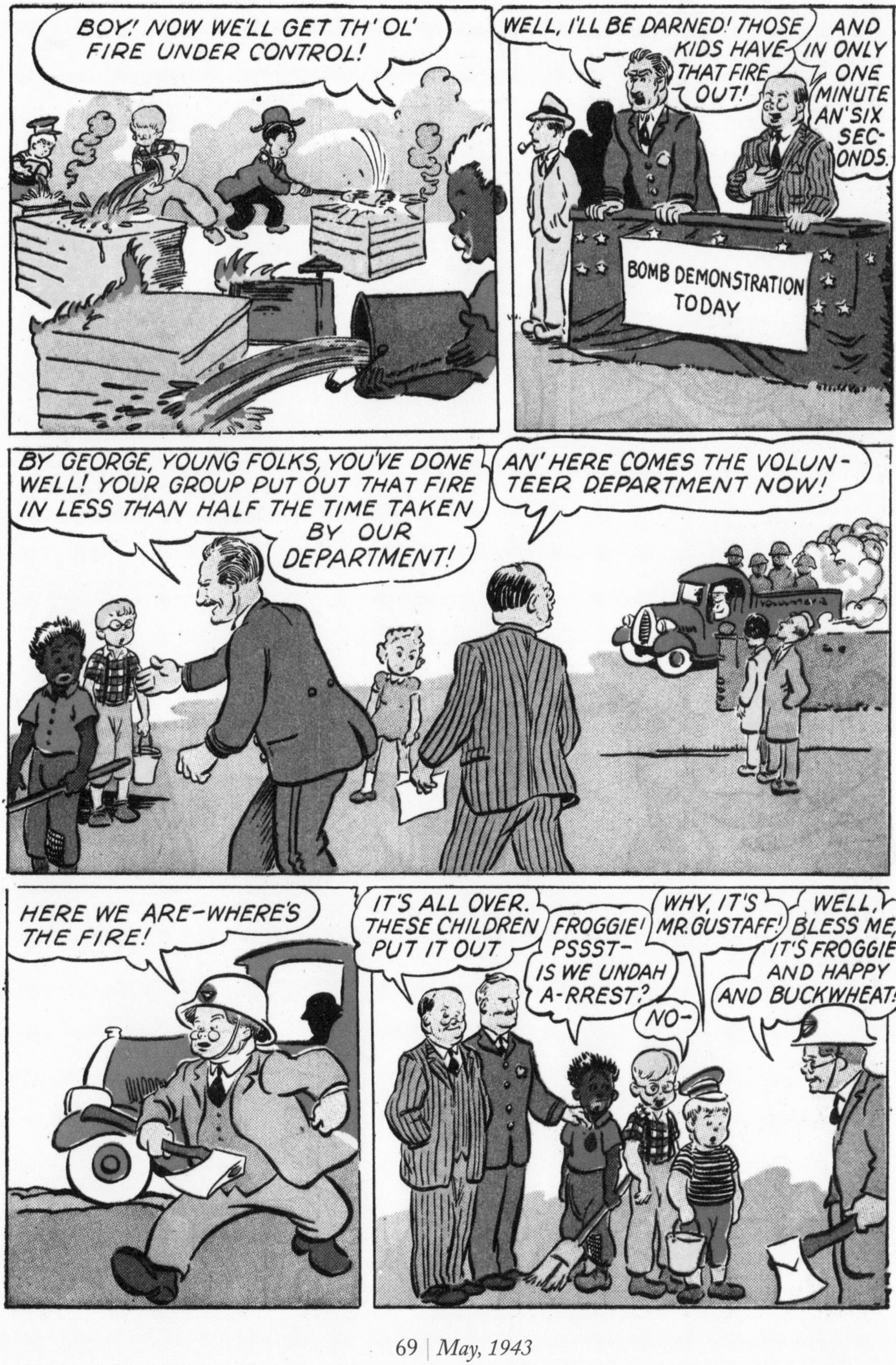
BOY! NOW WE'LL GET TH' OL' FIRE UNDER CONTROL!
WELL, I'LL BE DARNED! THOSE KIDS HAVE THAT FIRE OUT!
AND IN ONLY ONE MINUTE AN' SIX SEC-ONDS.
BOMB DEMONSTRATION TODAY
BY GEORGE, YOUNG FOLKS, YOU'VE DONE WELL! YOUR GROUP PUT OUT THAT FIRE IN LESS THAN HALF THE TIME TAKEN BY OUR DEPARTMENT!
AN' HERE COMES THE VOLUN-TEER DEPARTMENT NOW!
HERE WE ARE–WHERE'S THE FIRE!
IT'S ALL OVER. THESE CHILDREN PUT IT OUT
FROGGIE! PSSST– IS WE UNDAH A-RREST?
NO–
WHY, IT'S MR. GUSTAFF!
WELL, BLESS ME, IT'S FROGGIE AND HAPPY AND BUCKWHEAT!

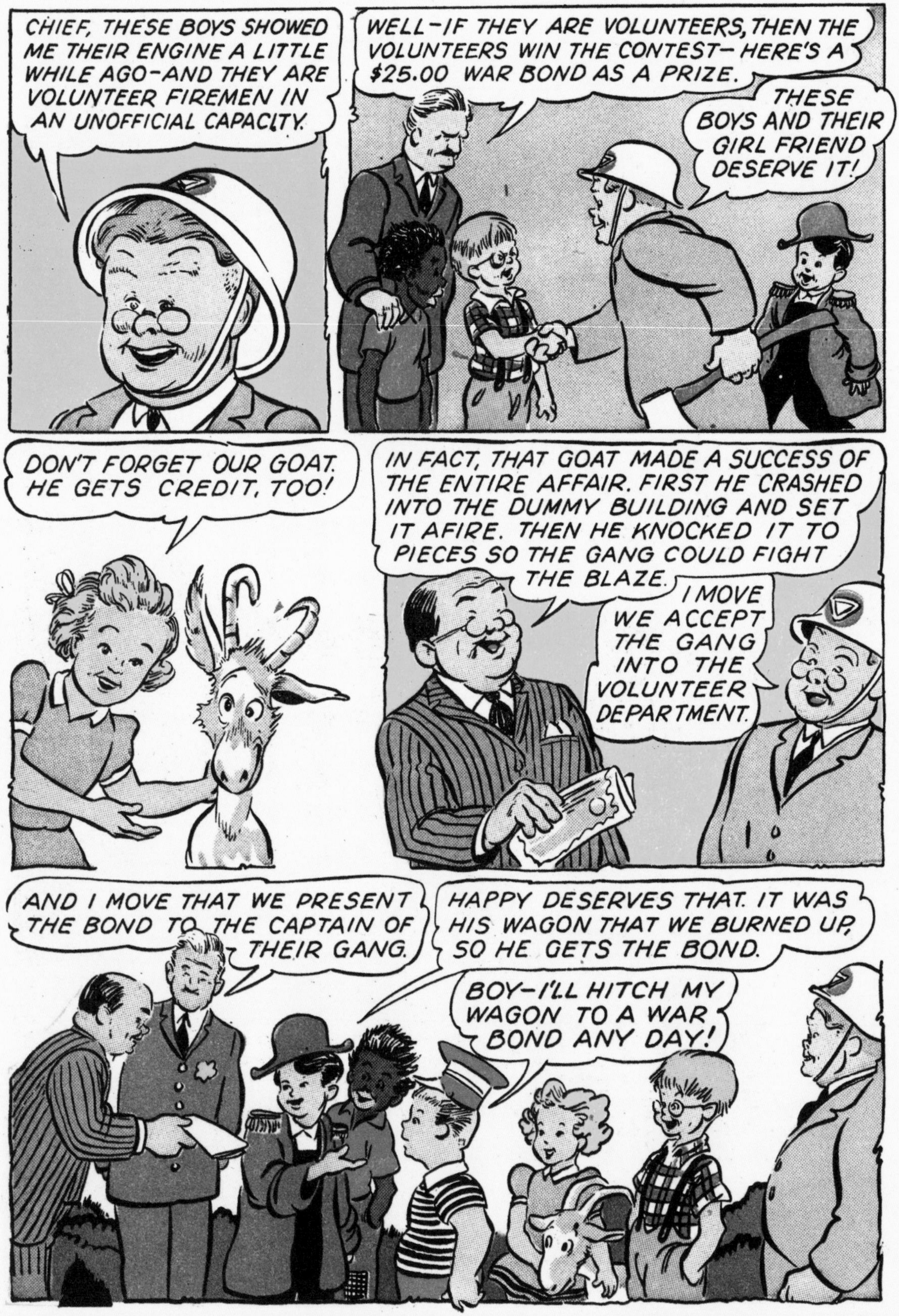
CHIEF, THESE BOYS SHOWED ME THEIR ENGINE A LITTLE WHILE AGO–AND THEY ARE VOLUNTEER FIREMEN IN AN UNOFFICIAL CAPACITY.
WELL–IF THEY ARE VOLUNTEERS, THEN THE VOLUNTEERS WIN THE CONTEST– HERE'S A $25.00 WAR BOND AS A PRIZE.
THESE BOYS AND THEIR GIRL FRIEND DESERVE IT!
DON'T FORGET OUR GOAT. HE GETS CREDIT, TOO!
IN FACT, THAT GOAT MADE A SUCCESS OF THE ENTIRE AFFAIR. FIRST HE CRASHED INTO THE DUMMY BUILDING AND SET IT AFIRE. THEN HE KNOCKED IT TO PIECES SO THE GANG COULD FIGHT THE BLAZE.
I MOVE WE ACCEPT THE GANG INTO THE VOLUNTEER DEPARTMENT.
AND I MOVE THAT WE PRESENT THE BOND TO THE CAPTAIN OF THEIR GANG.
HAPPY DESERVES THAT. IT WAS HIS WAGON THAT WE BURNED UP, SO HE GETS THE BOND.
BOY–I'LL HITCH MY WAGON TO A WAR BOND ANY DAY!

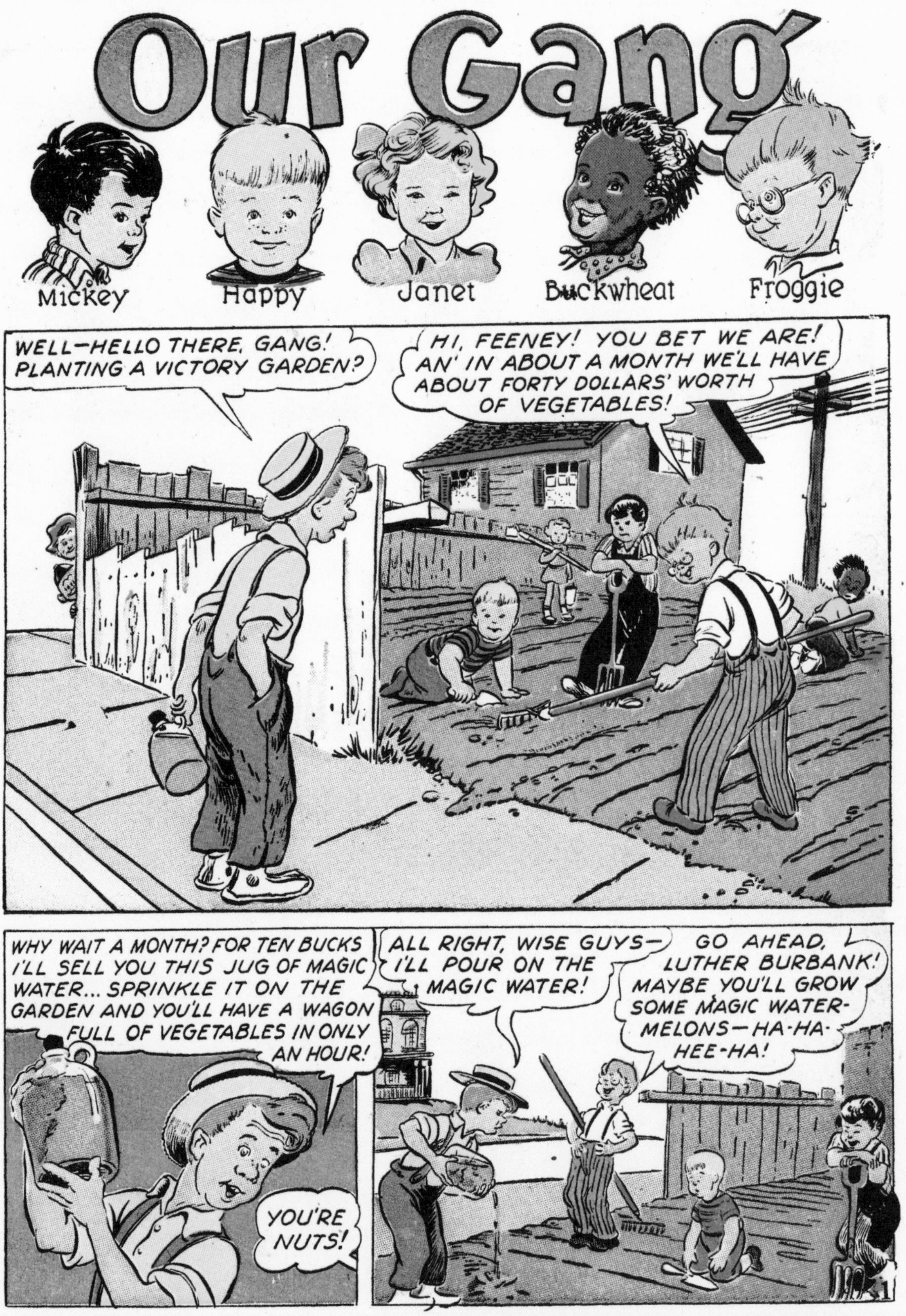
Our Gang
Mickey
Happy
Janet
Buckwheat
Froggie
WELL—HELLO THERE, GANG! PLANTING A VICTORY GARDEN?
HI, FEENEY! YOU BET WE ARE! AN' IN ABOUT A MONTH WE'LL HAVE ABOUT FORTY DOLLARS' WORTH OF VEGETABLES!
WHY WAIT A MONTH? FOR TEN BUCKS I'LL SELL YOU THIS JUG OF MAGIC WATER... SPRINKLE IT ON THE GARDEN AND YOU'LL HAVE A WAGON FULL OF VEGETABLES IN ONLY AN HOUR!
YOU'RE NUTS!
ALL RIGHT, WISE GUYS— I'LL POUR ON THE MAGIC WATER!
GO AHEAD, LUTHER BURBANK! MAYBE YOU'LL GROW SOME MAGIC WATER-MELONS—HA-HA-HEE-HA!

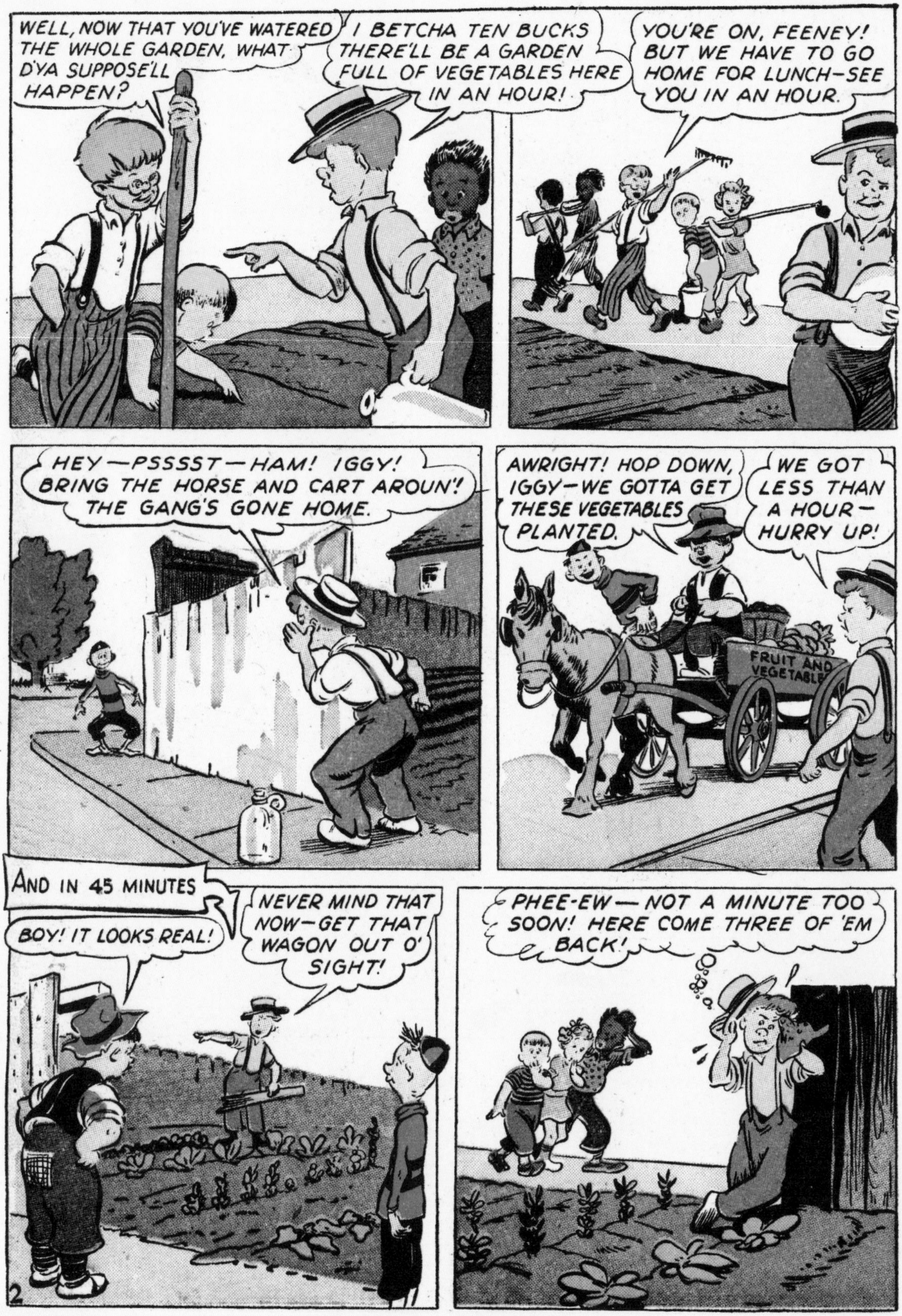
WELL, NOW THAT YOU'VE WATERED THE WHOLE GARDEN, WHAT D'YA SUPPOSE'LL HAPPEN?
I BETCHA TEN BUCKS THERE'LL BE A GARDEN FULL OF VEGETABLES HERE IN AN HOUR!
YOU'RE ON, FEENEY! BUT WE HAVE TO GO HOME FOR LUNCH—SEE YOU IN AN HOUR.
HEY—PSSSST—HAM! IGGY! BRING THE HORSE AND CART AROUN'! THE GANG'S GONE HOME.
AWRIGHT! HOP DOWN, IGGY—WE GOTTA GET THESE VEGETABLES PLANTED.
WE GOT LESS THAN A HOUR—HURRY UP!
FRUIT AND VEGETABLE
AND IN 45 MINUTES
BOY! IT LOOKS REAL!
NEVER MIND THAT NOW—GET THAT WAGON OUT O' SIGHT!
PHEE-EW—NOT A MINUTE TOO SOON! HERE COME THREE OF 'EM BACK!
2

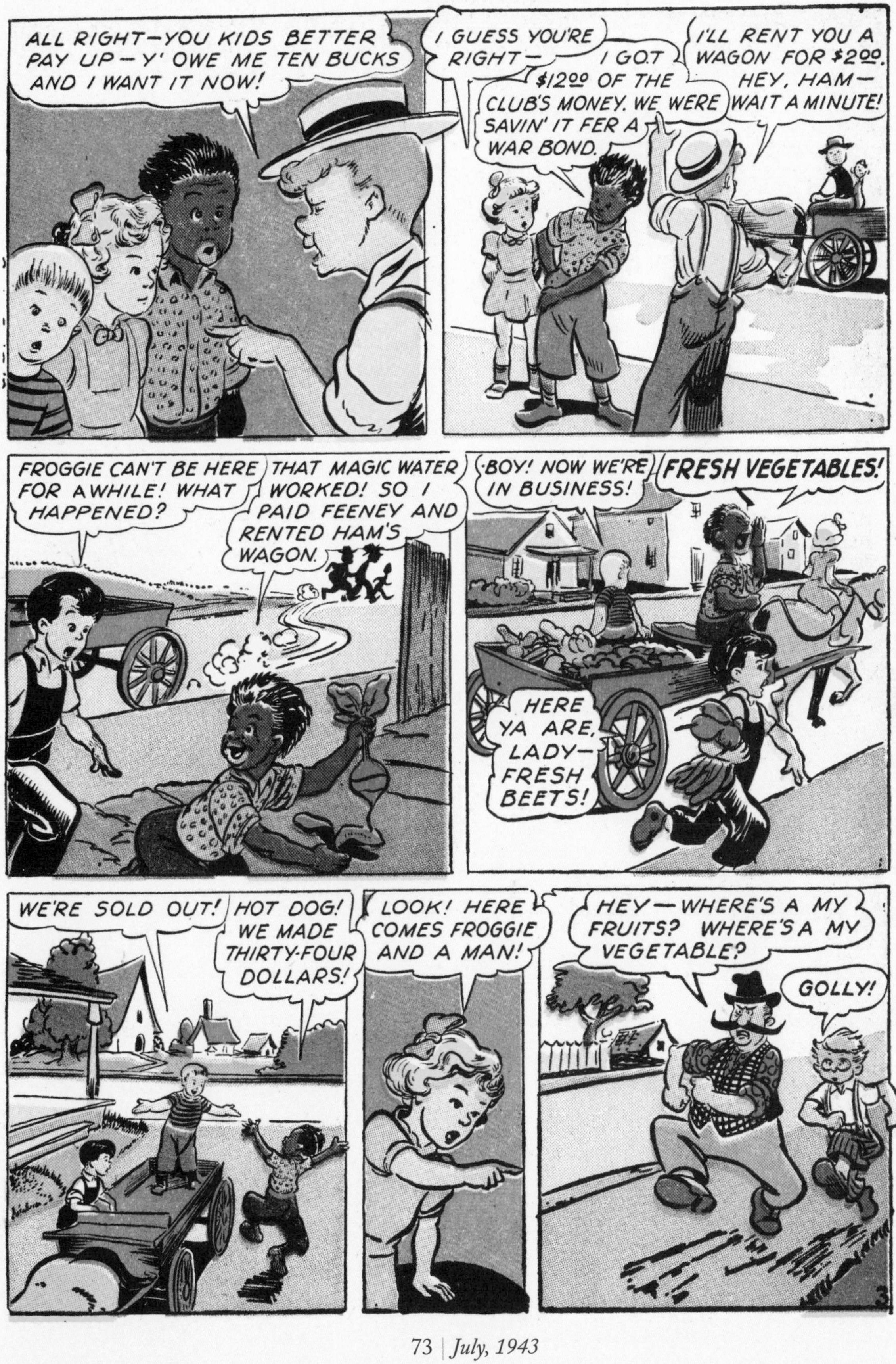
ALL RIGHT—YOU KIDS BETTER PAY UP—Y' OWE ME TEN BUCKS AND I WANT IT NOW!
I GUESS YOU'RE RIGHT—
I GOT $12.00 OF THE CLUB'S MONEY. WE WERE SAVIN' IT FER A WAR BOND.
I'LL RENT YOU A WAGON FOR $2.00.
HEY, HAM—WAIT A MINUTE!
FROGGIE CAN'T BE HERE FOR AWHILE! WHAT HAPPENED?
THAT MAGIC WATER WORKED! SO I PAID FEENEY AND RENTED HAM'S WAGON.
BOY! NOW WE'RE IN BUSINESS!
FRESH VEGETABLES!
HERE YA ARE, LADY—FRESH BEETS!
WE'RE SOLD OUT!
HOT DOG! WE MADE THIRTY-FOUR DOLLARS!
LOOK! HERE COMES FROGGIE AND A MAN!
HEY—WHERE'S A MY FRUITS? WHERE'S A MY VEGETABLE?
GOLLY!
3

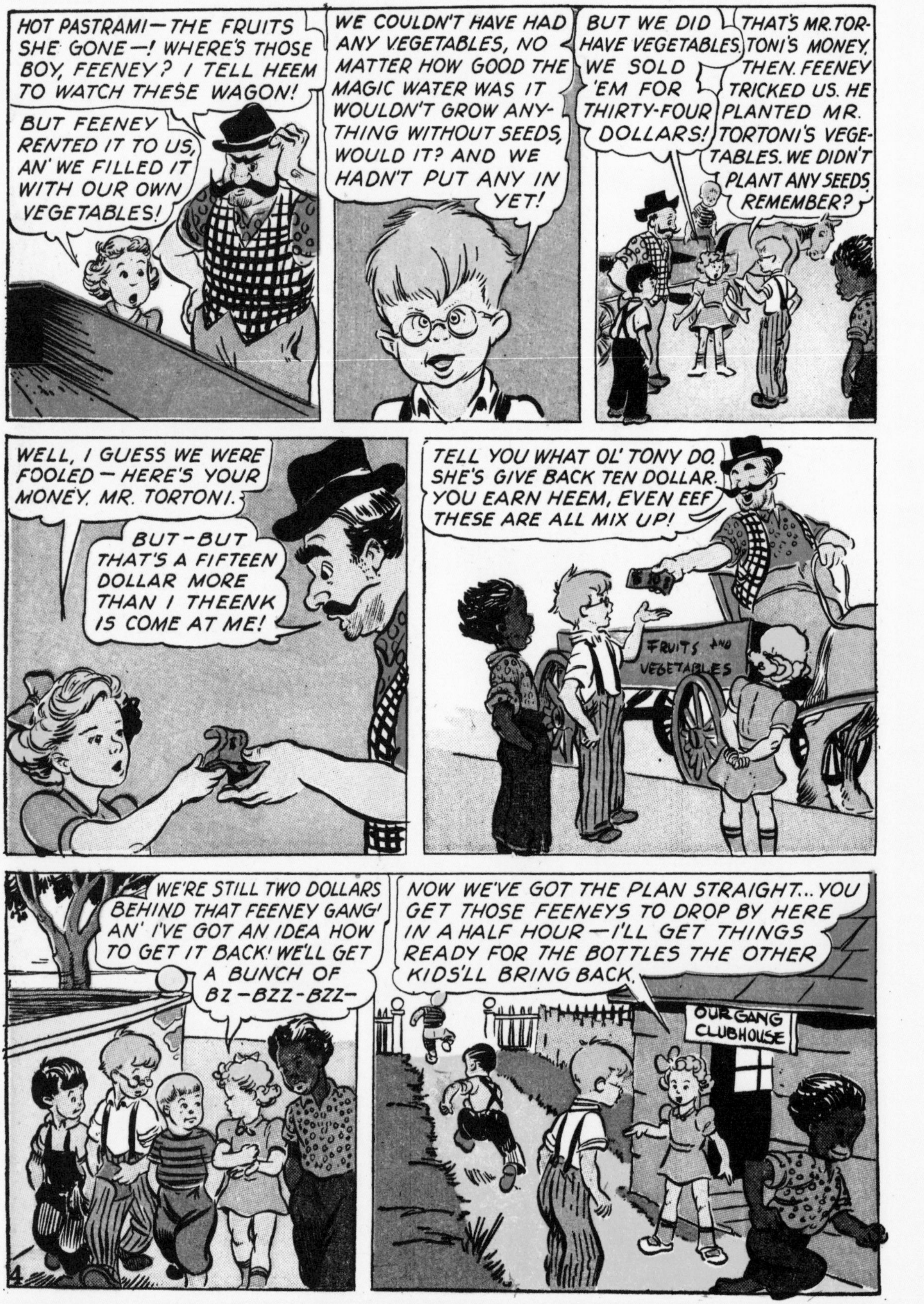
HOT PASTRAMI—THE FRUITS SHE GONE—! WHERE'S THOSE BOY, FEENEY? I TELL HEEM TO WATCH THESE WAGON!
BUT FEENEY RENTED IT TO US, AN' WE FILLED IT WITH OUR OWN VEGETABLES!
WE COULDN'T HAVE HAD ANY VEGETABLES, NO MATTER HOW GOOD THE MAGIC WATER WAS IT WOULDN'T GROW ANYTHING WITHOUT SEEDS, WOULD IT? AND WE HADN'T PUT ANY IN YET!
BUT WE DID HAVE VEGETABLES. WE SOLD 'EM FOR THIRTY-FOUR DOLLARS!
THAT'S MR. TORTONI'S MONEY, THEN. FEENEY TRICKED US. HE PLANTED MR. TORTONI'S VEGETABLES. WE DIDN'T PLANT ANY SEEDS, REMEMBER?
WELL, I GUESS WE WERE FOOLED—HERE'S YOUR MONEY, MR. TORTONI.
BUT-BUT THAT'S A FIFTEEN DOLLAR MORE THAN I THEENK IS COME AT ME!
TELL YOU WHAT OL' TONY DO. SHE'S GIVE BACK TEN DOLLAR. YOU EARN HEEM, EVEN EEF THESE ARE ALL MIX UP!
FRUITS AND VEGETABLES
WE'RE STILL TWO DOLLARS BEHIND THAT FEENEY GANG! AN' I'VE GOT AN IDEA HOW TO GET IT BACK! WE'LL GET A BUNCH OF BZ-BZZ-BZZ-
4
NOW WE'VE GOT THE PLAN STRAIGHT... YOU GET THOSE FEENEYS TO DROP BY HERE IN A HALF HOUR—I'LL GET THINGS READY FOR THE BOTTLES THE OTHER KIDS'LL BRING BACK.
OUR GANG CLUBHOUSE

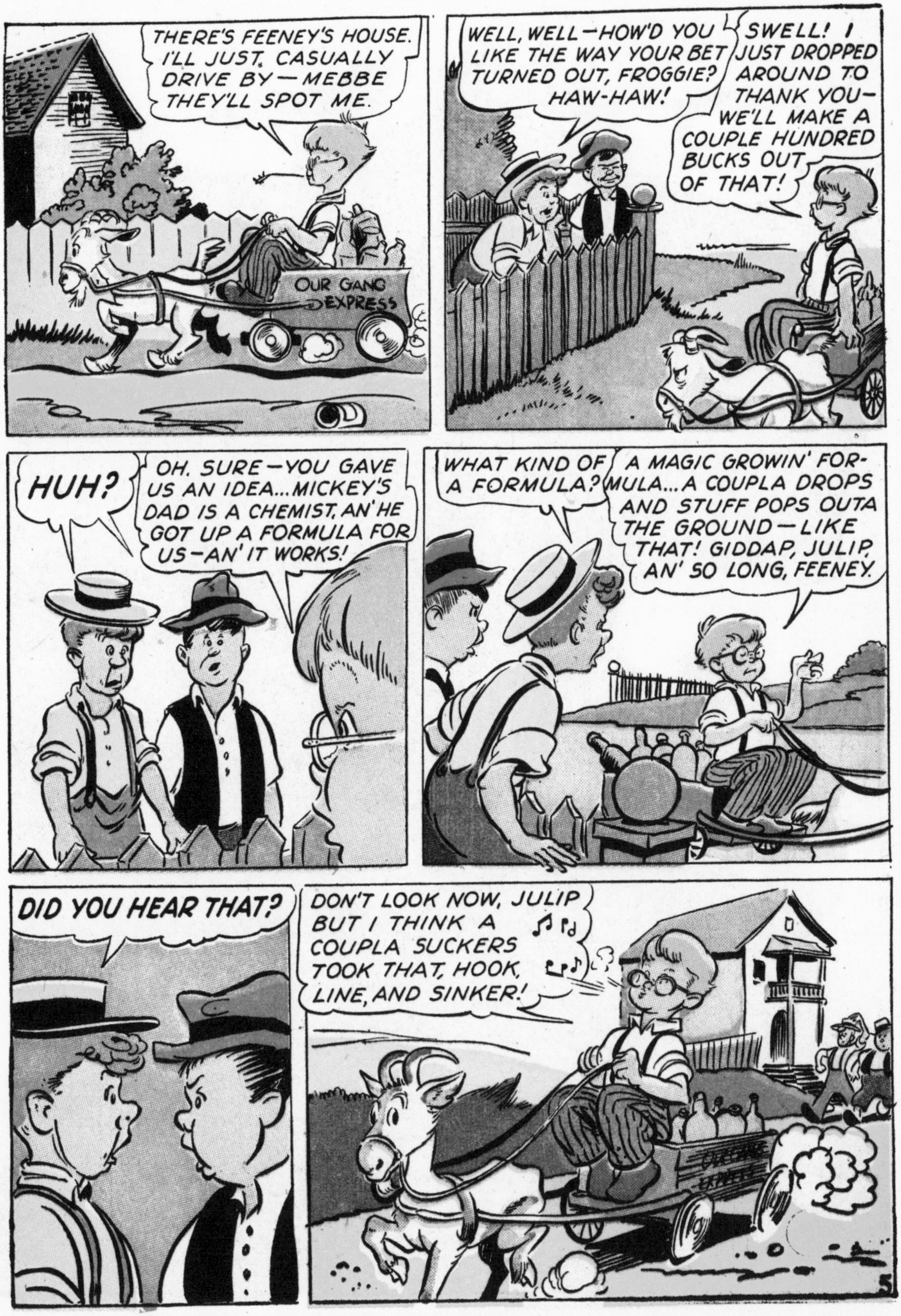
THERE'S FEENEY'S HOUSE. I'LL JUST CASUALLY DRIVE BY—MEBBE THEY'LL SPOT ME.
OUR GANG EXPRESS
WELL, WELL—HOW'D YOU LIKE THE WAY YOUR BET TURNED OUT, FROGGIE? HAW-HAW!
SWELL! I JUST DROPPED AROUND TO THANK YOU—WE'LL MAKE A COUPLE HUNDRED BUCKS OUT OF THAT!
HUH?
OH, SURE—YOU GAVE US AN IDEA...MICKEY'S DAD IS A CHEMIST, AN' HE GOT UP A FORMULA FOR US—AN' IT WORKS!
WHAT KIND OF A FORMULA?
A MAGIC GROWIN' FORMULA...A COUPLA DROPS AND STUFF POPS OUTA THE GROUND—LIKE THAT! GIDDAP, JULIP, AN' SO LONG, FEENEY.
DID YOU HEAR THAT?
DON'T LOOK NOW, JULIP BUT I THINK A COUPLA SUCKERS TOOK THAT, HOOK, LINE, AND SINKER!
5

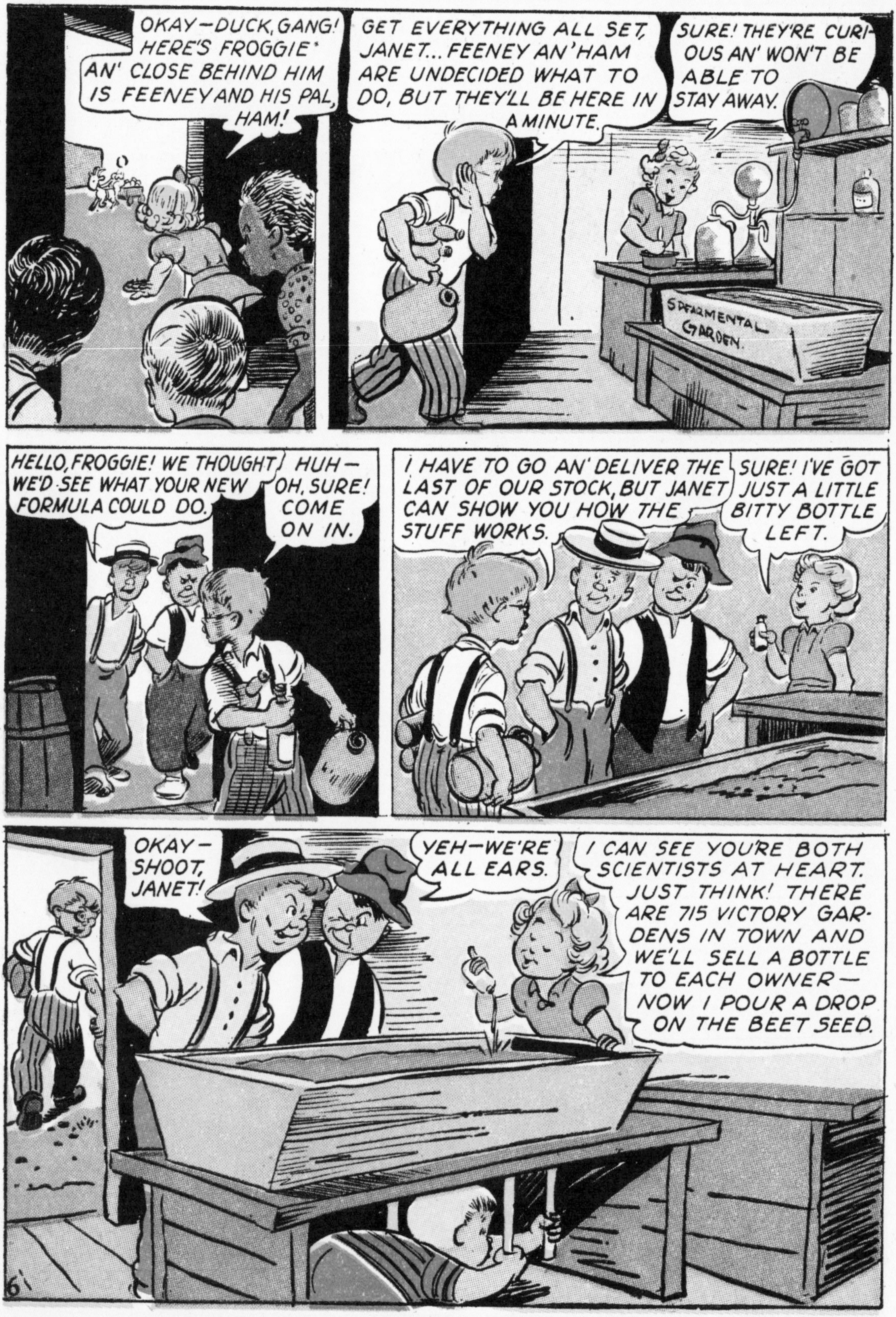

OKAY—DUCK, GANG! HERE'S FROGGIE* AN' CLOSE BEHIND HIM IS FEENEY AND HIS PAL, HAM!
GET EVERYTHING ALL SET, JANET... FEENEY AN' HAM ARE UNDECIDED WHAT TO DO, BUT THEY'LL BE HERE IN A MINUTE.
SURE! THEY'RE CURIOUS AN' WON'T BE ABLE TO STAY AWAY.
SPERMENTAL GARDEN
HELLO, FROGGIE! WE THOUGHT WE'D SEE WHAT YOUR NEW FORMULA COULD DO.
HUH— OH, SURE! COME ON IN.
I HAVE TO GO AN' DELIVER THE LAST OF OUR STOCK, BUT JANET CAN SHOW YOU HOW THE STUFF WORKS.
SURE! I'VE GOT JUST A LITTLE BITTY BOTTLE LEFT.
OKAY— SHOOT, JANET!
YEH—WE'RE ALL EARS.
I CAN SEE YOU'RE BOTH SCIENTISTS AT HEART. JUST THINK! THERE ARE 715 VICTORY GARDENS IN TOWN AND WE'LL SELL A BOTTLE TO EACH OWNER— NOW I POUR A DROP ON THE BEET SEED.
6

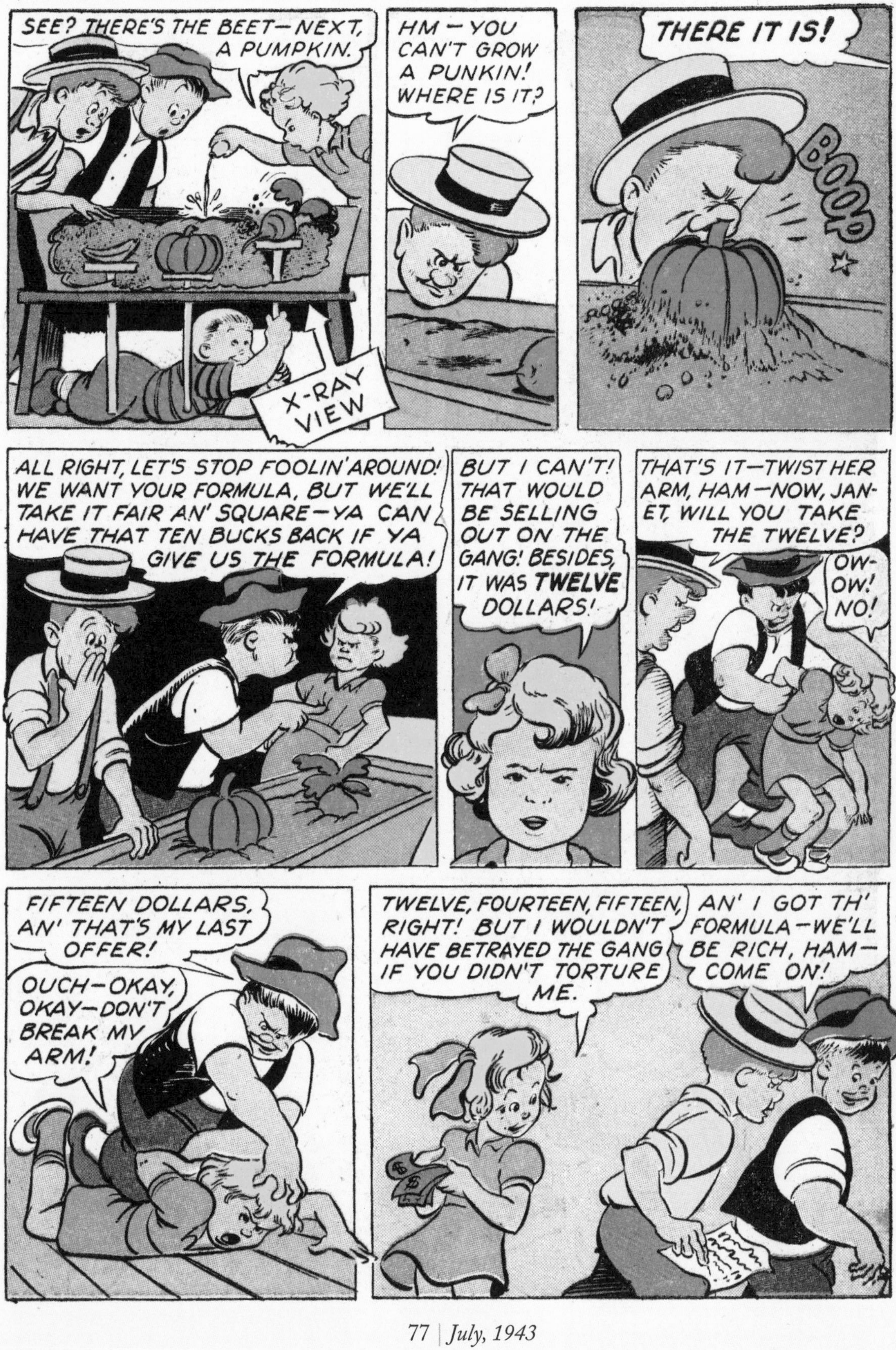
SEE? THERE'S THE BEET—NEXT, A PUMPKIN.
X-RAY VIEW
HM—YOU CAN'T GROW A PUNKIN! WHERE IS IT?
THERE IT IS!
BOOP
ALL RIGHT, LET'S STOP FOOLIN' AROUND! WE WANT YOUR FORMULA, BUT WE'LL TAKE IT FAIR AN' SQUARE—YA CAN HAVE THAT TEN BUCKS BACK IF YA GIVE US THE FORMULA!
BUT I CAN'T! THAT WOULD BE SELLING OUT ON THE GANG! BESIDES, IT WAS **TWELVE** DOLLARS!
THAT'S IT—TWIST HER ARM, HAM—NOW, JANET, WILL YOU TAKE THE TWELVE?
OW-OW! NO!
FIFTEEN DOLLARS, AN' THAT'S MY LAST OFFER!
OUCH—OKAY, OKAY—DON'T BREAK MY ARM!
TWELVE, FOURTEEN, FIFTEEN, RIGHT! BUT I WOULDN'T HAVE BETRAYED THE GANG IF YOU DIDN'T TORTURE ME.
AN' I GOT TH' FORMULA—WE'LL BE RICH, HAM—COME ON!

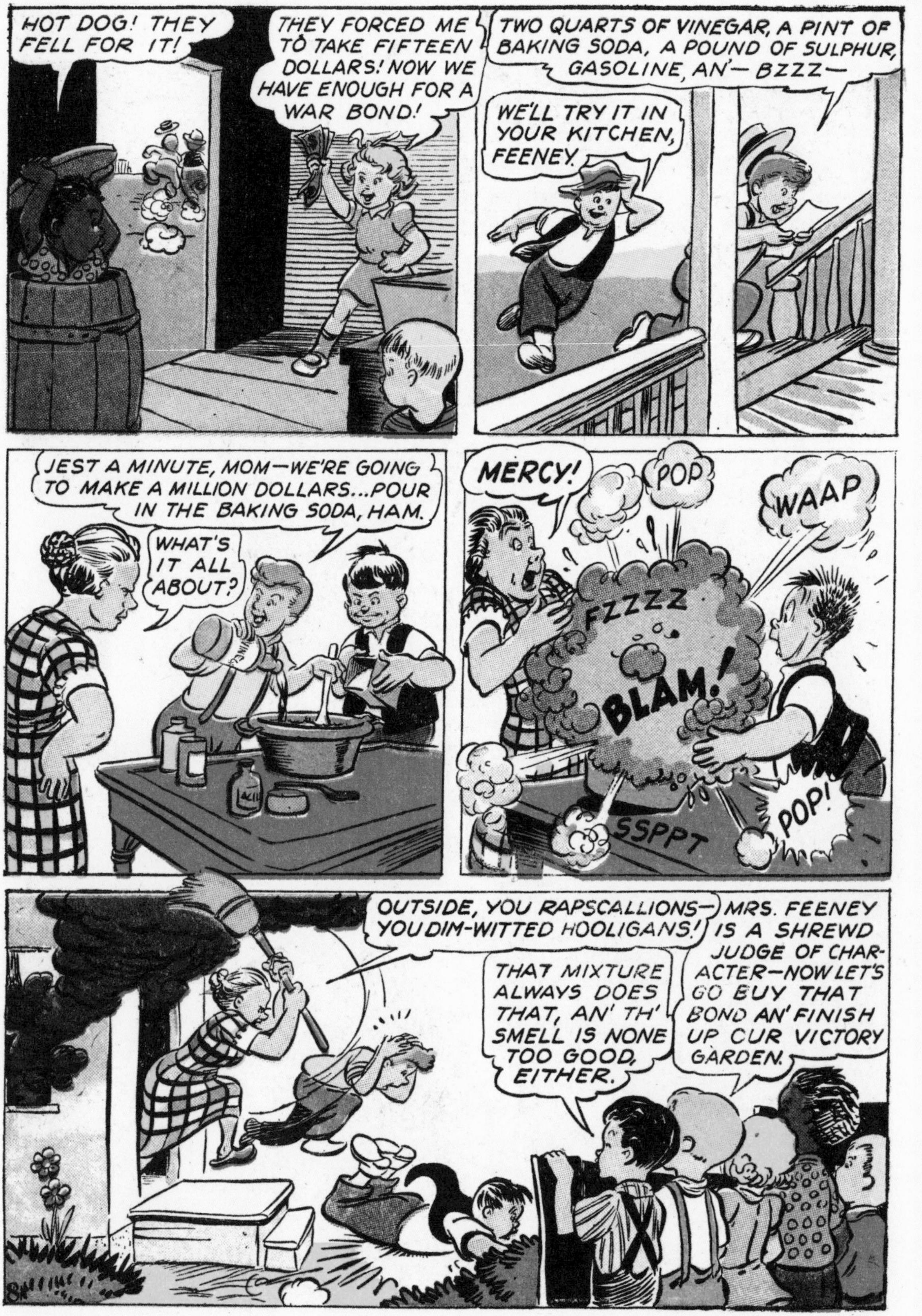
HOT DOG! THEY FELL FOR IT!
THEY FORCED ME TO TAKE FIFTEEN DOLLARS! NOW WE HAVE ENOUGH FOR A WAR BOND!
TWO QUARTS OF VINEGAR, A PINT OF BAKING SODA, A POUND OF SULPHUR, GASOLINE, AN'— BZZZ—
WE'LL TRY IT IN YOUR KITCHEN, FEENEY.
JEST A MINUTE, MOM—WE'RE GOING TO MAKE A MILLION DOLLARS...POUR IN THE BAKING SODA, HAM.
WHAT'S IT ALL ABOUT?
MERCY!
POP
WAAP
FZZZZ
BLAM!
SSPPT
POP!
OUTSIDE, YOU RAPSCALLIONS— YOU DIM-WITTED HOOLIGANS!
MRS. FEENEY IS A SHREWD JUDGE OF CHARACTER—NOW LET'S GO BUY THAT BOND AN' FINISH UP OUR VICTORY GARDEN.
THAT MIXTURE ALWAYS DOES THAT, AN' TH' SMELL IS NONE TOO GOOD, EITHER.

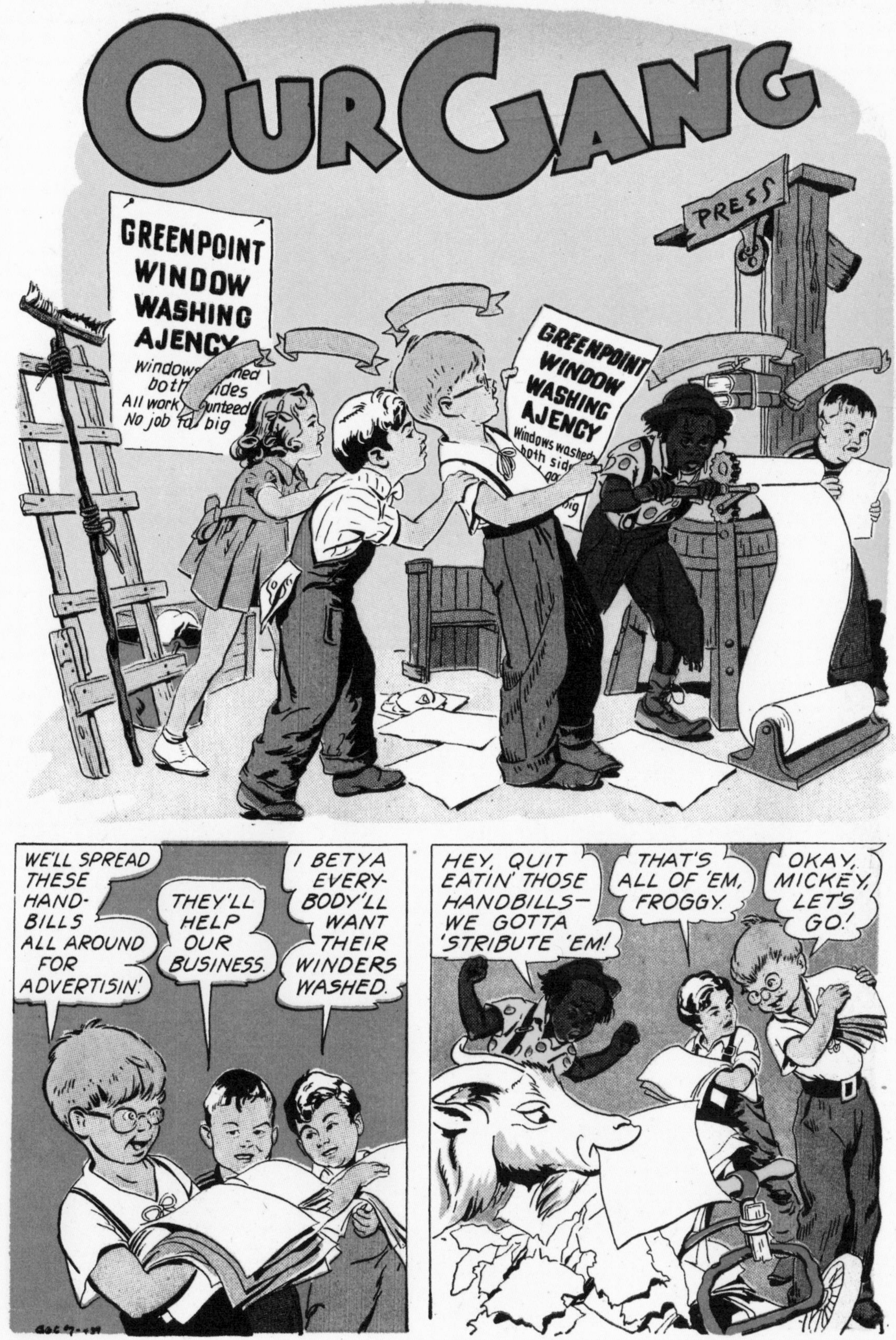
OUR GANG
GREENPOINT WINDOW WASHING AJENCY
Windows washed both sides
All work guaranteed
No job too big
PRESS
WE'LL SPREAD THESE HAND-BILLS ALL AROUND FOR ADVERTISIN'
THEY'LL HELP OUR BUSINESS.
I BETYA EVERY-BODY'LL WANT THEIR WINDERS WASHED.
HEY, QUIT EATIN' THOSE HANDBILLS— WE GOTTA 'STRIBUTE 'EM!
THAT'S ALL OF 'EM, FROGGY.
OKAY, MICKEY, LET'S GO!

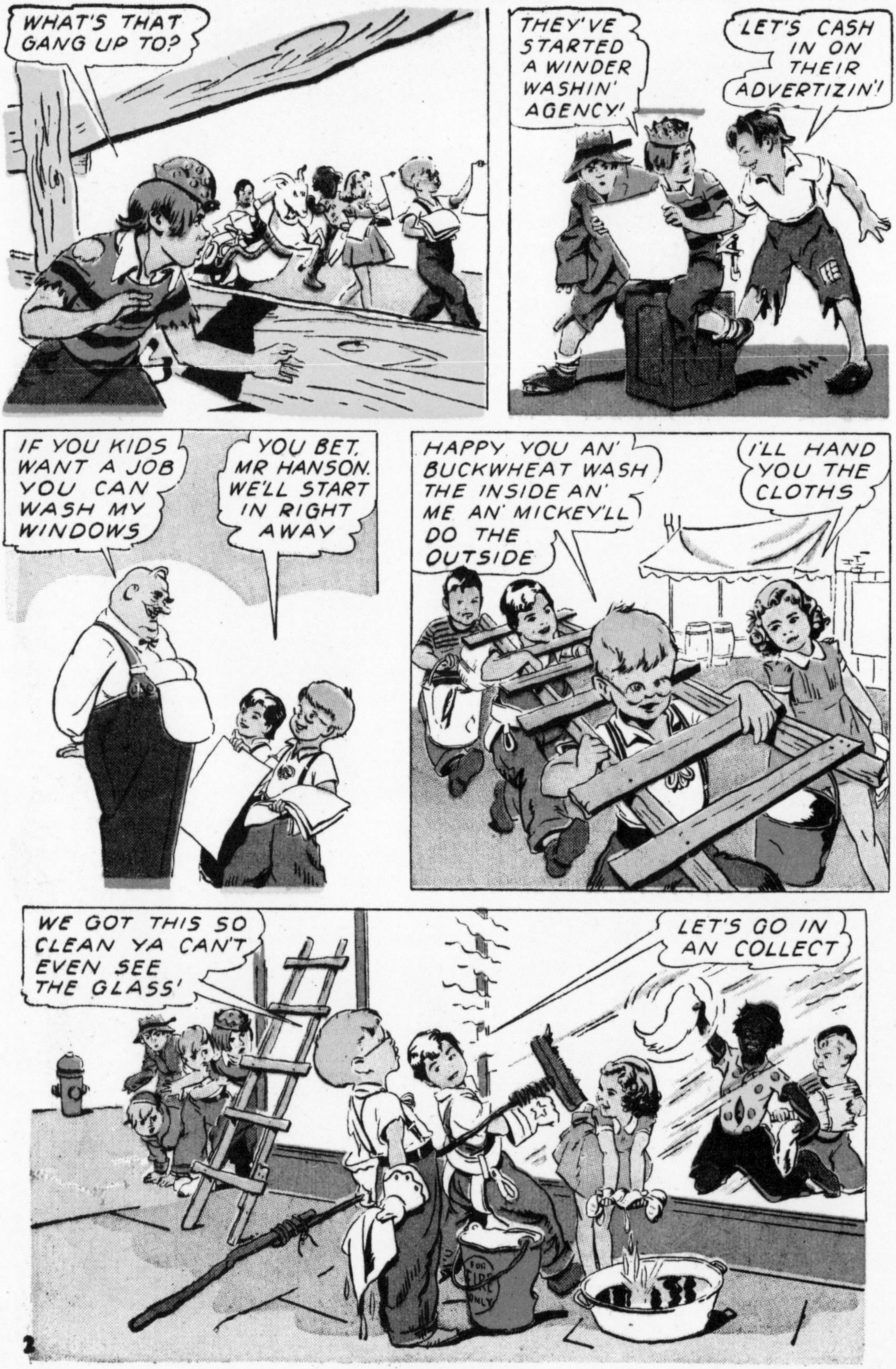
WHAT'S THAT GANG UP TO?
THEY'VE STARTED A WINDER WASHIN' AGENCY!
LET'S CASH IN ON THEIR ADVERTIZIN'!
IF YOU KIDS WANT A JOB YOU CAN WASH MY WINDOWS
YOU BET, MR HANSON. WE'LL START IN RIGHT AWAY
HAPPY YOU AN' BUCKWHEAT WASH THE INSIDE AN' ME AN' MICKEY'LL DO THE OUTSIDE
I'LL HAND YOU THE CLOTHS
WE GOT THIS SO CLEAN YA CAN'T EVEN SEE THE GLASS'
LET'S GO IN AN COLLECT
FOR FIRE ONLY
2

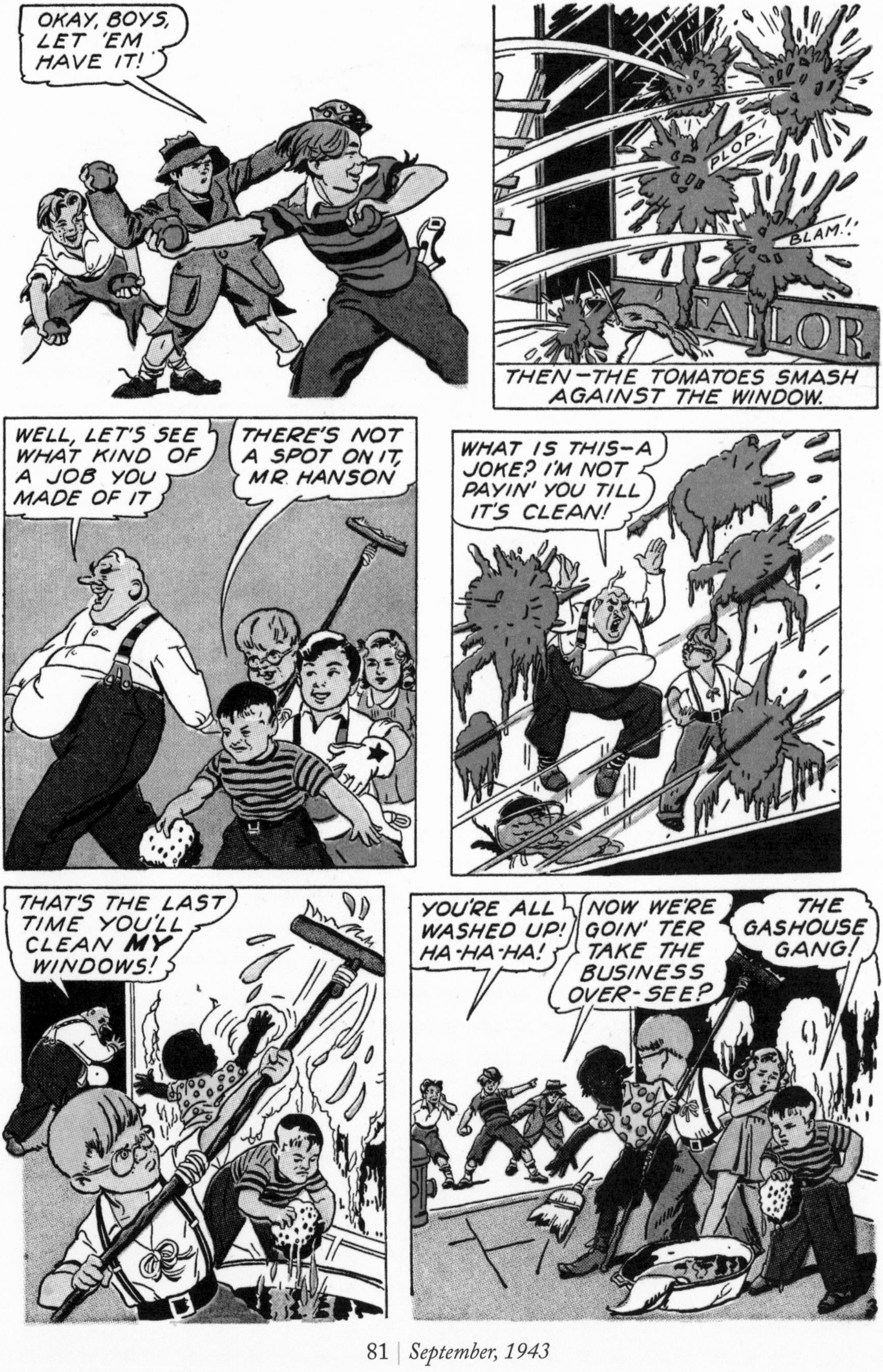
OKAY, BOYS, LET 'EM HAVE IT!
PLOP.
BLAM.!.
TAILOR
THEN—THE TOMATOES SMASH AGAINST THE WINDOW.
WELL, LET'S SEE WHAT KIND OF A JOB YOU MADE OF IT
THERE'S NOT A SPOT ON IT, MR. HANSON
WHAT IS THIS—A JOKE? I'M NOT PAYIN' YOU TILL IT'S CLEAN!
THAT'S THE LAST TIME YOU'LL CLEAN **MY** WINDOWS!
YOU'RE ALL WASHED UP! HA-HA-HA!
NOW WE'RE GOIN' TER TAKE THE BUSINESS OVER-SEE?
THE GASHOUSE GANG!

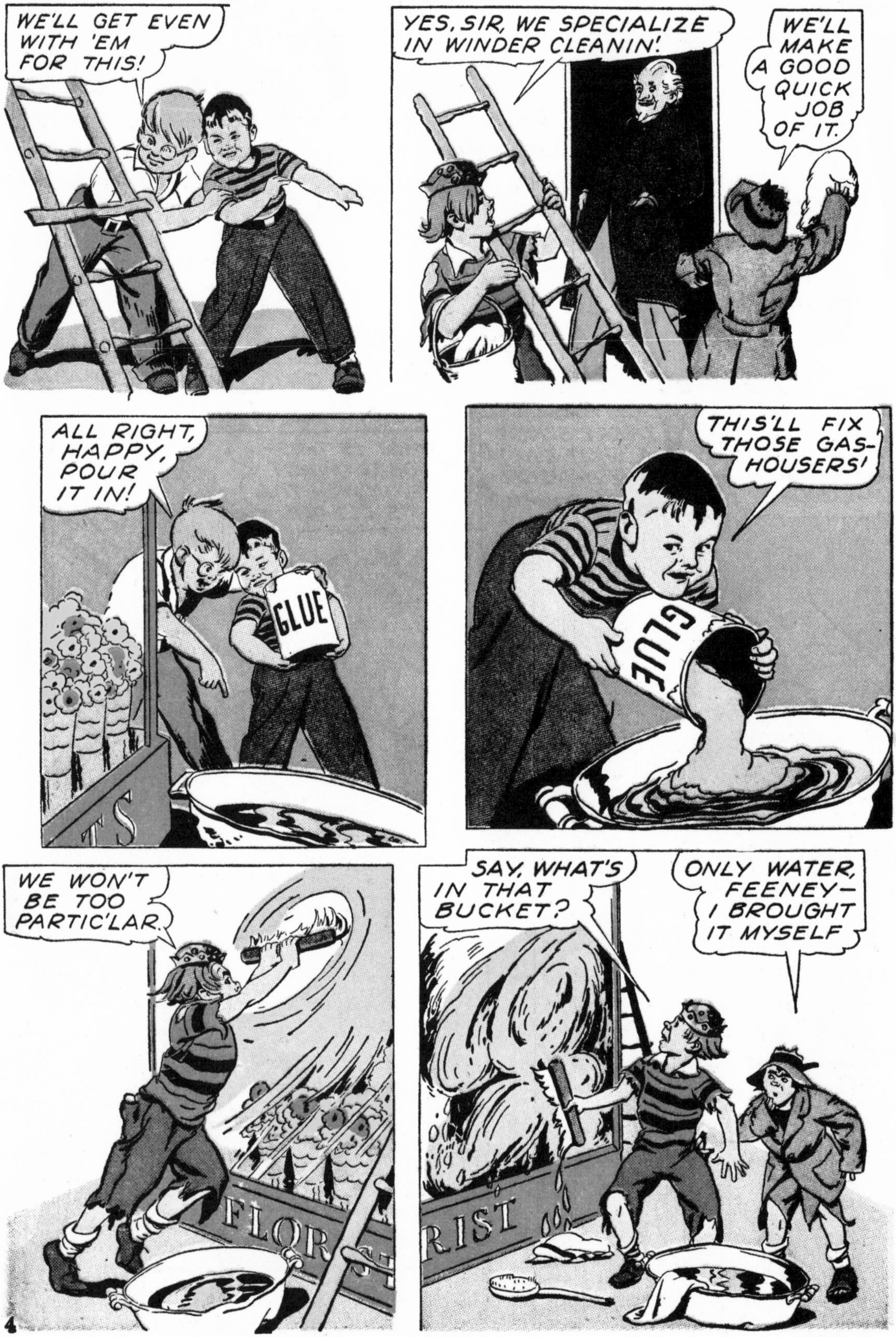

WE'LL GET EVEN WITH 'EM FOR THIS!
YES, SIR, WE SPECIALIZE IN WINDER CLEANIN!
WE'LL MAKE A GOOD QUICK JOB OF IT.
ALL RIGHT, HAPPY, POUR IT IN!
GLUE
THIS'LL FIX THOSE GAS-HOUSERS!
GLUE
TS
WE WON'T BE TOO PARTIC'LAR.
SAY, WHAT'S IN THAT BUCKET?
ONLY WATER, FEENEY— I BROUGHT IT MYSELF
FLOR
RIST
4

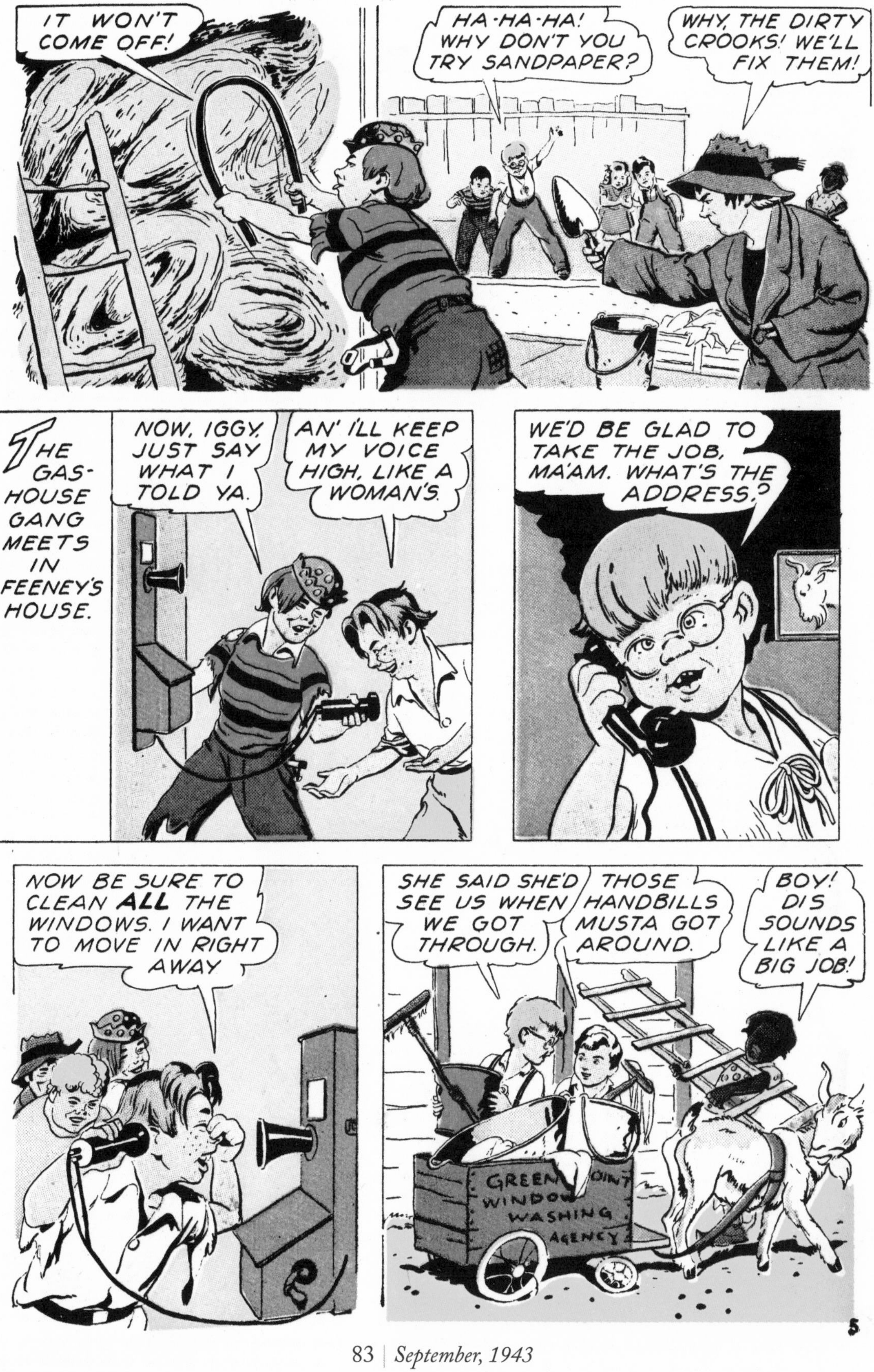

IT WON'T COME OFF!
HA-HA-HA! WHY DON'T YOU TRY SANDPAPER?
WHY, THE DIRTY CROOKS! WE'LL FIX THEM!
THE GAS-HOUSE GANG MEETS IN FEENEY'S HOUSE.
NOW, IGGY, JUST SAY WHAT I TOLD YA.
AN' I'LL KEEP MY VOICE HIGH, LIKE A WOMAN'S.
WE'D BE GLAD TO TAKE THE JOB, MA'AM. WHAT'S THE ADDRESS?
NOW BE SURE TO CLEAN ALL THE WINDOWS. I WANT TO MOVE IN RIGHT AWAY
SHE SAID SHE'D SEE US WHEN WE GOT THROUGH.
THOSE HANDBILLS MUSTA GOT AROUND.
BOY! DIS SOUNDS LIKE A BIG JOB!
GREENPOINT WINDOW WASHING AGENCY
5

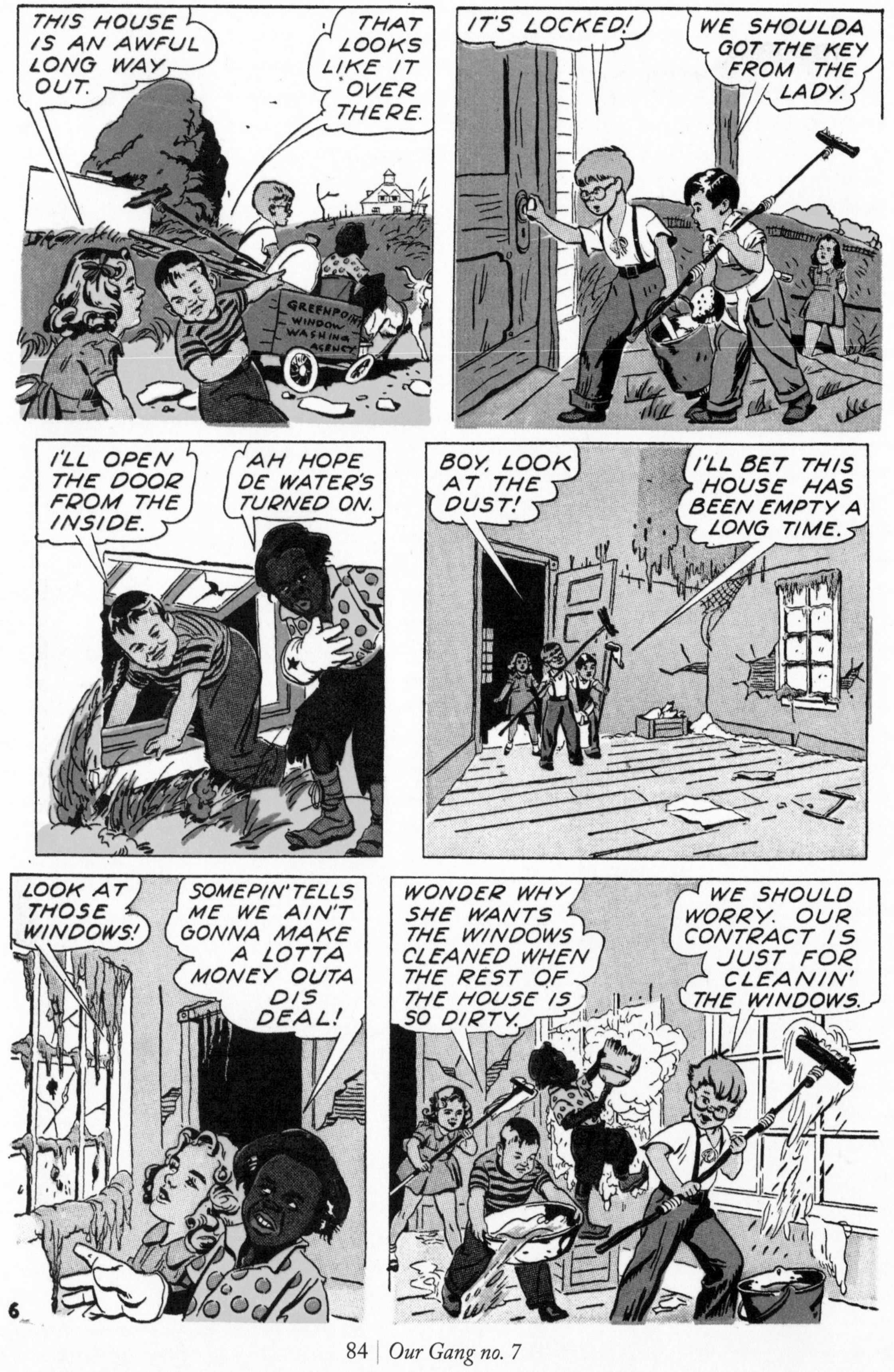
THIS HOUSE IS AN AWFUL LONG WAY OUT.
THAT LOOKS LIKE IT OVER THERE.
GREENPOINT WINDOW WASHING AGENCY
IT'S LOCKED!
WE SHOULDA GOT THE KEY FROM THE LADY.
I'LL OPEN THE DOOR FROM THE INSIDE.
AH HOPE DE WATER'S TURNED ON.
BOY, LOOK AT THE DUST!
I'LL BET THIS HOUSE HAS BEEN EMPTY A LONG TIME.
LOOK AT THOSE WINDOWS!
SOMEPIN' TELLS ME WE AIN'T GONNA MAKE A LOTTA MONEY OUTA DIS DEAL!
WONDER WHY SHE WANTS THE WINDOWS CLEANED WHEN THE REST OF THE HOUSE IS SO DIRTY.
WE SHOULD WORRY. OUR CONTRACT IS JUST FOR CLEANIN' THE WINDOWS.
6

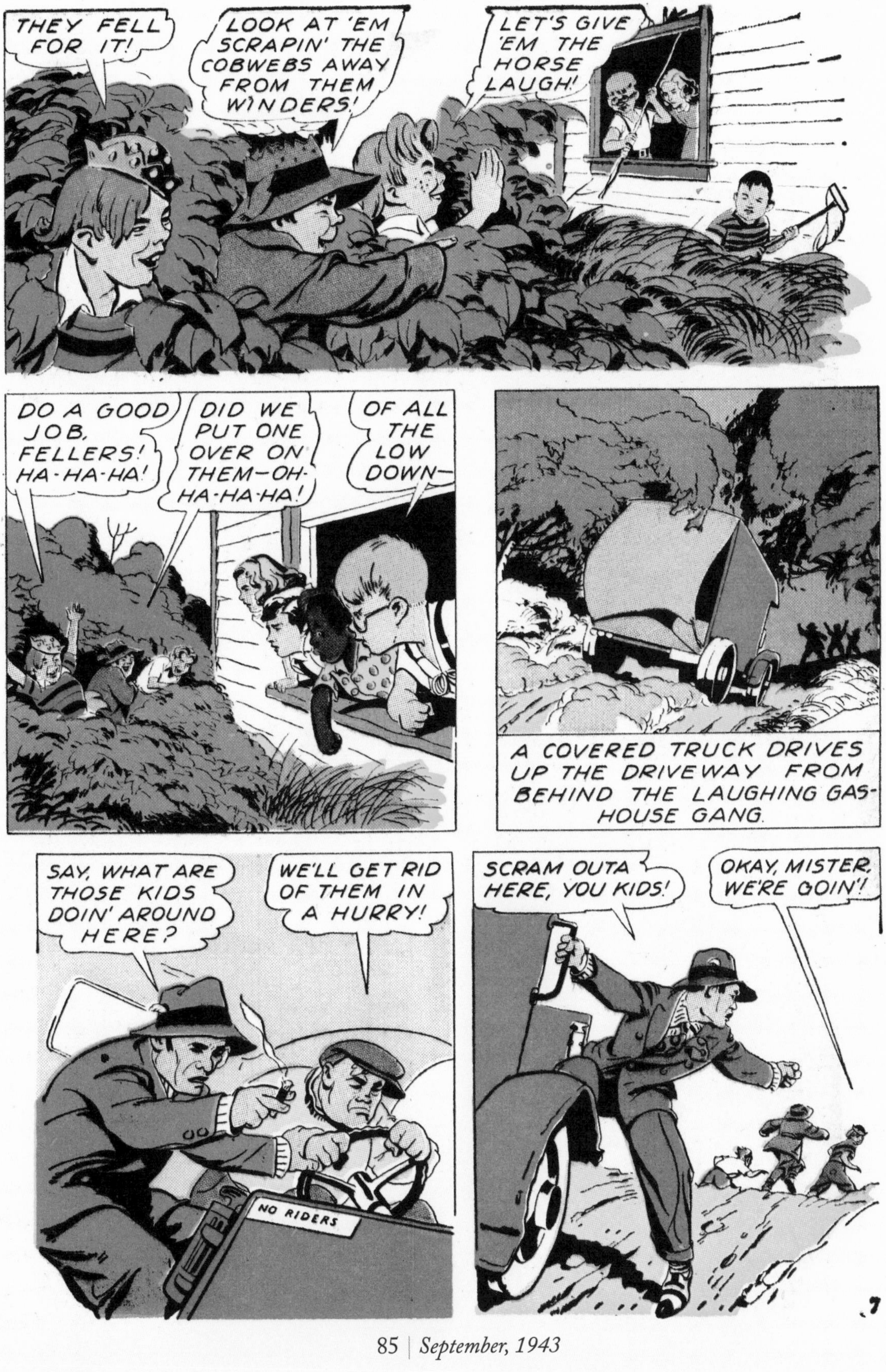
THEY FELL FOR IT!
LOOK AT 'EM SCRAPIN' THE COBWEBS AWAY FROM THEM WINDERS!
LET'S GIVE 'EM THE HORSE LAUGH!
DO A GOOD JOB, FELLERS! HA-HA-HA!
DID WE PUT ONE OVER ON THEM—OH-HA-HA-HA!
OF ALL THE LOW DOWN—
A COVERED TRUCK DRIVES UP THE DRIVEWAY FROM BEHIND THE LAUGHING GAS-HOUSE GANG.
SAY, WHAT ARE THOSE KIDS DOIN' AROUND HERE?
WE'LL GET RID OF THEM IN A HURRY!
NO RIDERS
SCRAM OUTA HERE, YOU KIDS!
OKAY, MISTER, WE'RE GOIN'!
7

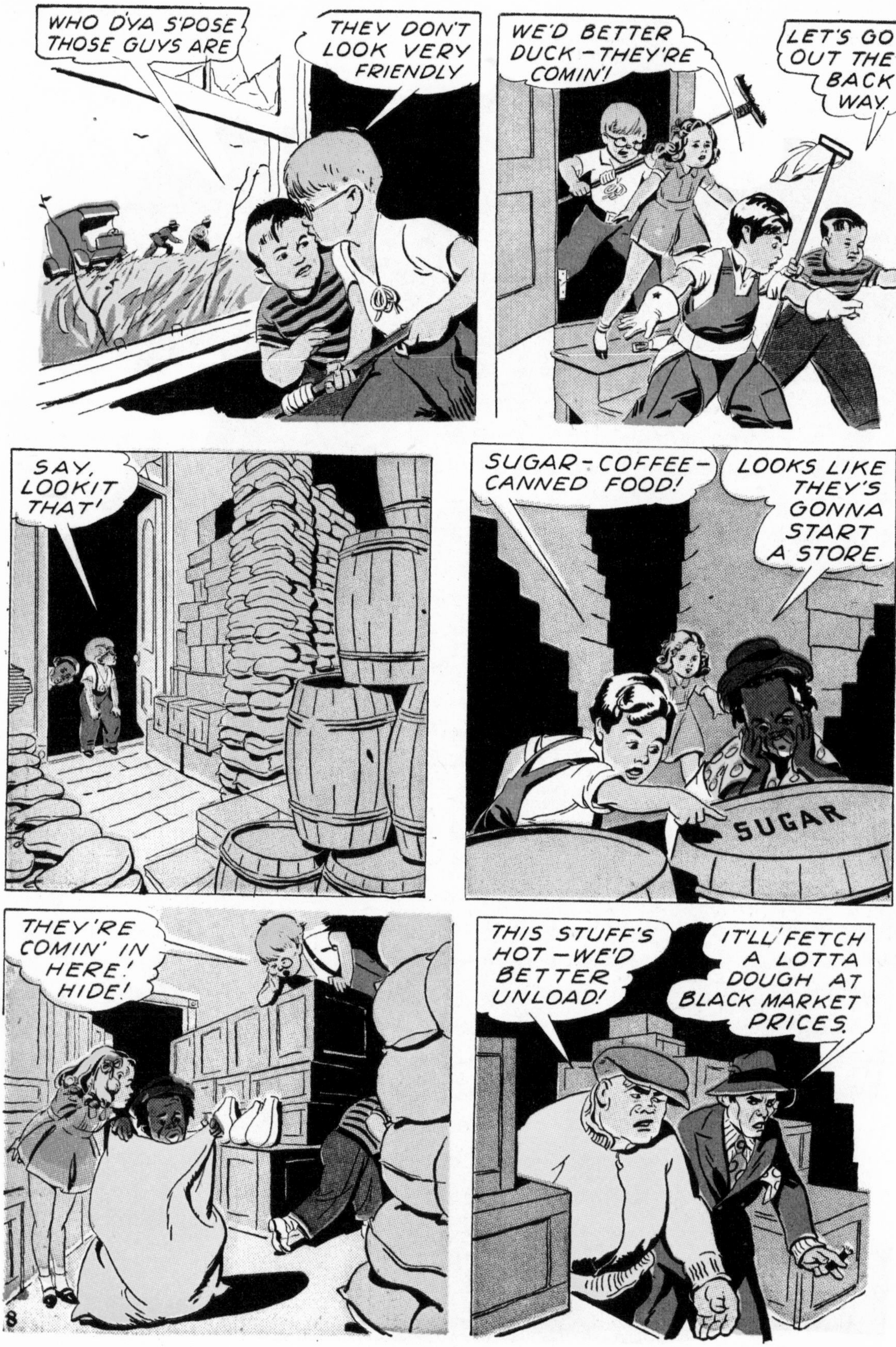
WHO D'YA S'POSE THOSE GUYS ARE
THEY DON'T LOOK VERY FRIENDLY
WE'D BETTER DUCK—THEY'RE COMIN'!
LET'S GO OUT THE BACK WAY.
SAY, LOOKIT THAT!
SUGAR—COFFEE—CANNED FOOD!
LOOKS LIKE THEY'S GONNA START A STORE.
SUGAR
THEY'RE COMIN' IN HERE! HIDE!
THIS STUFF'S HOT—WE'D BETTER UNLOAD!
IT'LL FETCH A LOTTA DOUGH AT BLACK MARKET PRICES.
8

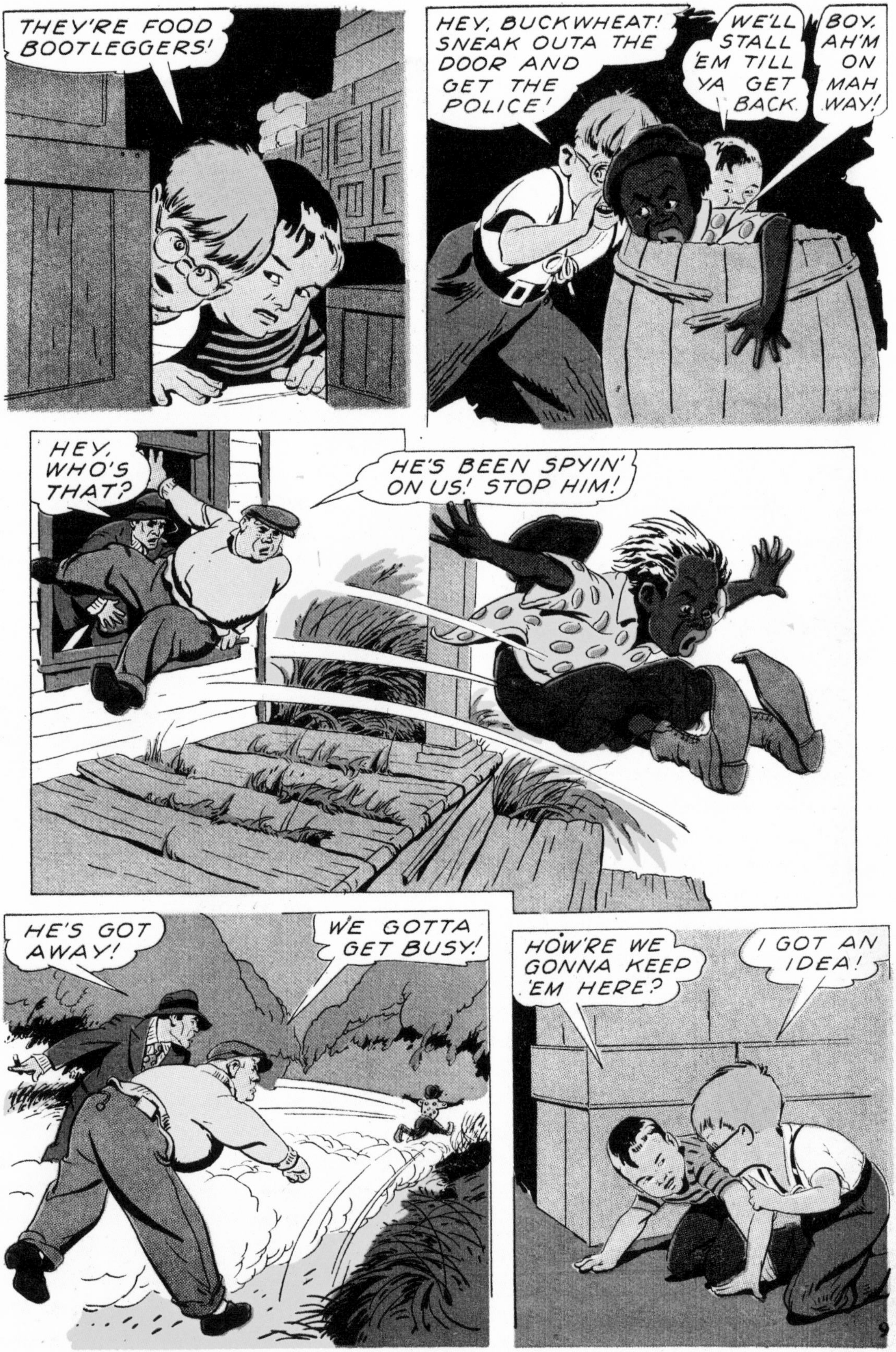
THEY'RE FOOD BOOTLEGGERS!
HEY, BUCKWHEAT! SNEAK OUTA THE DOOR AND GET THE POLICE!
WE'LL STALL 'EM TILL YA GET BACK.
BOY, AH'M ON MAH WAY!
HEY, WHO'S THAT?
HE'S BEEN SPYIN' ON US! STOP HIM!
HE'S GOT AWAY!
WE GOTTA GET BUSY!
HOW'RE WE GONNA KEEP 'EM HERE?
I GOT AN IDEA!
9

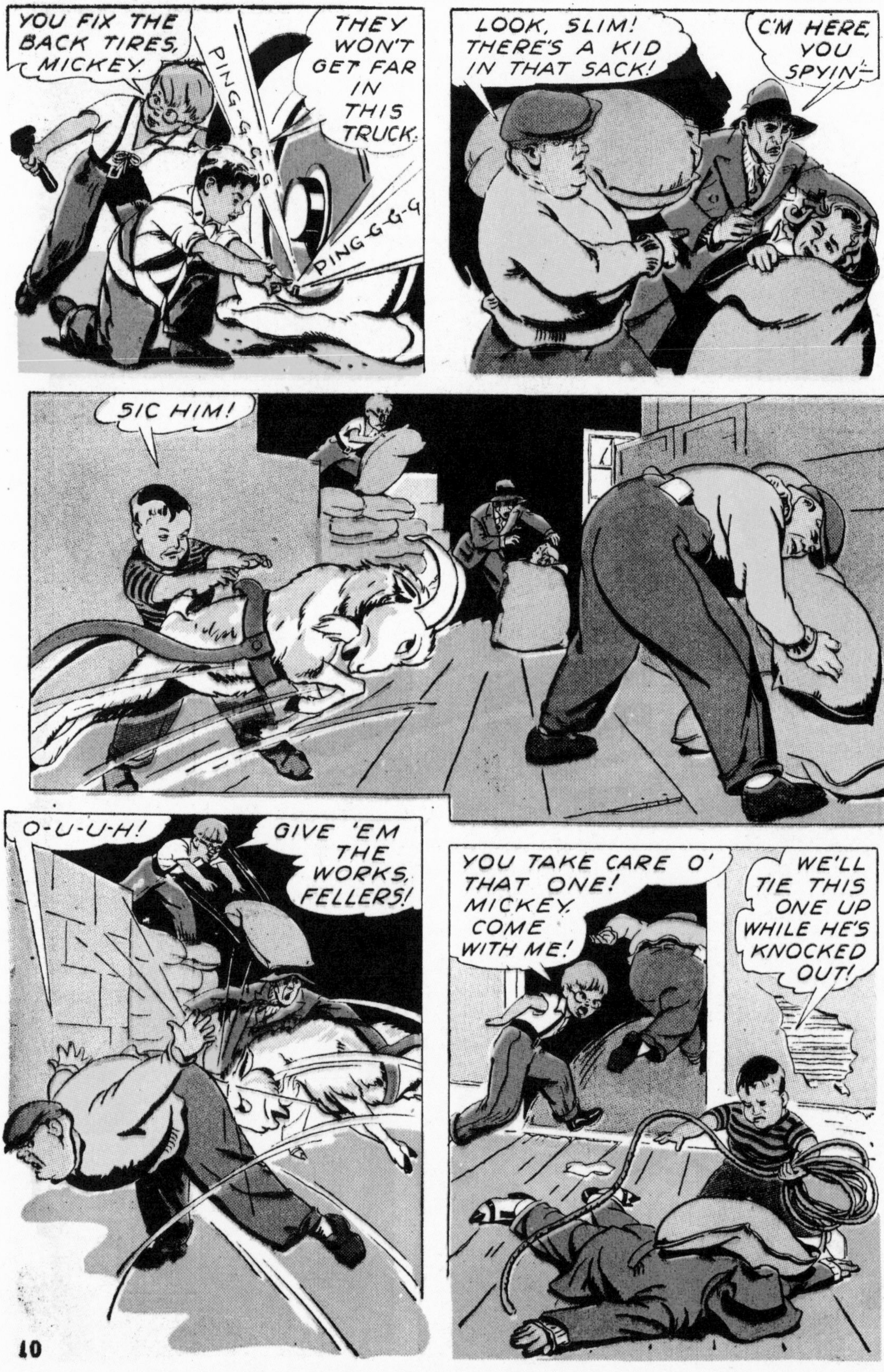
YOU FIX THE BACK TIRES, MICKEY.
PING-G-G-G
THEY WON'T GET FAR IN THIS TRUCK.
PING-G-G-G
LOOK, SLIM! THERE'S A KID IN THAT SACK!
C'M HERE, YOU SPYIN'–
SIC HIM!
O-U-U-H!
GIVE 'EM THE WORKS, FELLERS!
YOU TAKE CARE O' THAT ONE! MICKEY, COME WITH ME!
WE'LL TIE THIS ONE UP WHILE HE'S KNOCKED OUT!
10

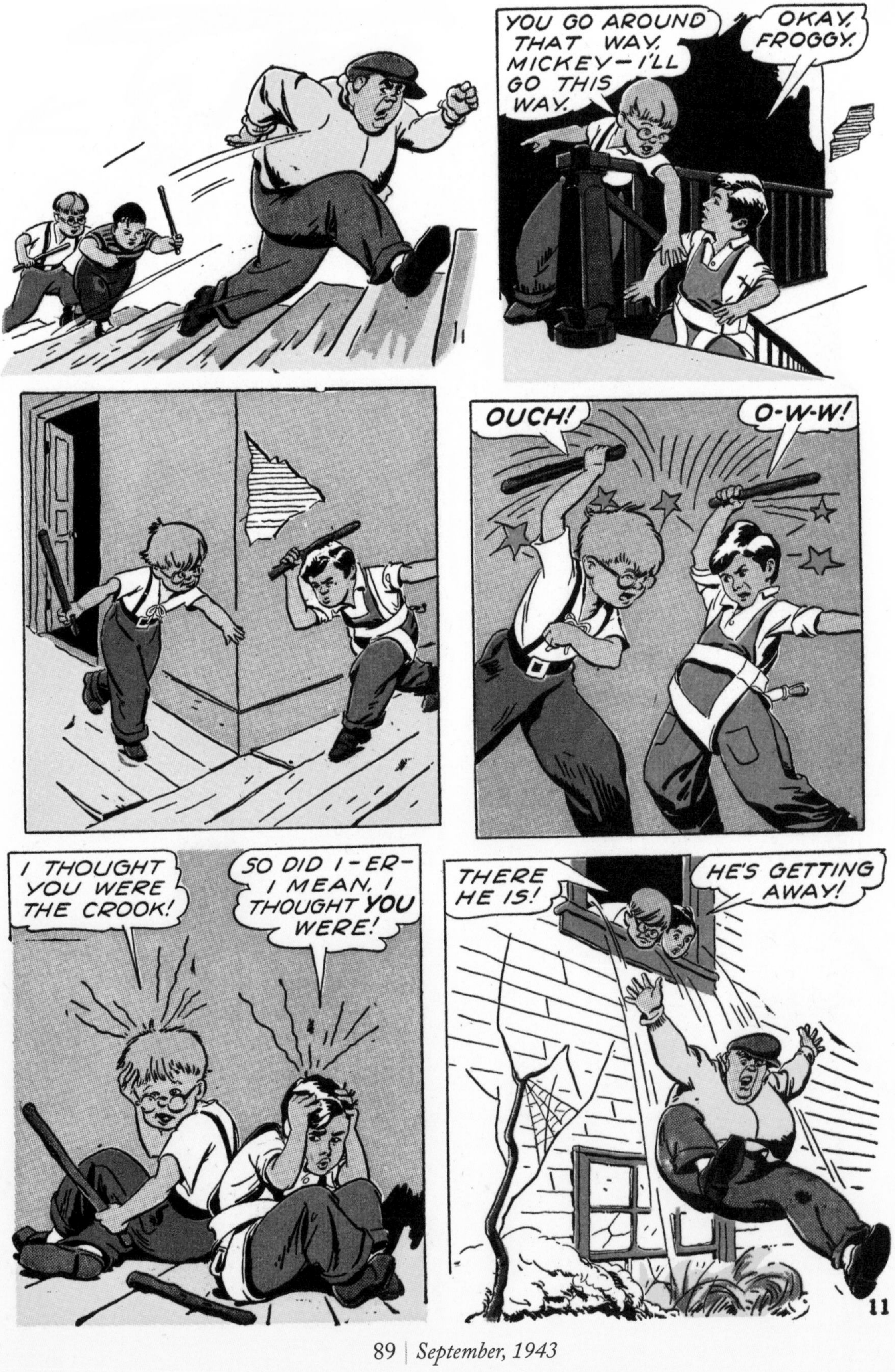
YOU GO AROUND THAT WAY, MICKEY—I'LL GO THIS WAY.
OKAY, FROGGY.
OUCH!
O-W-W!
I THOUGHT YOU WERE THE CROOK!
SO DID I—ER—I MEAN, I THOUGHT YOU WERE!
THERE HE IS!
HE'S GETTING AWAY!
11

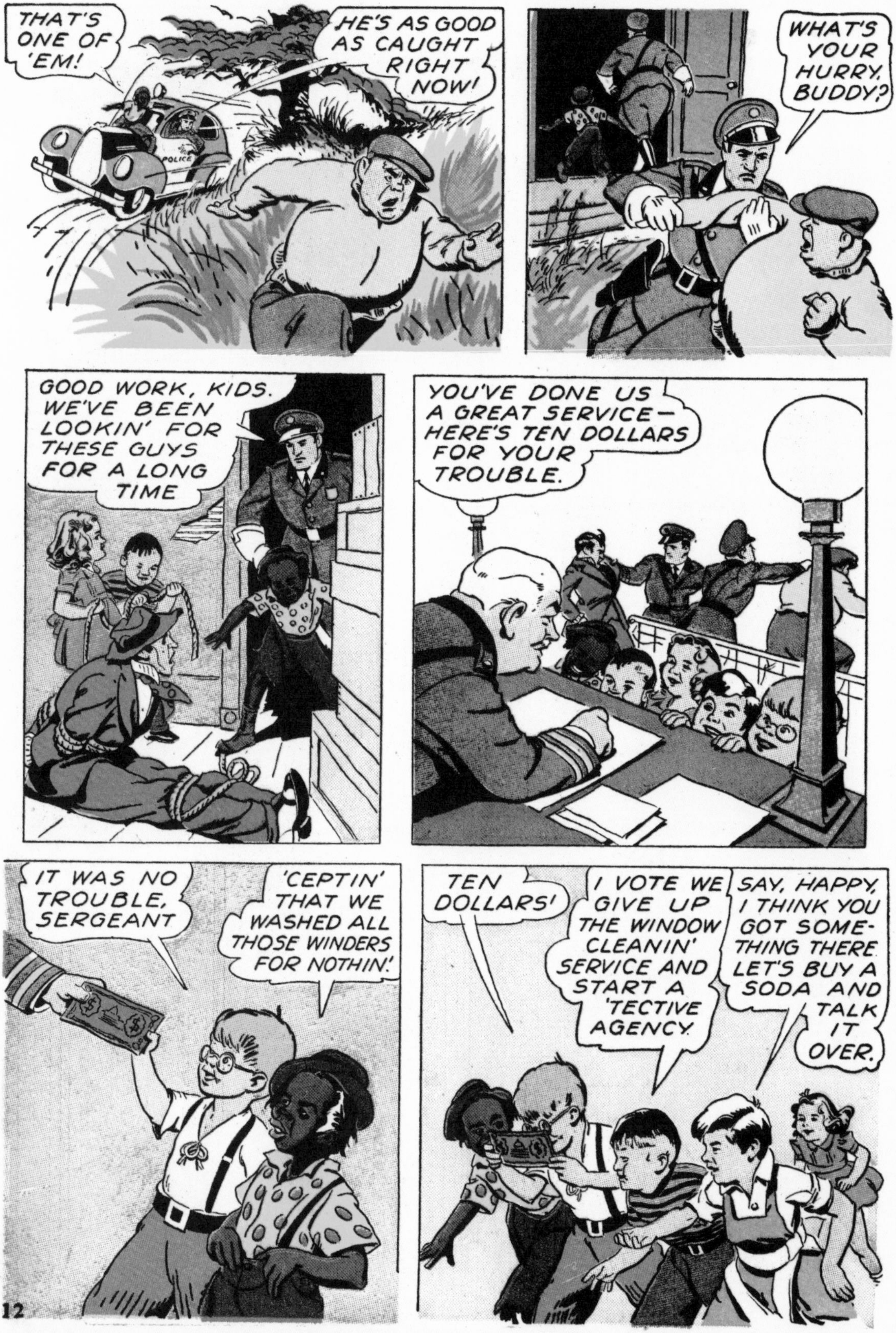
THAT'S ONE OF 'EM!
HE'S AS GOOD AS CAUGHT RIGHT NOW!
POLICE
WHAT'S YOUR HURRY, BUDDY?
GOOD WORK, KIDS. WE'VE BEEN LOOKIN' FOR THESE GUYS FOR A LONG TIME
YOU'VE DONE US A GREAT SERVICE— HERE'S TEN DOLLARS FOR YOUR TROUBLE.
IT WAS NO TROUBLE, SERGEANT
'CEPTIN' THAT WE WASHED ALL THOSE WINDERS FOR NOTHIN'!
12
TEN DOLLARS!
I VOTE WE GIVE UP THE WINDOW CLEANIN' SERVICE AND START A 'TECTIVE AGENCY.
SAY, HAPPY, I THINK YOU GOT SOME-THING THERE. LET'S BUY A SODA AND TALK IT OVER.

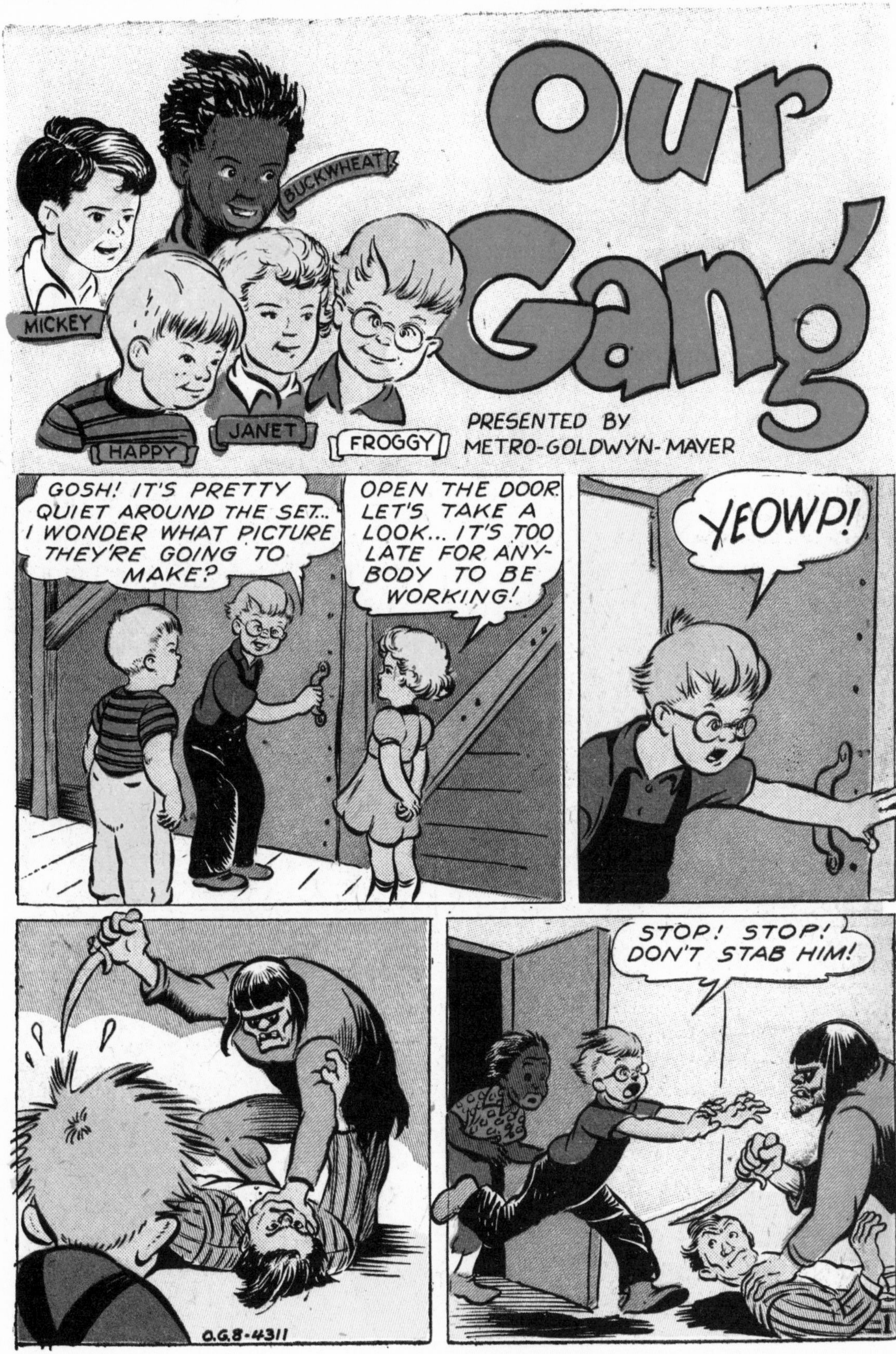
Our Gang
BUCKWHEAT
MICKEY
HAPPY
JANET
FROGGY
PRESENTED BY
METRO-GOLDWYN-MAYER
GOSH! IT'S PRETTY QUIET AROUND THE SET... I WONDER WHAT PICTURE THEY'RE GOING TO MAKE?
OPEN THE DOOR. LET'S TAKE A LOOK... IT'S TOO LATE FOR ANY-BODY TO BE WORKING!
YEOWP!
STOP! STOP! DON'T STAB HIM!
O.G.8-4311

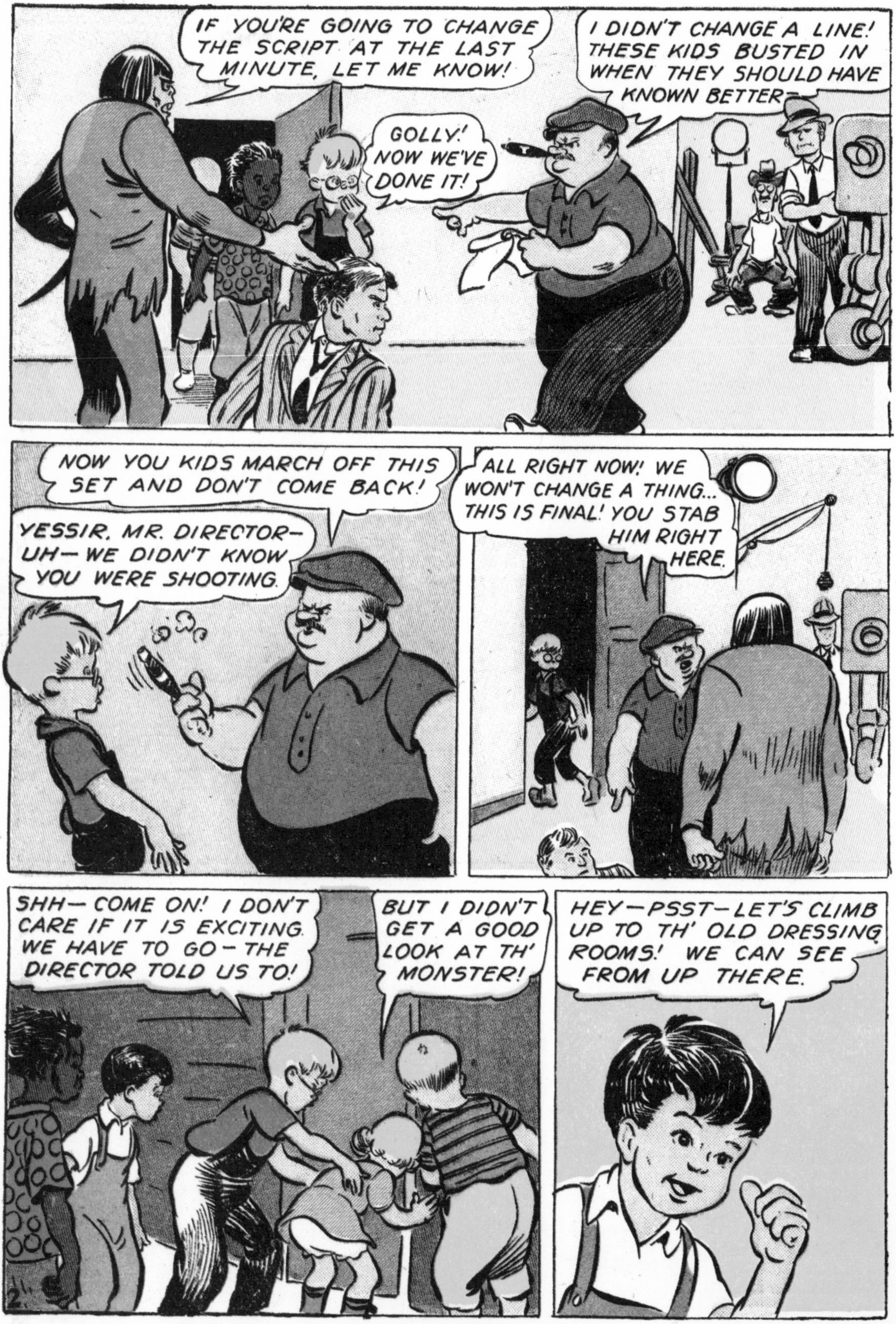
IF YOU'RE GOING TO CHANGE THE SCRIPT AT THE LAST MINUTE, LET ME KNOW!
I DIDN'T CHANGE A LINE! THESE KIDS BUSTED IN WHEN THEY SHOULD HAVE KNOWN BETTER—
GOLLY! NOW WE'VE DONE IT!
NOW YOU KIDS MARCH OFF THIS SET AND DON'T COME BACK!
YESSIR, MR. DIRECTOR— UH— WE DIDN'T KNOW YOU WERE SHOOTING.
ALL RIGHT NOW! WE WON'T CHANGE A THING... THIS IS FINAL! YOU STAB HIM RIGHT HERE.
SHH— COME ON! I DON'T CARE IF IT IS EXCITING. WE HAVE TO GO— THE DIRECTOR TOLD US TO!
BUT I DIDN'T GET A GOOD LOOK AT TH' MONSTER!
HEY— PSST— LET'S CLIMB UP TO TH' OLD DRESSING ROOMS! WE CAN SEE FROM UP THERE.

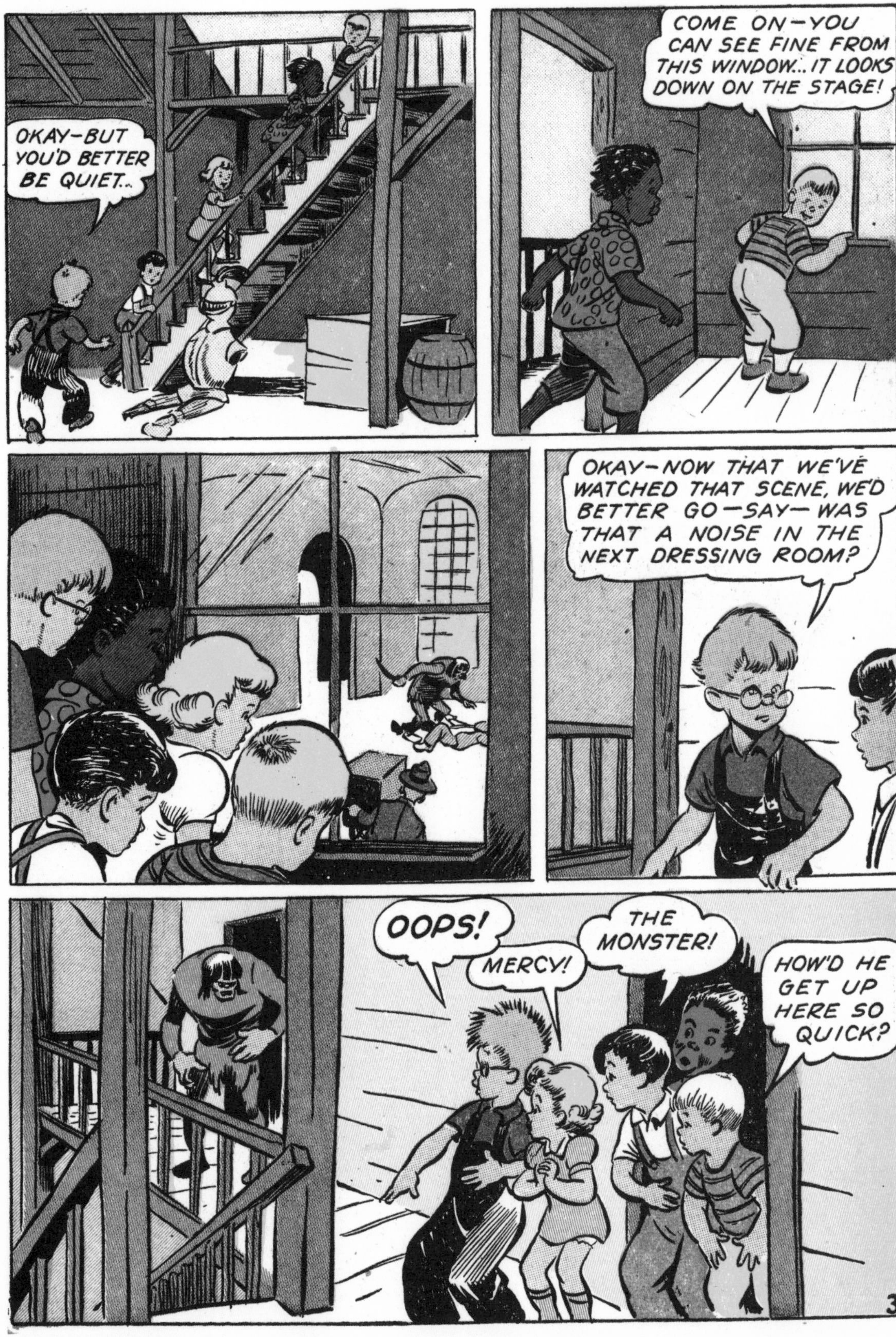
OKAY—BUT YOU'D BETTER BE QUIET...
COME ON—YOU CAN SEE FINE FROM THIS WINDOW... IT LOOKS DOWN ON THE STAGE!
OKAY—NOW THAT WE'VE WATCHED THAT SCENE, WE'D BETTER GO—SAY—WAS THAT A NOISE IN THE NEXT DRESSING ROOM?
OOPS!
MERCY!
THE MONSTER!
HOW'D HE GET UP HERE SO QUICK?
3

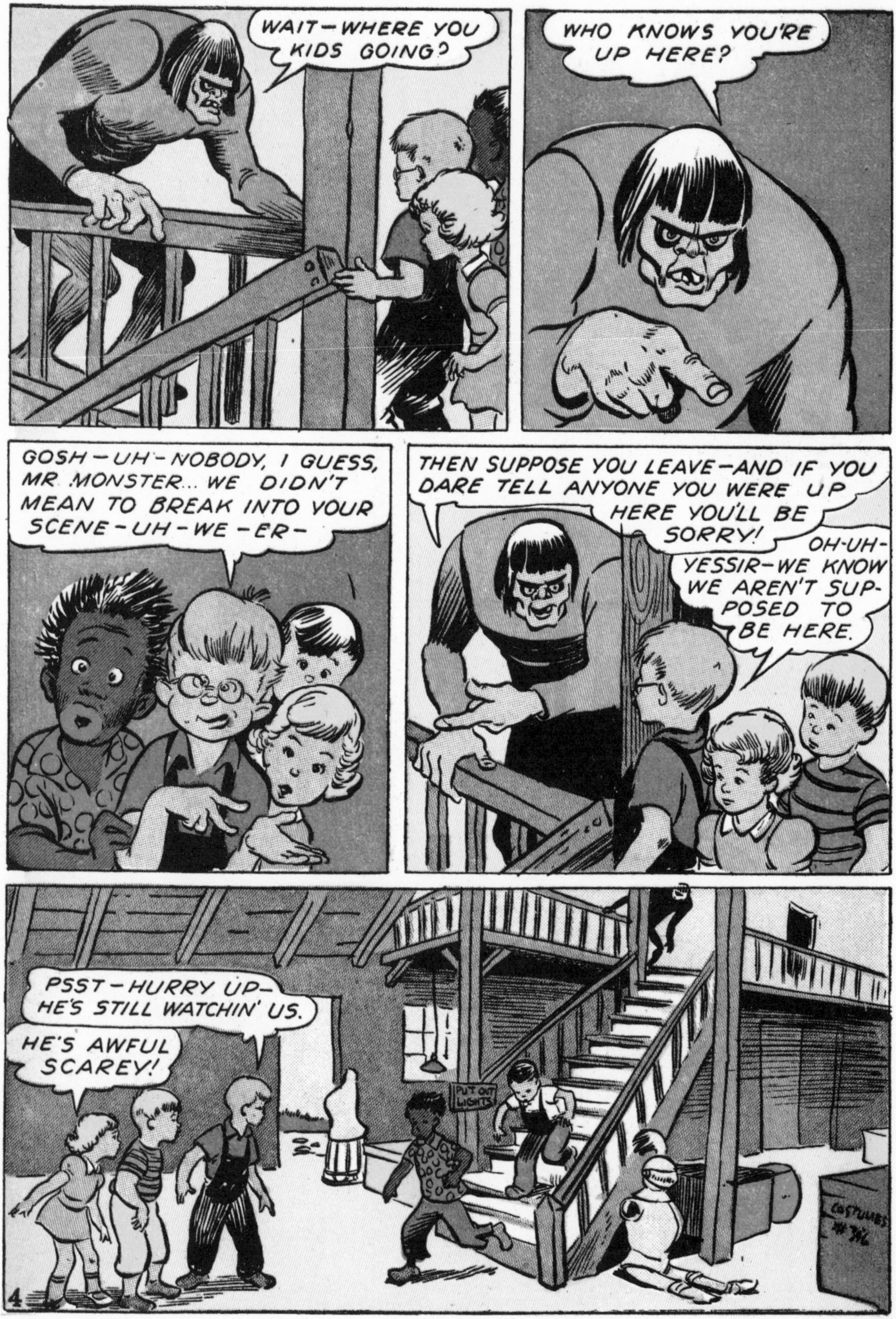
WAIT—WHERE YOU KIDS GOING?
WHO KNOWS YOU'RE UP HERE?
GOSH—UH—NOBODY, I GUESS, MR. MONSTER... WE DIDN'T MEAN TO BREAK INTO YOUR SCENE—UH—WE—ER—
THEN SUPPOSE YOU LEAVE—AND IF YOU DARE TELL ANYONE YOU WERE UP HERE YOU'LL BE SORRY!
OH-UH-YESSIR—WE KNOW WE AREN'T SUPPOSED TO BE HERE.
PSST—HURRY UP—HE'S STILL WATCHIN' US.
HE'S AWFUL SCAREY!
PUT OUT LIGHTS
COSTUMES
4

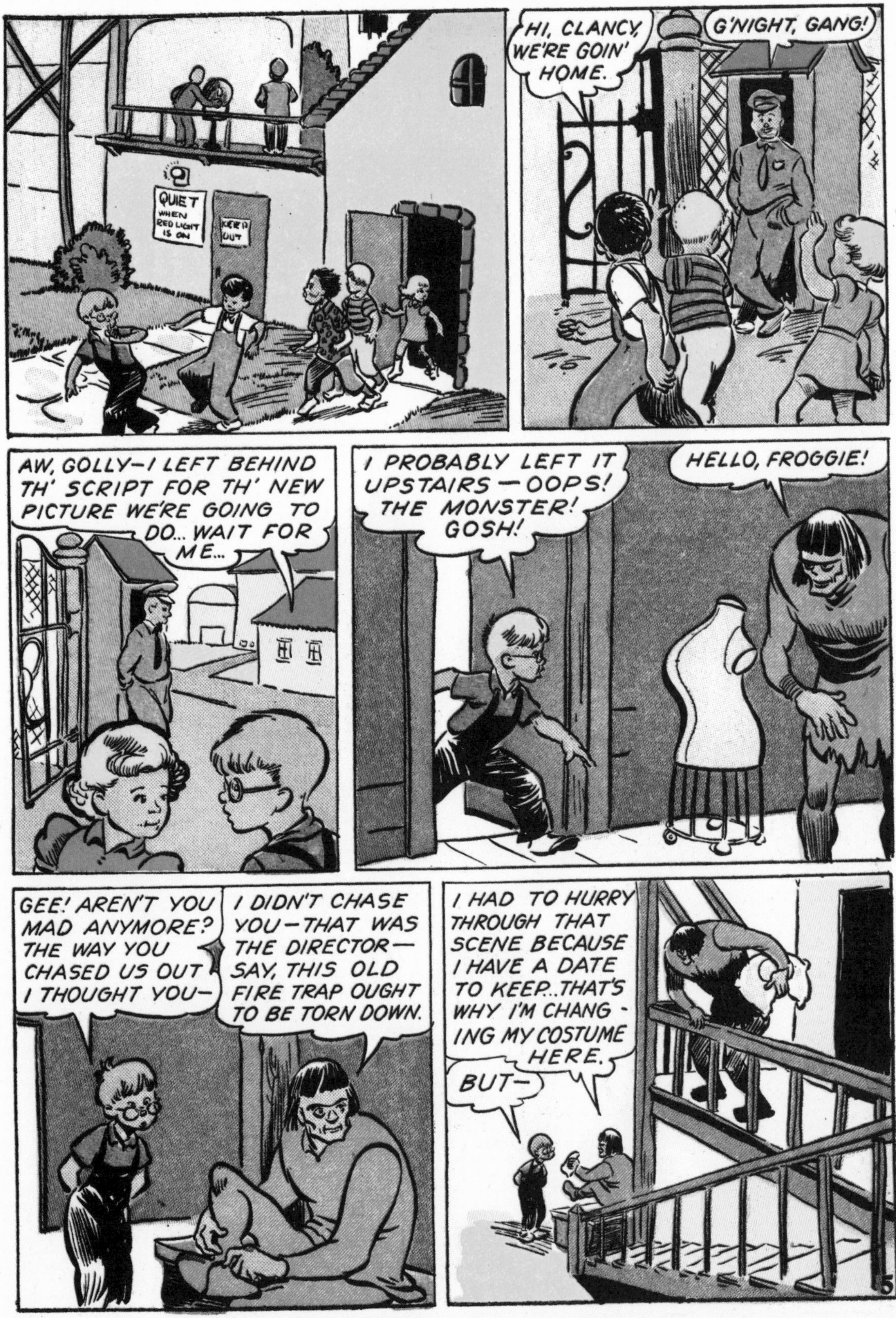
QUIET WHEN RED LIGHT IS ON
KEEP OUT
HI, CLANCY, WE'RE GOIN' HOME.
G'NIGHT, GANG!
AW, GOLLY—I LEFT BEHIND TH' SCRIPT FOR TH' NEW PICTURE WE'RE GOING TO DO... WAIT FOR ME...
I PROBABLY LEFT IT UPSTAIRS — OOPS! THE MONSTER! GOSH!
HELLO, FROGGIE!
GEE! AREN'T YOU MAD ANYMORE? THE WAY YOU CHASED US OUT I THOUGHT YOU—
I DIDN'T CHASE YOU—THAT WAS THE DIRECTOR— SAY, THIS OLD FIRE TRAP OUGHT TO BE TORN DOWN.
I HAD TO HURRY THROUGH THAT SCENE BECAUSE I HAVE A DATE TO KEEP...THAT'S WHY I'M CHANGING MY COSTUME HERE.
BUT—
5

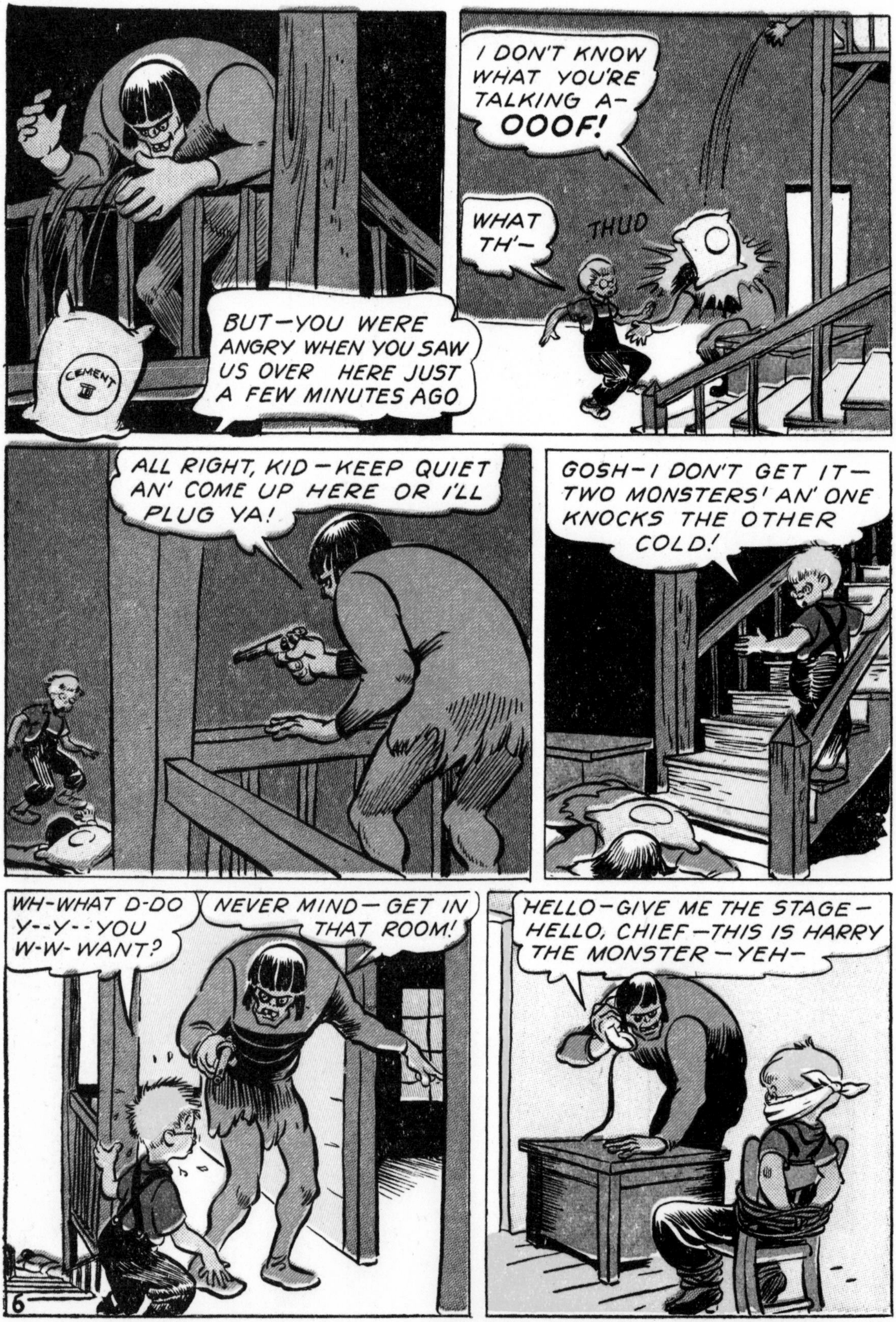
BUT—YOU WERE ANGRY WHEN YOU SAW US OVER HERE JUST A FEW MINUTES AGO
CEMENT
I DON'T KNOW WHAT YOU'RE TALKING A- OOOF!
WHAT TH'-
THUD
ALL RIGHT, KID—KEEP QUIET AN' COME UP HERE OR I'LL PLUG YA!
GOSH—I DON'T GET IT—TWO MONSTERS' AN' ONE KNOCKS THE OTHER COLD!
WH-WHAT D-DO Y--Y--YOU W-W-WANT?
NEVER MIND—GET IN THAT ROOM!
HELLO—GIVE ME THE STAGE—HELLO, CHIEF—THIS IS HARRY THE MONSTER—YEH—
6

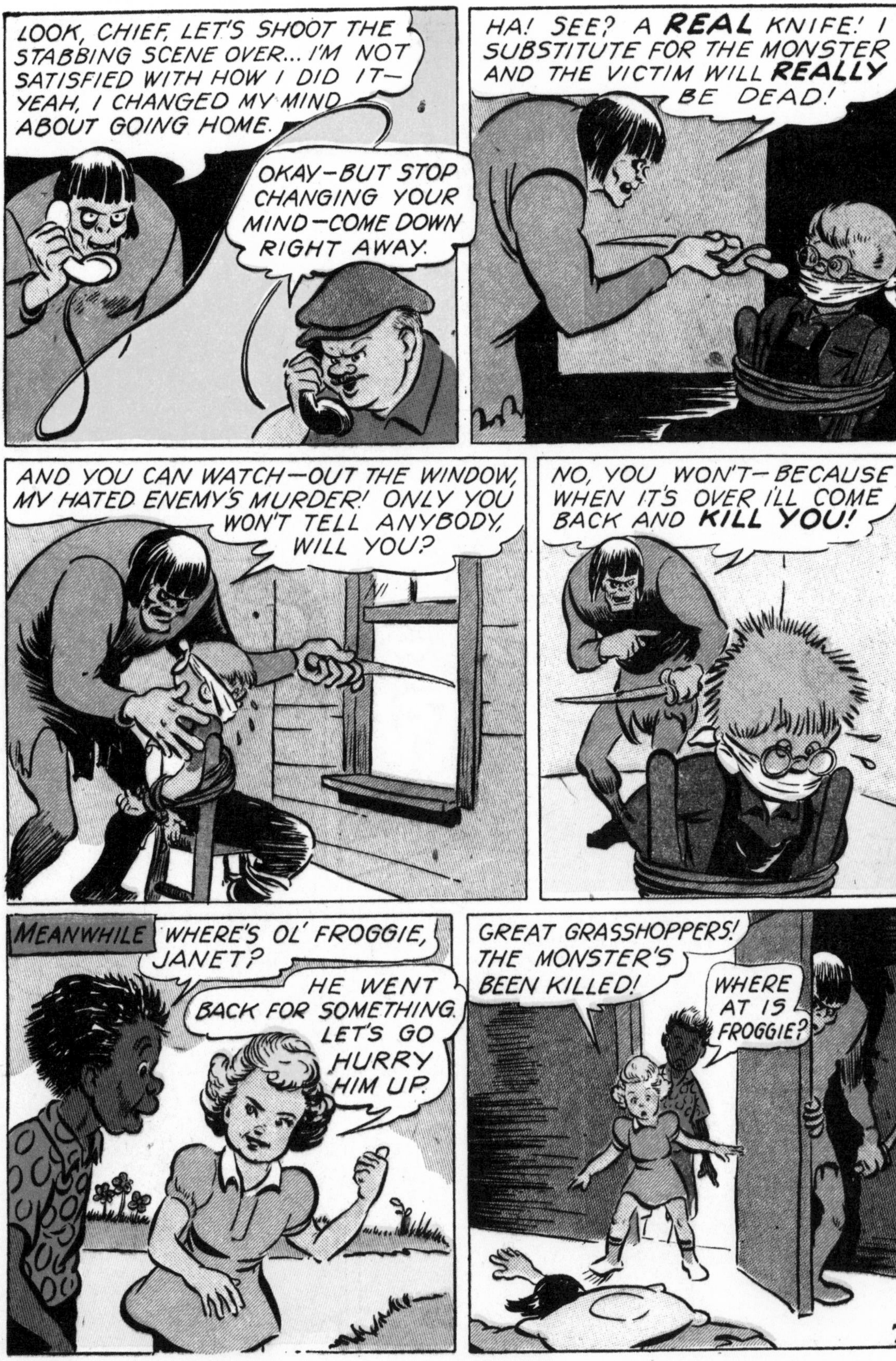

LOOK, CHIEF, LET'S SHOOT THE STABBING SCENE OVER... I'M NOT SATISFIED WITH HOW I DID IT— YEAH, I CHANGED MY MIND ABOUT GOING HOME.
OKAY—BUT STOP CHANGING YOUR MIND—COME DOWN RIGHT AWAY.
HA! SEE? A REAL KNIFE! I SUBSTITUTE FOR THE MONSTER AND THE VICTIM WILL REALLY BE DEAD!
AND YOU CAN WATCH—OUT THE WINDOW, MY HATED ENEMY'S MURDER! ONLY YOU WON'T TELL ANYBODY, WILL YOU?
NO, YOU WON'T—BECAUSE WHEN IT'S OVER I'LL COME BACK AND KILL YOU!
MEANWHILE
WHERE'S OL' FROGGIE, JANET?
HE WENT BACK FOR SOMETHING. LET'S GO HURRY HIM UP.
GREAT GRASSHOPPERS! THE MONSTER'S BEEN KILLED!
WHERE AT IS FROGGIE?
7

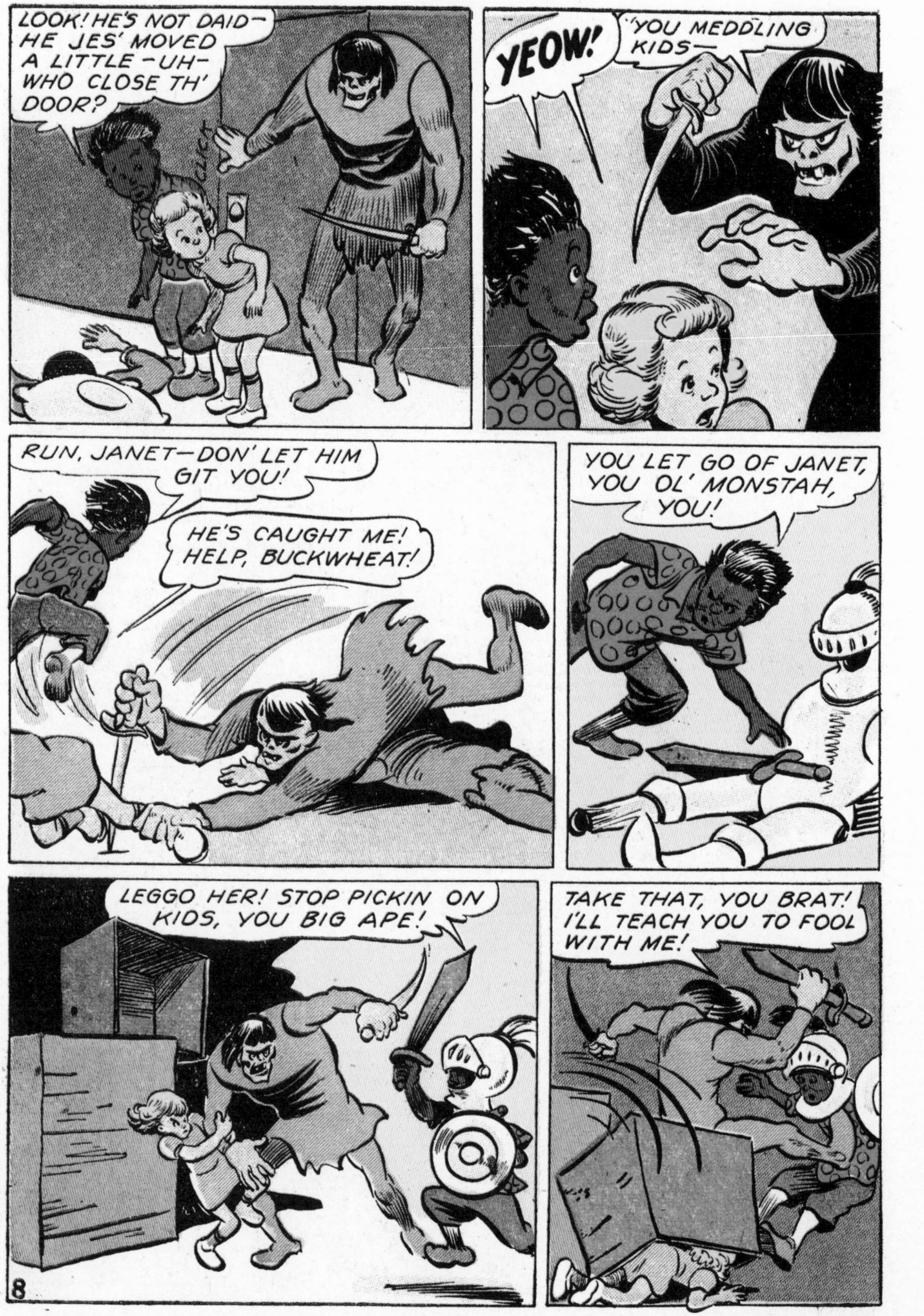
LOOK! HE'S NOT DAID— HE JES' MOVED A LITTLE—UH— WHO CLOSE TH' DOOR?
YEOW!
"YOU MEDDLING KIDS—
RUN, JANET—DON' LET HIM GIT YOU!
HE'S CAUGHT ME! HELP, BUCKWHEAT!
YOU LET GO OF JANET, YOU OL' MONSTAH, YOU!
LEGGO HER! STOP PICKIN ON KIDS, YOU BIG APE!
TAKE THAT, YOU BRAT! I'LL TEACH YOU TO FOOL WITH ME!
8

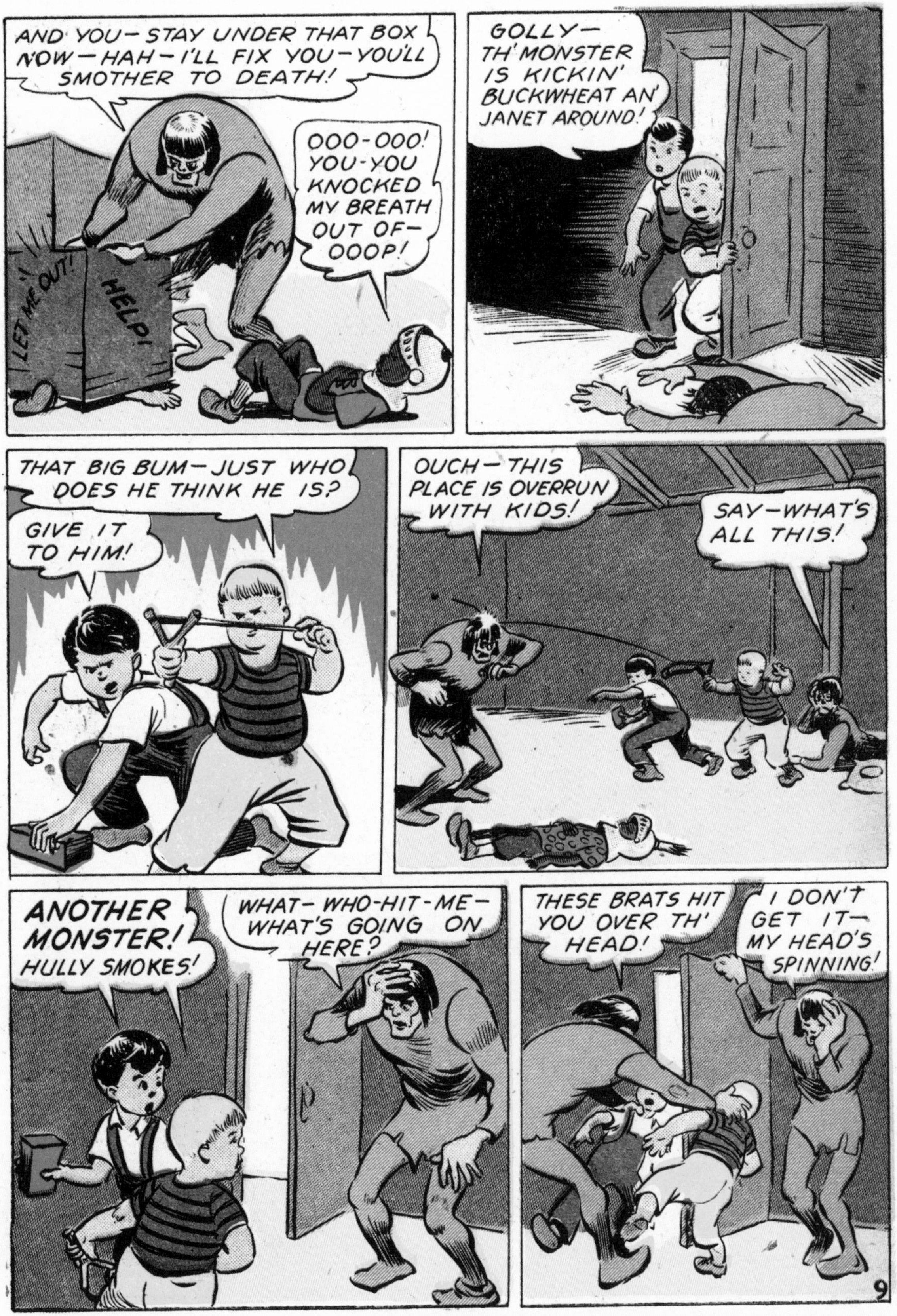
AND YOU—STAY UNDER THAT BOX NOW—HAH—I'LL FIX YOU—YOU'LL SMOTHER TO DEATH!
OOO-OOO! YOU-YOU KNOCKED MY BREATH OUT OF—OOOP!
LET ME OUT!
HELP!
GOLLY—TH' MONSTER IS KICKIN' BUCKWHEAT AN' JANET AROUND!
THAT BIG BUM—JUST WHO DOES HE THINK HE IS?
GIVE IT TO HIM!
OUCH—THIS PLACE IS OVERRUN WITH KIDS!
SAY—WHAT'S ALL THIS!
ANOTHER MONSTER! HULLY SMOKES!
WHAT—WHO-HIT-ME—WHAT'S GOING ON HERE?
THESE BRATS HIT YOU OVER TH' HEAD!
I DON'T GET IT—MY HEAD'S SPINNING!
9

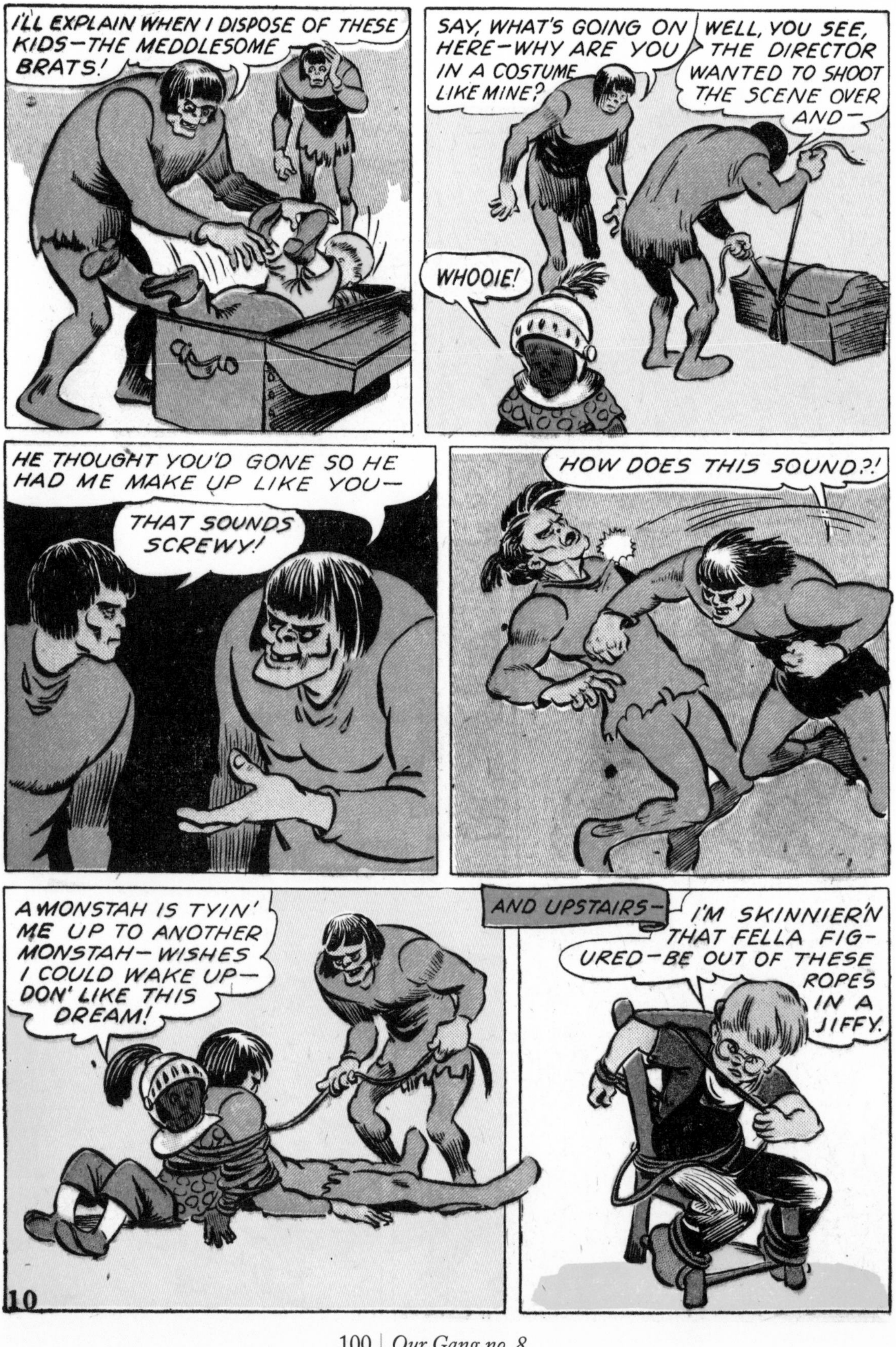
I'LL EXPLAIN WHEN I DISPOSE OF THESE KIDS—THE MEDDLESOME BRATS!
SAY, WHAT'S GOING ON HERE—WHY ARE YOU IN A COSTUME LIKE MINE?
WELL, YOU SEE, THE DIRECTOR WANTED TO SHOOT THE SCENE OVER AND—
WHOOIE!
HE THOUGHT YOU'D GONE SO HE HAD ME MAKE UP LIKE YOU—
THAT SOUNDS SCREWY!
HOW DOES THIS SOUND?!
A MONSTAH IS TYIN' ME UP TO ANOTHER MONSTAH—WISHES I COULD WAKE UP—DON' LIKE THIS DREAM!
AND UPSTAIRS—
I'M SKINNIER'N THAT FELLA FIG-URED—BE OUT OF THESE ROPES IN A JIFFY.
10

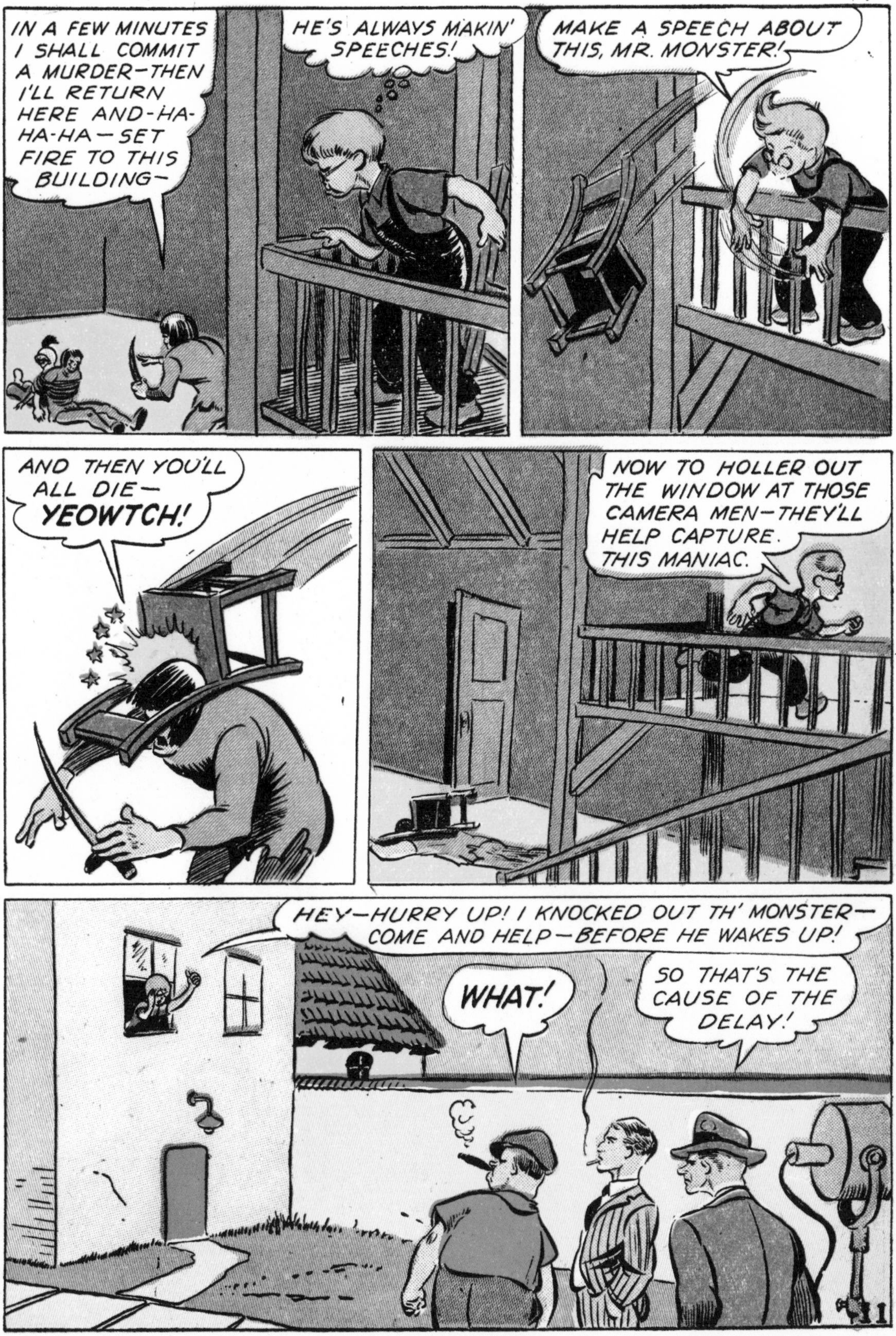
IN A FEW MINUTES I SHALL COMMIT A MURDER—THEN I'LL RETURN HERE AND-HA-HA-HA—SET FIRE TO THIS BUILDING—
HE'S ALWAYS MAKIN' SPEECHES!
MAKE A SPEECH ABOUT THIS, MR. MONSTER!
AND THEN YOU'LL ALL DIE—YEOWTCH!
NOW TO HOLLER OUT THE WINDOW AT THOSE CAMERA MEN—THEY'LL HELP CAPTURE THIS MANIAC.
HEY—HURRY UP! I KNOCKED OUT TH' MONSTER—COME AND HELP—BEFORE HE WAKES UP!
WHAT!
SO THAT'S THE CAUSE OF THE DELAY!
11

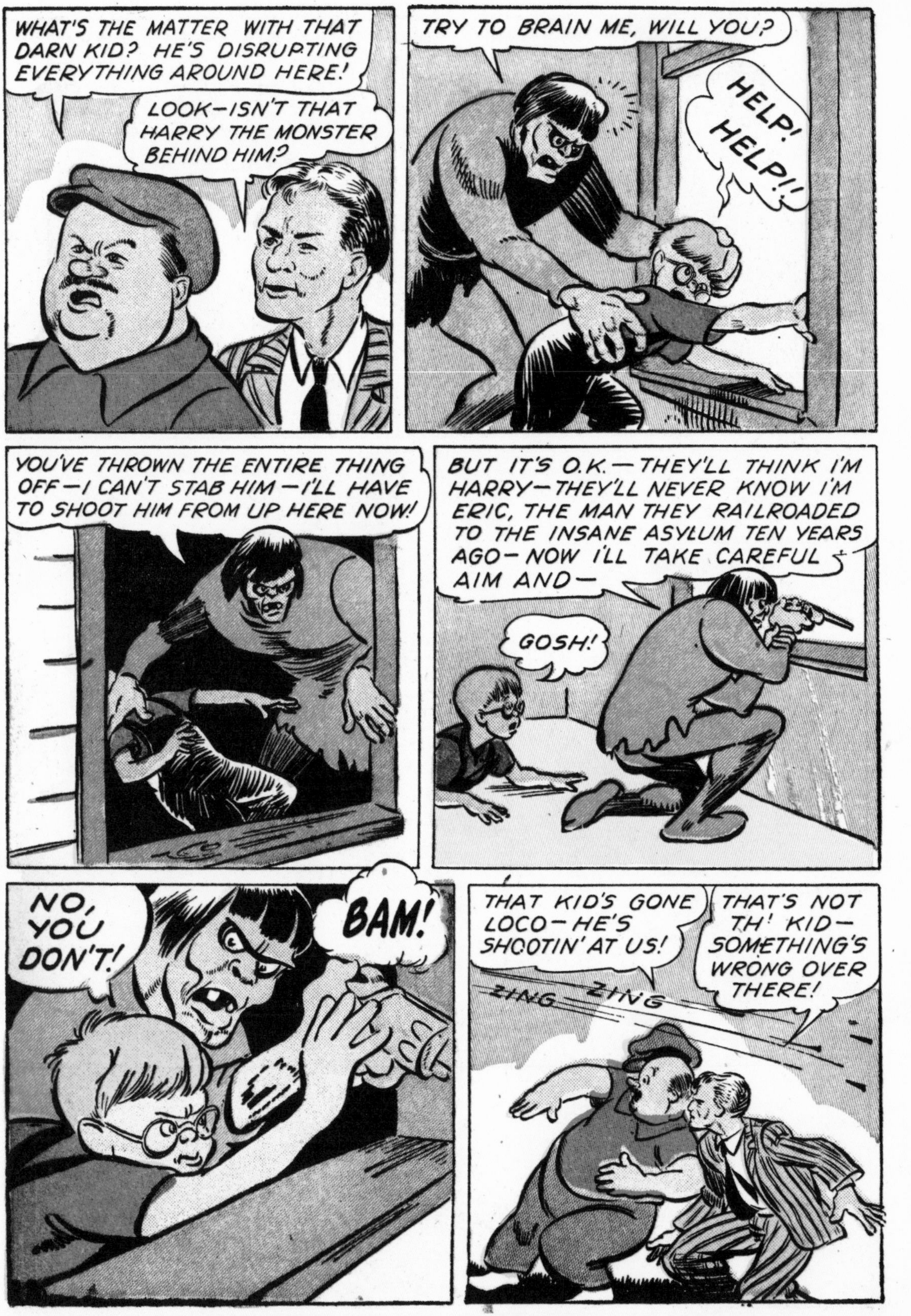
WHAT'S THE MATTER WITH THAT DARN KID? HE'S DISRUPTING EVERYTHING AROUND HERE!
LOOK—ISN'T THAT HARRY THE MONSTER BEHIND HIM?
TRY TO BRAIN ME, WILL YOU?
HELP! HELP!!
YOU'VE THROWN THE ENTIRE THING OFF—I CAN'T STAB HIM—I'LL HAVE TO SHOOT HIM FROM UP HERE NOW!
BUT IT'S O.K.—THEY'LL THINK I'M HARRY—THEY'LL NEVER KNOW I'M ERIC, THE MAN THEY RAILROADED TO THE INSANE ASYLUM TEN YEARS AGO—NOW I'LL TAKE CAREFUL AIM AND—
GOSH!
NO, YOU DON'T!
BAM!
THAT KID'S GONE LOCO—HE'S SHOOTIN' AT US!
THAT'S NOT TH' KID—SOMETHING'S WRONG OVER THERE!
ZING ZING

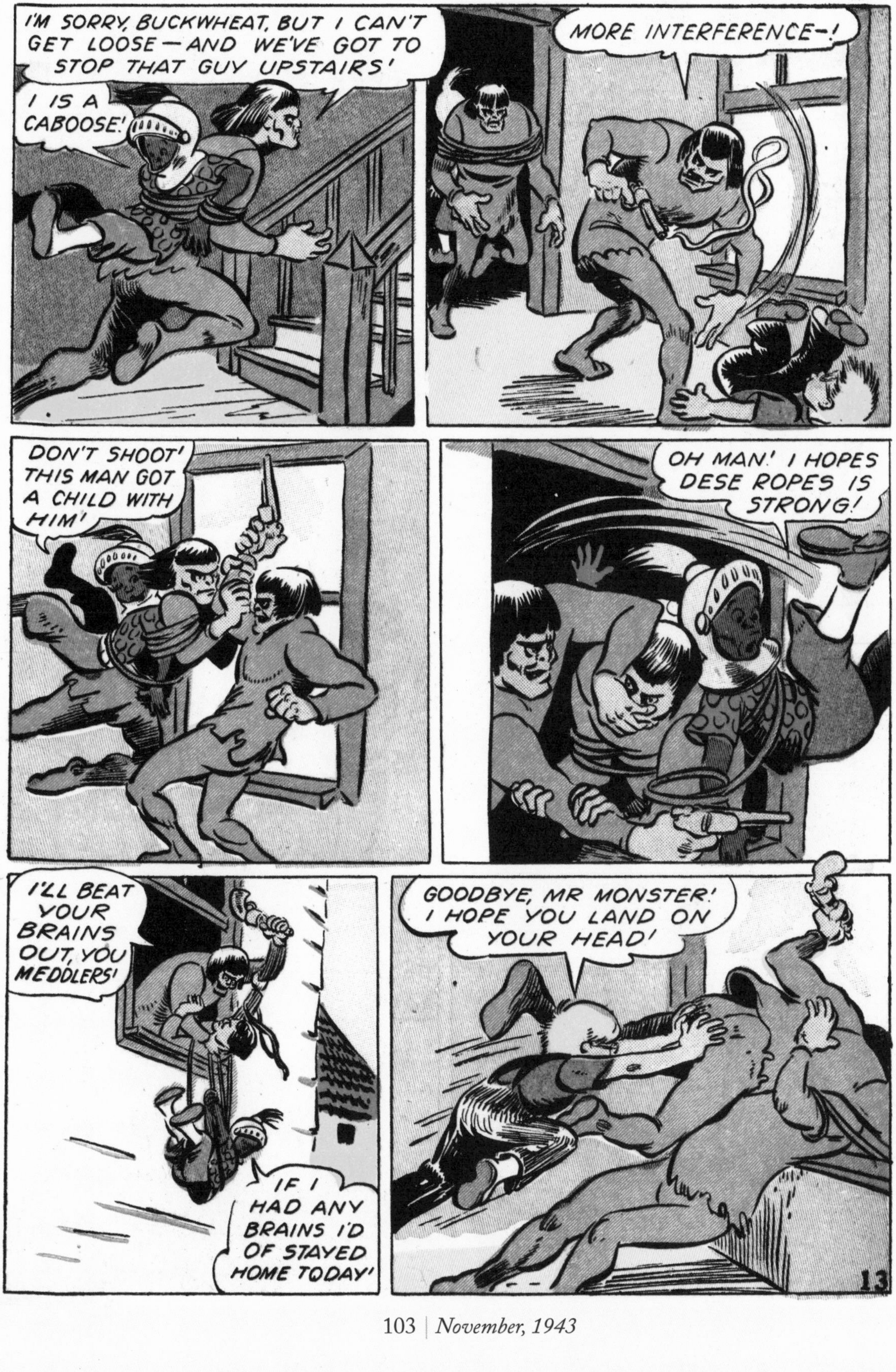
I'M SORRY, BUCKWHEAT, BUT I CAN'T GET LOOSE — AND WE'VE GOT TO STOP THAT GUY UPSTAIRS!
I IS A CABOOSE!
MORE INTERFERENCE-!
DON'T SHOOT! THIS MAN GOT A CHILD WITH HIM!
OH MAN! I HOPES DESE ROPES IS STRONG!
I'LL BEAT YOUR BRAINS OUT, YOU MEDDLERS!
IF I HAD ANY BRAINS I'D OF STAYED HOME TODAY!
GOODBYE, MR MONSTER! I HOPE YOU LAND ON YOUR HEAD!
13

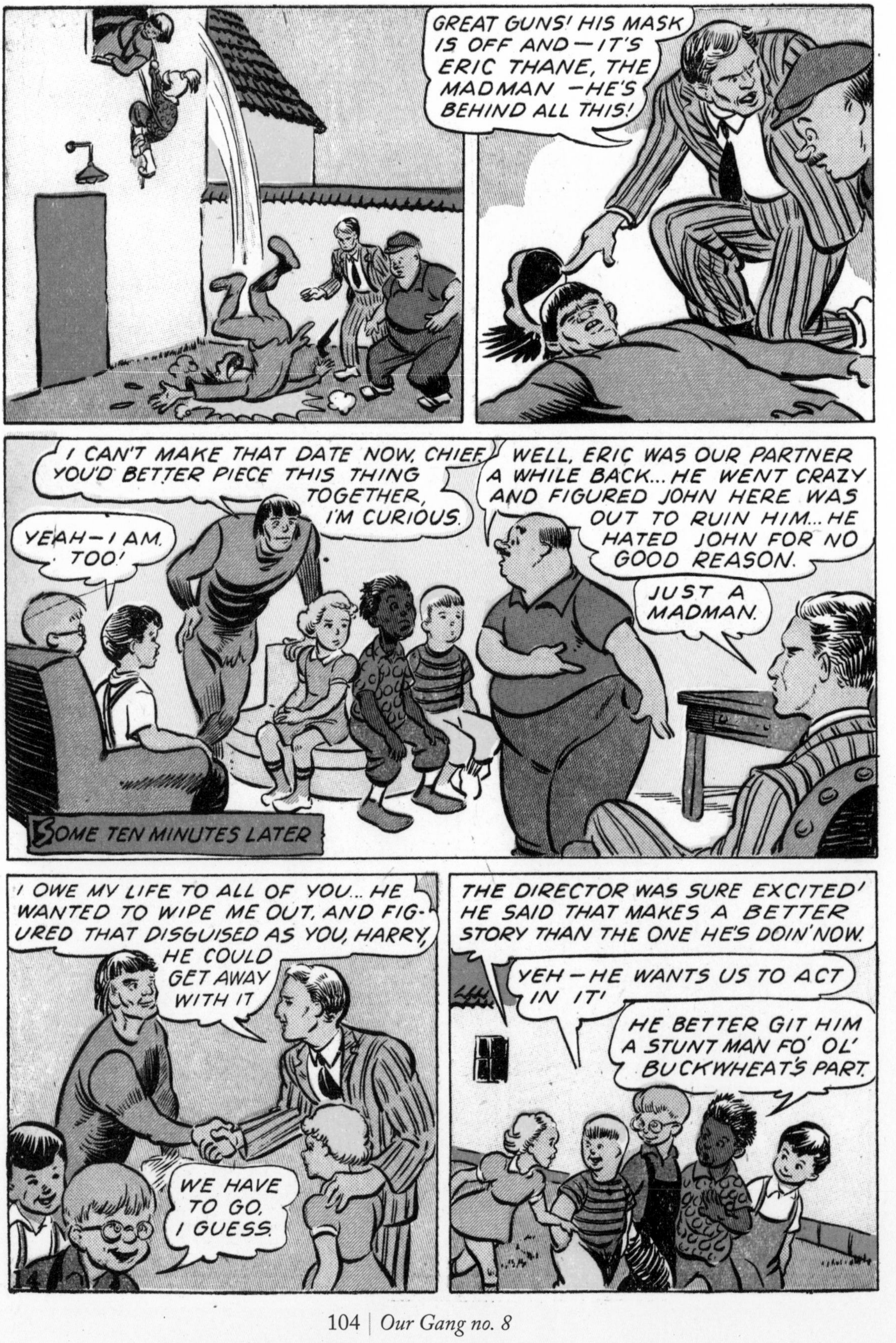
GREAT GUNS! HIS MASK IS OFF AND—IT'S ERIC THANE, THE MADMAN—HE'S BEHIND ALL THIS!
SOME TEN MINUTES LATER
I CAN'T MAKE THAT DATE NOW, CHIEF. YOU'D BETTER PIECE THIS THING TOGETHER, I'M CURIOUS.
YEAH—I AM, TOO!
WELL, ERIC WAS OUR PARTNER A WHILE BACK... HE WENT CRAZY AND FIGURED JOHN HERE WAS OUT TO RUIN HIM... HE HATED JOHN FOR NO GOOD REASON.
JUST A MADMAN.
I OWE MY LIFE TO ALL OF YOU... HE WANTED TO WIPE ME OUT, AND FIGURED THAT DISGUISED AS YOU, HARRY, HE COULD GET AWAY WITH IT
WE HAVE TO GO, I GUESS.
14
THE DIRECTOR WAS SURE EXCITED! HE SAID THAT MAKES A BETTER STORY THAN THE ONE HE'S DOIN' NOW.
YEH—HE WANTS US TO ACT IN IT!
HE BETTER GIT HIM A STUNT MAN FO' OL' BUCKWHEAT'S PART.